Translation and Cultural Identity: Selected Essays on Translation and Cross-Cultural Communication

Translation and Cultural Identity: Selected Essays on Translation and Cross-Cultural Communication

Edited by

Micaela Muñoz-Calvo
and Carmen Buesa-Gómez

Translation and Cultural Identity: Selected Essays on Translation and Cross-Cultural Communication,
Edited by Micaela Muñoz-Calvo and Carmen Buesa-Gómez

This book first published 2010

Cambridge Scholars Publishing

12 Back Chapman Street, Newcastle upon Tyne, NE6 2XX, UK

British Library Cataloguing in Publication Data
A catalogue record for this book is available from the British Library

Copyright © 2010 by Micaela Muñoz-Calvo and Carmen Buesa-Gómez and contributors

All rights for this book reserved. No part of this book may be reproduced, stored in a retrieval system, or transmitted, in any form or by any means, electronic, mechanical, photocopying, recording or otherwise, without the prior permission of the copyright owner.

ISBN (10): 1-4438-1989-1, ISBN (13): 978-1-4438-1989-3

TABLE OF CONTENTS

Acknowledgements.. VII

Introduction.. 1
Translation and Cross-Cultural Communication
Micaela Muñoz-Calvo ~ University of Zaragoza, Spain

Chapter One... 13
Translation and Cultural Identity: Competence and
Performance of the Author-Translator
Julio-César Santoyo ~ University of Leon, Spain

Chapter Two... 33
The Languages of Translation. Keys to the Dynamics
of Culture
José Lambert ~ CETRA/Catholic University
of Louvain, Belgium

Chapter Three.. 61
Linguistic Preferences in Translation from English into
Spanish: A Case of "Missing Identity"?
Rosa Rabadán ~ University of Leon, Spain

Chapter Four.. 83
A Map and a Compass for Navigating through
Translation
Patrick Zabalbeascoa ~ Pompeu Fabra University,
Barcelona, Spain

Chapter Five... 107
Crosscultural Translation and Conflicting Ideologies
Christina Schäffner ~ Aston University, Birmingham,
United Kingdom

Chapter Six 129
   Building TRACE (Translations Censored) Theatre
   Corpus: some Methodological Questions on Text
   Selection
   Raquel Merino Álvarez ~ The University of the Basque
   Country, Spain

Chapter Seven 155
   Some Recent (and More Recent) Myths in Translation
   Studies: An Essay on the Present and Future of the
   Discipline.
   Gideon Toury ~ Tel-Aviv University, Israel

Notes on Contributors 173

Notes on Editors 177

Index 179

ACKNOWLEDGEMENTS

We wish to express our gratitude to the distinguished scholars who have participated in this volume and who honour us with their contributions: José Lambert (CETRA/Catholic University of Louvain, Belgium), Raquel Merino Álvarez (University of the Basque Country, Spain), Rosa Rabadán (University of Leon, Spain), Julio-César Santoyo (University of Leon, Spain), Christina Schäffner (Aston University, Birmingham, United Kingdom), Gideon Toury (Tel-Aviv University, Israel) and Patrick Zabalbeascoa (Pompeu Fabra University, Barcelona, Spain). These eminent specialists, together with Dirk Delabastita (University of Namur, Belgium), Theo Hermans (University College London, United Kingdom) and José Miguel Santamaría (University of the Basque Country, Spain) formed the Scientific Committee of the *XIII Susanne Hübner: Seminar Translation and Cultural Identity*, held in Zaragoza, Spain, in 2005. Together, they constituted the panel of reviewers of the papers finally published in the companion piece *New Trends in Translation and Cultural Identity,* published in 2008 by Cambridge Scholars Publishing.

We would like to thank Tim Bozman for his careful and meticulous revision of the text, José Ignacio Perruca for the design of the cover and Flor Rincón and Pablo Cisneros for their help in the production of this volume.

Finally, we are greatly indebted to Miguel Bayón (journalist and writer), to our colleagues Beatriz Penas and José Ángel García-Landa (English and German Department, University of Zaragoza) and to Javier Muñoz-Basols (University of Oxford) for their support and for their valuable and selfless help.

Introduction

Translation and Cross-Cultural Communication

Micaela Muñoz-Calvo

In the course of millions of years of evolution, the genus *homo* was the only primate to develop language. Eudald Carbonell and Robert Sala (2000:146) state:

> Our brain transformed itself to formulate and transmit language, but since then our brain has not stopped creating new ways of communication: writing, architecture, theatre, the *jongleur* world, illuminated manuscripts, contemporary comics, cinema, computing and virtual universes, to communicate a physical reality and other "fictitious" and symbolic realities. Language, to develop itself, evolves within the forms it has adopted that become more and more complex, powerful and universal.[1]

Those ancestors not only had to adapt their brain but also their vocal apparatus to produce speech since they certainly used non-verbal as well as verbal codes for successful communication; communication that resulted in natural selection and survival. Translation must have been implicit in their most primitive acts of communication if, as Steiner stated (1975: 47), "Inside or between languages, human communication equals translation*"*.

So, our ancestors communicated, talked, painted, traded...and survived thanks to that successful communication, thanks to translation.

According to Xaverio Ballester (2002), we may situate the origin of speech about 6 million years ago. Forty-five thousand years ago man must have talked languages perfectly comparable with the present ones and "if not all languages, at least the immense majority of languages would have a common origin" (2002:116)[2].

---

1   My translation
2   My translation

That common origin has produced a large number of languages. The total number of languages in the world is between 5,000 and 10,000, although, as the Wikipedia[3] puts it, "It is probably impossible to accurately enumerate the living languages because our worldwide knowledge is incomplete, and it is a 'moving target'".

It seems our brain contains innate norms to understand, acquire and reproduce patterns of use of any language. The space in our brain devoted to our mother tongue is smaller than the space and activity devoted to any other language. The reason is that learning/acquiring another language is more difficult and requires more effort from us than the system we develop naturally when we are about two years old. (Eudald Carbonell and Robert Sala, 2000:158-159).

After tens of thousands of years of evolution through which language was fundamental for the development of mankind, we have reached the age of globalization. Though nowadays there are few borders left that have not been breached by the great Internet, electronic mail, and telecommunication, language may still be an important barrier in communication and translation is still necessary for successful communication.

A language postulates in itself a model of reality and a phonic association with the universe it describes, so we cannot separate language from culture. Both linguistic equivalence and cultural transfer are at stake when translating. Translation is a cultural fact that means necessarily cross-cultural communication because translation enables language to cross borders and helps intercultural exchange and understanding.

The complexity and multiplicity of cultures and languages, the empire of quantity, makes it impossible for an individual to cope with even fundamental references of literary or scientific works within different languages. For these reasons, we need bicultural translators and interpreters to translate across diverse languages and cultures, to act as mediators/ambassadors across cultures and as necessary intercultural communicators in a world where language access has become a right that is, or should be, protected by international laws in all parts of the world. Translators need cultural literacy, communicative language competences and cross-cultural compe-

---

3   Wikipedia, 26th April, 2009: "As of early 2007, there are 6,912 known languages. A 'living language' is simply one which is in wide use by a specific group of living people. The exact number of known living languages vary from 5,000 to 10,000 depending generally on the precision of one's definition of 'language', and in particular on how one classifies dialects. There are also many dead or extinct languages".

tence as well, because they have to interpret socio-cultural meaning in cross-cultural encounters, contributing to the transfer of knowledge across cultures and to cultural development as well.

Is cultural identity in danger in a world which is progressively less diverse? Is respect for the peculiarities of diverse cultures with different sets of norms and values in conflict with globalization? Or, on the contrary, will globalization bring cultures closer and support their rich cultural diversity to enhance communication and to help towards a global understanding?

We live in an increasingly globalized world. We talk about global agriculture, global warming, international global financial architecture, global market, business on a global scale, global minds[4], global actions, global humour, global classroom, global education, …and even a global university that will certainly help cultures to build bridges across cultural boundaries.

The UN presented[5] the first online global university, with free registration, thereby promoting access to Higher Education for students from the less developed regions of the world. This new education project is called the University of the People and it is framed within the UN's Global Alliance on Technology of Communication and Development (GAID) to help to bridge the gulf between one nation and another in educational matters by means of new technologies. The requirements for registering and participating in this virtual campus are: access to a computer, a secondary education certificate and a certain level of English.

Statistics show why "a certain level of English" is required: between 300 and 500 million persons have English as their mother tongue[6] (people from USA, Canada, United Kingdom, New Zealand, Australia…); moreover, English is the official language of 52[7] countries that include high growth rate countries like South Africa or India and is the most widely spoken foreign language for communicating both with native and non-native speakers of English.

---

4 You may even become a part of the BBC Global Minds Community, contributing to shaping the BBC's programming, giving insights into their output: sharing your thoughts on programmes, participating in forum debates and Web chats, taking part in fascinating discussions held in their Global Minds Community.
5 "Educación para todos. La ONU presenta la primera universidad global online y de matrícula gratuita". *Ibercampus.es*, 20/5/09
6 Wikipedia's "List of Languages by number of native speakers" (30/05/09): Encarta's estimate is 341,000,000; Ethnologue's 2005 estimate: 508,350,000.
7 Navarro 1997:6

Even though English is the second most widely spoken language[8] in the world, 75% of printed information is written in English and 85% of the information you find in the Internet uses English as a vehicle. According to these percentages[9], English is the most widely used language not only when traditional means of learning and communicating, like books, are used, but also when more universal and effective means of communication, like the Internet, are available. If communication and information are the key to progress and the bases for technological development and if information is power, we can state, beyond any doubt, that English is the most actively influential international language.

We live in a "global village" (McLuhan 1962), in which English is considered a *lingua franca*. This has given rise to specific phenomena of linguistic simplification and standardization. Snell-Hornby (2000: 17) says:

> ...there is the free-floating *lingua franca* ("International English") that has largely lost track of its original cultural identity, its idioms, its hidden connotations, its grammatical subtleties, and has become a reduced standardised form of language for supra-cultural communication—the "McLanguage" of our globalised "McWorld"...

Other widely spoken languages would include Hindi, Spanish[10] and Arabic; they are also used in this globalised world, although their global influence is far below that of English.

Should we be afraid of this global phenomenon? Will this phenomenon lead us to a world of uniformity in thought, sameness in education, a single value system...?

The fact is that globalization is fraught with real dangers due to the fact that problems may spread overnight all over this interconnected world, over all countries, rich and poor. Think of the AIDS pandemic, for instance, the outbreak of swine flu; think of the international financial downturn...

We witness global problems that require global solutions every day. The international financial downturn, the impact of the crisis on a global scale, the so-called "greatest crisis since the Great Depression" has made

---

8 According to Wikipedia (30/05/09), the first most widely used language is Mandarin.
9 Data given by Thomas Schmidt at a lecture delivered at the British Council in Barcelona (28/5/09)
10 Wikipedia's "List of Languages by number of native speakers" (30/05/09): Spanish is the fourth on the list: Ethnologue's estimate: 438,300,000; Encarta's: 322,200,000.

people talk of saving the "world's economy" because the recovery has to be global and actions have to be taken jointly to solve global problems.

Can countries step out of this global phenomenon?

It seems anti-globalization is not a solution to global financial problems, on the contrary, the introduction of barriers like protectionism, nationalism and economic isolation may be considered to be the dangers of today. We cannot close frontiers. Even if we wanted to, there is no way we can do so because people communicate, travel, trade... Survival is a global matter nowadays that still depends on successful communication and that still depends on translation. Translation plays a vital role in this new global framework that demands that actions be taken jointly to solve global problems.

We have to accept that the old world has gone. Cultural/ethnical/regional identity and globalization interface and there are political, economic, social and linguistic implications. Translation plays an undeniable role in the shaping of cultures, of national identities, and it is the vehicle that may make compatible the strengthening of our group identity and consequent knowledge of our own culture with the sharing and learning of other cultures; cultures and their texts becoming accessible and available to international audiences in their own language.

In this cross-cultural communication, interstellar communication has also to be mentioned. Spacecraft were launched carrying on board interstellar messages: pictorial messages (Pioneer plaques) and phonograph records containing sounds and messages that show the diversity of life and culture on Earth. Electromagnetic signals, radio messages (Cosmic Calls) and long distance radio signals are also used in the attempt to communicate with outer space. The SETI Projects (Search for Extraterrestrial Intelligence) try to detect intelligent extraterrestrial life, to find evidence of civilizations on distant planets. Well-known science fiction films dealt with this interstellar communication like "Close Encounters of the Third Kind", released in 1977 and directed by Steven Spielberg, or "Contact" directed by Robert Zemeckis in 1997, adapted from the Carl Sagan novel of the same name. Sagan, an astronomer and astrochemist, promoted the Search for Extraterrestrial Intelligence. It seems that, so far, this interstellar communication between planetary systems has not been successful.

The highly interdisciplinary and multifaceted title of the book I am introducing refers to complex concepts and involves a great variety of disciplines that cover several different fields of research with approaches that complement and interact with one another: Translation Studies, Cultural

Studies, Communication Studies, Philology, Linguistics, Applied Linguistics, Pragmatics, Discourse Analysis, Literary Studies, Psycho- and Socio-linguistics, Philosophy, Sociology, Psychology, History, Anthropology, Ethnography, Ethnology, Artificial Intelligence, Palaeontology, Neurology, Biology, Genetics, Political Science...

Thus, this interdisciplinarity needs an interdisciplinary approach and interdisciplinary competences have to be used. Over the last few years, scholars from different disciplines and from different approaches have been discussing translation and cultural identity and translation and cross-cultural communication. The concepts behind these abstract terms are complex and have different senses and definitions depending on the discipline from which they are taken.

Many interesting books[11], reviews[12] and journals[13] have been published on translation, culture, cultural identity and cross-cultural communication. These questions are among the concerns of many international conferences[14],

---

11 To quote but a few: Blommaert and Verschueren 1991, Snell-Hornby *et al.* 1995, Hatim 1997, Hatim and Mason 1997, Katan 1999/2004, Shäffner 2000, Hermans 2002, Hernando 2002, Holliday *et al.* 2004, Penas Ibáñez and López Sáenz 2006, González and Tolron 2006, Castillo García 2006, Cronin 2006, Monaghan and Goodman 2007, Muñoz-Calvo *et al.* 2008, Nikcevic-Batricevic and Knezevic 2008, Gentzler 2008, etc.
12 Like *Interculturality & Translation. International Review* 2005, *I & T:* Revista Internacional *Interculturalidad & Traducción*. Servicio de Publicaciones de la Universidad de León.
13 Like *Cultus: The Journal of Intercultural mediation and communication,* and *The Translator: Studies in Intercultural Communication.*
14 Among recent ones: *The III Conferences on Cross-Cultural Capability*, Leeds Metropolitan University, December 1998; *Translation and cultural Identity*, University of Zaragoza, November 2005; *Languages and Cultures in Contact.* Institute of Foreign Languages, University of Montenegro, September 2007; *Metaphor in Cross-Cultural Communication.* Seventh International Conference on Researching and Applying Metaphor. University of Extremadura, Cáceres, May 2008; *Translation and Cultural Diversity*, XVIII World Congress of the International Federation of Translators. Shanghai, China, August 2008; *Bridging the gap in cultural studies: From meaning construction to (inter-)cultural communicative competence* Language, Culture and Mind III Conference, Odense, July 2008; *International Conference on Translation in the Era of Information.* Universidad de Oviedo, Spain. 22-24 October 2008; *Identity, Diversity and Intercultural Dialogue.* 5th International WEEK of ESEC (IWE), Coimbra, Portugal, March 2008; *Translation, Language Contact and Multilingual Communication*, August 2008, City University of Hong Kong; Multilingualism: Challenges and Opportunities. AILA World Congress in Europe 2008; *Mediation and Conflict: Translation and Culture in a Global Context.* 3rd Conference of the International Association for Translation and Intercultural Studies (IATIS). Monash University, Melbourne, Australia July 2009.

associations[15], research working groups[16], and even advertisements for university posts[17].

This volume tackles the complexity of the concepts mentioned in its title through seven essays, written by most highly regarded experts in the field of Translation Studies. The essays are varied and innovative. Their common feature is that they deal with various aspects of translation and cultural identity and that they contribute to the enrichment of the study of communication across cultures.

The first four essays focus on how language, culture and translation are fundamental in the literary communicative process across cultures.

Julio-César Santoyo (University of Leon, Spain) highlights the importance of self-translation as an interesting phenomenon which has been neglected up till now by Translation Studies, even though it is frequently found in universal literature. Using his own experience, Santoyo explains that the elements which are most heavily marked culturally in a text cause translators and self-translators many problems in the cross-language exchange, though self-translators enjoy the freedom to reconstruct a second version of the original.

José Lambert (CETRA/Catholic University of Louvain, Belgium) stresses the importance of interdisciplinarity and multiperspectivism in an analysis of translated verbal communication and the dynamics of translating at any given cultural moment, in any cultural/social situation.

Lambert contemplates the exact position and goals of the speaker as one of the traditional difficulties in any scholarly discourse on "translation" in any cultural environment. The author reflects on issues as relevant as the languages of translation, the language of translators and the dynamics of languages.

---

15 International Association for Translation and Intercultural Studies (IATIS); the Globalization and Localization Association (GALA)
16 *MCCC (Multilingualism and Cross-Cultural Communication)*, Compostela Group of Universities.
17 "Applications are invited for the position of Professor or Assistant Professor in English-Chinese and Chinese-English translation in the Translation Programme. The Programme was established in 1990 with the aim of training sophisticated cross-cultural communicators to serve the local community and the Mainland of China". Hong Kong Baptist University. Faculty of Arts. Department of English Language and Literature. Professor/Assistant Professor in Translation (PR042/07-08). Closing date: 29 September 2007. (Taken from Mona Baker's e-mail 5/9/07).

Rosa Rabadán (University of Leon, Spain) considers that not much attention has been paid so far to the way in which the processes undergone by texts in their encounter with the target language readership are related to language roles and linguistic choices. Rabadán discusses language and identity issues and also the role of translation in the construction of identities. She uses two corpus-based empirical studies to provide evidence of how identities are reflected in translated as opposed to nontranslated Spanish and presents the translation strategies and linguistic preferences in translated Spanish for identity marking.

Patrick Zabalbeascoa (Pompeu Fabra University, Barcelona, Spain) helps us navigate the tumultuous seas of translation by providing us with conceptual tools for identifying and discriminating translation problems, and by supplying us with a binary-tree mapping model useful for establishing translational criteria by which possible solutions to a given translation problem can be found.

Zabalbeascoa uses examples of analysis to show how one can examine translation problems and find translational solutions in the light of a given interpretation of the source text and in relation to theoretically possible solutions that are plausible or not depending on the aims of the target text. He gives us a compass to navigate our way through translational norms.

The next two essays enlighten us on the ideological, political and cultural implications of translation: in our daily life, in the international exchange of news, in shaping our way of thinking—through different means like text selection or censorship.

Christina Schäffner (Aston University, Birmingham, UK) looks at the role of translation in the production and dissemination of news. She considers translation a component of news production, even if this is not always explicitly indicated. Schäffner illustrates the translation policies and practices of news translation on the basis of two case studies: *Spiegel International* and *BBC Monitoring Service*.

The analysis of the translation practices in the two media corporations leads her to raise the question: whose voice do we hear in the translations? Translation in major media corporations is a process which is determined by the values of news journalism. This becomes particularly obvious whenever information transfer involves conflicting ideologies (as, for example, in the reporting on the "war on terror").

In Spain, a research group called TRACE has been carrying out studies on censored translations in Franco's time from a historical standpoint. TRACE split the fifty-year period of translations into subperiods and has tackled research on a subperiod and/or (sub)genre in a descriptive fashion (Merino, 2005). They have compiled catalogues of censored (narrative, theatre, cinema...) translations from censorship archives and have derived criteria for selecting sets of representative texts, from the analysis of such catalogues. These fragments/sets of texts have become object(s) of study, in tune with the notion of "well-defined corpus" (Toury 2004: 77-80). **Raquel Merino Álvarez** (University of the Basque Country, Spain) uses a TRACE theatre case study to pinpoint the various methodological issues at stake in such descriptive studies. Merino examines in detail a "well-defined" corpus of drama texts dealing with homosexuality, and the abundant contextual information that illustrates how this topic found its way onto Spanish stages through translation.

Gideon Toury (Tel-Aviv University, Israel) closes the book with an enlightening meta-theoretical essay devoted to myths in Translation Studies.

The concept of myth he applies is taken from modern sociology and anthropology —not from classical studies. Using a number of exemplary cases, he tackles some issues of cultural identity but shifts the spotlight from Translation to Translation Studies.

Toury, who has himself taken an active part in the creation of a number of myths in Translation Studies, shows how the notion of myth is appropriate for the discussion of the present and future of the discipline. He does so in a way that "may sound provocative" and that may trigger some discussion amongst specialists in the field, but which is, at the same time, engaging.

These major readings in translation studies will give readers food for thought and reflection and will promote research on translation, cultural identity and cross-cultural communication.

References

Arsuaga, Juan Luis and Ignacio Martínez. 1998. "El origen del lenguaje humano". *La especie elegida.* Madrid: Ediciones temas de hoy. 301-319.
Ballester, Xaverio. 2002. *Las Primeras Palabras de la Humanidad.* Valencia: Tilde.

Bassnett, Susan and André Lefevere. 1998. *Constructing Cultures.* Clevedon: Multilingual Matters.
Blommaert, Jan and Jef Verschueren. Eds. 1991. *The Pragmatics of Intercultural and International Communication.* Amsterdam/ Philadelphia: John Benjamins Publishing Company.
Carbonell, Eudald and Robert Sala. 2000. *Planeta humano.* Barcelona: Ediciones Península.
— 2002. "El chat y la evolución". *Aún no somos humanos. Propuestas de humanización para el tercer milenio.* Barcelona: Ediciones Península. 85-92.
Castillo García, Gema Soledad. 2006. *La (auto) traducción como mediación entre culturas.* Alcalá de Henares: Universidad de Alcalá de Henares.
Corbella, Josep, Eudald Carbonell, Salvador Moyá and Robert Sala. 2000. *Sapiens. El largo camino de los homínidos hacia la inteligencia.* Barcelona: Ediciones Península.
Cronin, Michael. 2006. *Translation and Identity.* London and New York: Routledge.
Gentzler, Edwin. 2008. *Translation and Identity in the Americas. New Directions in Translation Theory.* London and New York: Routledge.
González, Madelena and Francine Touron. 2006. *Translating Identity and the Identity of Translation.* Newcastle: Cambridge Scholars Publishing.
Hatim, Basil. 1997. *Communication Across Cultures.* Devon: The University of Exeter Press.
— 2001. *Teaching and Researching in Translation.* Harlow: Longman.
Hatim, Basil and Ian Mason. 1997. *The Translator as Communicator.* London and New York: Routledge.
Hermans, Theo. Ed. 2002. *Crosscultural Transgressions.* Manchester: St. Jerome Publishing.
Hernando, Almudena. 2002. *Arqueología de la Identidad.* Madrid: Akal.
Holliday, Adrian, Martin Hyde and John Kullman. 2004. *Intercultural Communication. An Advanced Resource Book.* London and New York: Routledge.
Interculturality and Translation. International Review. I & T. Interculturalidad y Traducción. 2005. Universidad de León. Departamento de Filología Moderna. www3.unileon.es/dp/dfm/i&t
Katan, David. 2004. (1999). *Translating Cultures. An Introduction for Translators, Interpreters and Mediators.* Manchester: St. Jerome Publishing.
Koskinen, Kaisa. 2004. "Shared culture? Reflections on recent trends in Translation Studies." *Target* 16.1: 143-156.

McLuhan, Marshall. 1962. *The Gutenberg Galaxy: The Making of Typographic Man*. Canada: University of Toronto Press.
Merino Álvarez, Raquel. 2005. "From catalogue to corpus in DTS. Translations censored under Franco: the TRACE Project". In *Revista Canaria de Estudios Ingleses* 29. Ed. C. Toledano. 129-138.
Monaghan, Leila and Jane E. Goodman. 2007. *A Cultural Approach to Interpersonal Communication*. Oxford: Blackwell Publishing.
Muñoz-Calvo, Micaela, Carmina Buesa-Gómez and María Ángeles Ruiz-Moneva. Eds. 2008. *New Trends in Translation and Cultural Identity*. Newcastle: Cambridge Scholars Publishing.
Navarro, F. 1997. "Which is the world's most important language?". *Lebende Sparchen* XLII: 5-10.
Nikcevic-Batricevic, Aleksandra and Marija Knezevic. 2008. *Culture-Bound Translation and Language in the Global Era*. Newcastle: Cambridge Scholars Publishing.
Penas Ibáñez, Beatriz and María Carmen López Sáenz. 2006. *Interculturalism: Between Identity and Diversity*. Bern/New York: Peter Lang.
Poyatos, Fernando. 2002. "Culture, Communication, and Cultural Fluency". In *Nonverbal Communication across Disciplines*. Amsterdam/Philadelphia: John Benjamins. 1-29.
Schäffner, Christina. ed. 2000. *Translation in the Global Village*. Clevedon/Buffalo/Toronto/Sidney: Multilingual Matters Ltd.
Schmidt, Thomas. 2009. "El inglés en el mundo de hoy -¿Cómo preparar a nuestros alumnos para mañana?" Lecture delivered at the British Council of Barcelona: 28/5/09.
Snell-Hornby, M. 2000. "Communicating in the Global Village: On Language, Translation and Cultural Identity". In *Translating in the Global Village*. Ed. Christina Schäeffner. Clevedon, Buffalo, Toronto, Sydney: Multilingual Matters. 11-28.
Snell-Hornby, Mary, Zuzana Jettmarová and Klaus Kaindl. 1995. *Translation as Intercultural Communication*. Amsterdam/Philadelphia: John Benjamins.
Steiner, George. 1975. *After Babel. Aspects of Language and Translation*. New York and London: Oxford University Press.
Toury, Gideon. 2004. *Los estudios descriptivos de traducción, y más allá. Metodología de la investigación en estudios de traducción*. Translation, introduction and notes by R. Rabadán and R. Merino. Madrid: Cátedra.
Venuti, Lawrence. 1994. "Translation and the Formation of Cultural Identities". *Current Issues in Language and Society* 1: 201-217.

CHAPTER ONE

TRANSLATION AND CULTURAL IDENTITY: COMPETENCE AND PERFORMANCE OF THE AUTHOR-TRANSLATOR

J. C. SANTOYO

> Self-translation is a topic that could do with far more analysis, generally being relegated to some asides in studies dealing primarily with translators who do not translate their own work....[It is] a thinly inhabited field...
> (Sinéad Mooney 2002: 288)

While preparing this text, I could not resist looking up the term "identidad cultural" on the Internet just to see how many pages came up. I was surprised by the results: 462,000. I asked for the same in English, "cultural identity", and I was even more surprised to find 2,610,000 pages. Quite clearly the topic is of significant relevance at present, in Spanish but particularly in English. And it has been so for many years: when, for example, in December 1992, Erich S. Gruen (1993:1) as President of the American Philological Association addressed its annual congress the first words of his speech were these:

> Cultural identity is a hot topic in the academy these days: the phenomenon has swept through the halls of ivy... In fact, the reshaping of academic disciplines in terms of cultural identity is a nationwide development, firmly entrenched in numerous institutions and in process of implementation in many others.

Once again my curiosity drove me to cross the two topics, "traducción" and "identidad cultural", and I obtained 61,100 pages which is not bad. But when I changed to English and crossed "translation" and "cultural identity", the results quadrupled with 342,000 entries. A subject, therefore, of great relevance today.

*

"Translating has shown me, quite definitively, that the transference between two cultural identities is impossible." The statement is by the Puerto Rican writer Rosario Ferré (1991: 157), after years of translating her own work from Spanish into English and *vice versa*.

It is, in my opinion, perhaps arguable, that the concept of "cultural identity" presupposes shared elements firmly localized in time and space. They do not even have to coincide with the frontiers of a state or nation, so that, when we refer to a culture, we do so with reference to the individual, local peculiarity of any group of individuals, with clearly defined spatial and temporal characteristics. I cannot be too far off the mark when the current dictionary of the Royal Spanish Academy defines the term as "group of lifestyles and customs, degree of development… in a certain epoch or social group; group of signs by which the traditional life of a population is expressed".

Evidently, the Holy Grail of translation is the creation of an equivalent text, however imprecise or even inappropriate the term "equivalent". Even so, culture is by nature whatever makes us who we are and whatever we enjoy uniquely (that is why the word "culture" is usually found in the company of an adjective). It is what differentiates and identifies us and for this reason cannot be compared with anything beyond our human experience and language.

It has been said more than once that it is the difference, difference from others, that determines cultural identity. Consequently, in such cases, the only thing that bilingual dictionaries can give us is not equivalences, which are absent from the target language and its culture, but mere definitions, with long explanatory phrases, which, without translation, fill the vacuum with sterile verbiage.

I have already presented the case and example on other occasions: when we try to find the equivalent term in a Spanish-English bilingual dictionary of a word as culturally marked as the bullfighting term *alternativa (dar la alternativa)*, we discover that there is no translation at all, at least not an "equivalent" one. There is only a definition: "Ceremony—says the dictionary—in which the senior matador confers professional status on the novice (*novillero*) thus accepting him as a professional equal capable of dispatching any bull in the proper manner". If all that were the translation of *alternative*, a sentence such as "ayer le dieron la alternative" would automatically convert to "yesterday he was given the ceremony in which the senior matador confers professional status on the novice (*novillero*) thus accepting him as a professional equal capable of dispatching any bull in the proper manner", which would of course be totally absurd.

Within the cultural area, and by the same token, the translation into English that a bilingual dictionary provides for the term *banderilla* is the following: "Small dart with a banderole placed into the nape of a bull during the second part of a bullfight". Once again there is a convoluted explanation used to define and describe but not to translate.

Moreover, in many cases you will not even find these roundabout explanations in the dictionary, but just silence, a void. Another example: in French culture there is a character in traditional infant folklore, called *el marchand de sable*, which has no equivalent in Spanish culture. This is a kind person who visits children at night to help them sleep peacefully, "he scatters a fine veil of sand on the children's eyelids until they close completely" (Félix 2002:67). In Spain we have nothing like that: neither *el coco*, nor *el hombre del saco*, who are more or less sinister characters fit the bill, even less so *el ratoncito Pérez*. The result of all this is hesitation and indecision when having to translate *marchand de sable* into Spanish. The French film with this title, directed by André Hugon in 1931, is known here as *El Mercador de Arena*, but various web pages refer to it as *el vendedor de arena*. And then, in a recent translation of the song by Celine Dion "Petit Papa Noel": "El *comerciante de arena* ha pasado, los niños van a dormir..." / "Le marchand de sable est passé, les enfants vont faire dodo..."

These are only three out of thousands of "culture bound" examples, rooted in culture, which every translator comes across in their daily work. What is more, the areas of culture which differentiate and separate us from other cultural groups are far more numerous than the first year student or inexpert translator could even begin to imagine. In 1964 Catford noted such areas as coins, measurements, institutions ("college" or "high school" in English), clothing, etc. All of which, he adds, differentiate one culture from another and can cause difficulty in translating. Vinay and Darbelnet had already mentioned earlier (1958) the areas of time division, jobs, positions and professions, food, drink, baking, particular aspects of social life, etc. Gastronomy not only responds to individual methods of preparation, but also frequently to the use of ingredients which are closely linked to a culture. To such "areas of culture" could be added certain sports, dances, musical and artistic terms..., specific areas of activity which correspond in the end to actions which are unique to a person or social group, subject to a very specific place and time.

In fact, if we could make an exhaustive compilation of everything that at one point cannot be translated naturally from one language to another, then we would have drawn the individualized profile of the *cultural identity* of that language: a large range of "aspects" that are peculiar to it and make up the idiosyncrasies and individual profiles of those who speak that language in a given time and place.

It is important not to make the mistake of thinking that such areas of culture are watertight compartments, when on the contrary they are for the most part permeable as traditionally distinct cultures draw closer and closer. Think of a sub-group as multiple and complex as Italian pasta, which was almost completely unknown to the Spanish culture fifty years ago. I remember as a child that the only pasta in the house was either *fideos* (fine noodles) or macaroni. Today with all the new fashion and styles, with travel, frozen food and increased international commerce, the "cultural" realm of Italian pasta is gradually becoming familiar in our culinary habits, as is the French, German and English cuisine. In addition to the traditional *fideos* and macaroni, we can now add *tallarines, lasagna, spaghetti, ravioli, pizza* and more.

This produces a complex phenomenon: when this unique area of unshared activity begins to be assimilated by another culture, which knew nothing of it up to that point, the importing culture, logically, lacks the terms necessary for the designation of the new activity, event or foreign object. For the first adaptation of the new cultural activity, the importing culture uses the original terms, and when it does not, it tries to translate them as best it can. At this early stage it rarely renames things. This happened with the importing of football, at the beginning of the 20th century. The football culture of 1910 or 1920, as can be seen in the Spanish press of the time, was not only full of, but teeming with terms which were imported directly from English culture and language, such as "referee", "score", "team", "match", "goal-keeper", "back", etc. Now football has become universal and has not only become perfectly assimilated to our sports culture, but has also become assimilated to a lexical system which is quite different from the one it emerged from, so "referee" has been replaced by the word *árbitro*, "team" by *equipo*, "match" by *partido* or *encuentro*, "goal-keeper" by *portero*, and on it goes. Only a few of the original terms remain, although transformed, such as *fútbol* and *gol*, and they have become so completely ours that a whole range of terms have been derived from the originals: *futbolín, futbolístico, futbolista, futbolísticamente, goleada, golazo, golear, goleador*, etc.

Nothing is stopping cultural areas that were once separate from becoming integrated in a world which is increasingly shared. On the contrary, everything favours such integration. Football, for example, used to be a sport with peculiarly British cultural characteristics for us, just like cricket: today it is just another factor resulting from a general tendency towards globalisation. As a matter of fact, specifically defined areas of culture are becoming fewer and fewer, because of an increasingly universal homogeneity. The "global village" is fleshing out thanks to the increasing globalisation of communication, thanks to translation too, which is its natural vehicle and the primary and perhaps unique factor in that communication.

*

My experience over the years of translating the work of Christopher Marlowe, Tolkien, Oscar Wilde, Edgar Allan Poe, Washington Irving, Willa Cather or Flannery O´Connor, amongst others, has shown me, sometimes to my dismay, that the elements which are most culturally marked in a text are those which have caused me the greatest problems in the cross-language transference.

As a translator I have always wondered what the author would have done at those moments, had they known Spanish and were in the position of having to translate their own work into our language. I do not know whether theirs would have been the best solution, but it certainly would have been the ideal solution, for at least they would surely be invested with what Brian T. Fitch (1988: 125) has termed "authorial intentionality": "authorial intentionality, something denied to versions made by other translators". Definitively, nobody knows the significance of their words better than the actual author, and particularly when it comes to applying their own criteria as author in choosing the "equivalent" alternative for the target language.

In this respect, and contrary to what is generally thought, a surprising number of authors have written their work in one language and then translated it themselves into a second language: authors who, for one reason or another, after publishing their work in one language for one set of readers, have then rewritten it for another readership of a different language and culture. I will not go as far back as the first century, nor even to the many authors from the Middle Ages or Renaissance to illustrate this point. I will limit myself to well known authors from our times.

Frédéric Mistral composed his epic pastoral *Mireio* in Provençal around the middle of the 19th century, later translated it into French and published it in a unique bilingual edition in 1859 ("avec la traduction littérale en regard"). He did the same with his three other works: *Calendau* (1867), *Lou Felibrige* (1883) and *Le Poème du Rhône* (1897). In 1904 he was awarded the Nobel Prize in Literature.

Rabindranath Tagore translated his Bengali poems into English for which he received the Nobel Prize in Literature in 1913. On this occasion the Swedish

Academy gave the award for the English translations that Tagore had done himself and not for the originals in Bengali, to which they had no access. The Institution's official statement made clear their reasons for giving the award:

> ... For the author himself, who by education and practice is a poet in his native Indian tongue, has bestowed upon the poems a new dress, alike perfect in form... This has made them accessible to all in England, America, and the entire Western world...; because... with consummate skill, he has made his poetic thought, expressed in his own English words, a part of the literature of the West.

Luigi Pirandello, the Sicilian novelist, playwright and author of *Six Characters in Search of an Author*, amongst other titles, wrote many of his works in Sicilian dialect which he later translated into Italian. He was the Nobel Prize winner for Literature in 1934.

The Irish novelist and playwright Samuel Beckett, voluntarily exiled in Paris, started by writing in English which he later translated into French, but ended up writing in French and translating himself back into English. He was the Nobel Prize winner for Literature in 1969.

The Polish writer, Isaac Bashevis Singer, who had emigrated to the United States in 1935 and translated many of his works from Yiddish to English at times with the help of another translator, was the Nobel Prize winner for Literature in 1978.

The Polish writer and poet of Lithuanian origin, Czeslaw Milosz, who lived in the United States for many years and translated his own work from Polish into English, received the Nobel Prize for Literature in 1980.

Joseph Brodsky, who in the USA translated many of his poems from Russian into English, was awarded the Nobel Prize for Literature in 1987.

It is true that neither James Joyce, Vladimir Nobokov, Julien Green, Chingiz Aitmatov, nor Karen Blixen or even Giuseppe Ungaretti, all self-translators, were ever distinguished by the Nobel Prize, but it is without question that they were equally if not more deserving of the prize than many of those honoured by the Swedish Academy. With or without the award, their names form an integral part of their national literature and often of the universal literature of the 20th century.

Aitmatov wrote in Kirghiz and Russian ("I write my books in Kirghiz and Russian: if a book is first written in Kirghiz, I translate it into Russian, and *vice versa*"); Vladimir Nabokov turned a large part of his work from Russian into English (or the reverse, as in the case of his novel *Lolita*); Julien Green went from French into English, Karen Blixen from Danish into English (and *vice versa*), Giuseppe Ungaretti from Italian into French; James Joyce translated part of *Finnegans Wake* into Italian (two large parts from the chapter "Anna Livia Plurabelle").

The seven Nobel Prize winners mentioned above, together with those the Swedish Academy forgot, should be enough to show that translations done by the author himself deserve more attention than they are actually given either by Descriptive Translation Studies or in the actual history of translation.

It has been said (and repeatedly, which is worse) that self-translations are *exceptions* (Berman 1984, Balliu 2001), that they are *infrequent in universal literature* (Elvira 2001), that they are *rarissimes dans le domaine littéraire* (Balliu 2001), that they are *rare enough* (Sylvester 1963), that they are *few, very few indeed* (Grady Miller 1999, Helena Tanqueiro 2000) and even that they are *borderline cases*, and *abnormal or special phenomena* (Kálmán 1993). In 1989 Steven Conner described self-translation as a *strange phenomenon* and in 1993 Miguel Sáenz spoke of the self-translator as *an odd creature*.

I totally disagree with such critics, considering the fact that the English poet John Donne translated his own work into a second language, as did the philosopher Baruch Spinoza, the Italian playwright Carlo Goldini, the poet Gabriele D´Annunzio, and the poet and film director Pier Paolo Pasolini, to quote just five names.

In Spain, names like the Marquis of Villena, Nebrija, Luis de León, Arias Montano, Sánchez de las Brozas, Feijoo, Francisco Martínez de la Rosa, Ramiro de Maeztu, Salvador de Madariaga and Alvaro Cunqueiro, to name just a few, fill the history of our literature with self-translations.

This is the same cross-linguistic (and cross-cultural) journey on which hundreds of Catalan, Basque, Asturian and Galician authors have nowadays embarked, all self-translators into Spanish and at times into French. In Galicia, it is enough to mention such names as Manuel Rivas, Alfredo Conde, Suso de Toro or the recently deceased Carlos Casares; in Catalonia, Pere Gimferrer, Quim Monzó, Carme Riera, Valentí Puig or Antoni Marí; and in the Basque Country, Bernardo Atxaga[1] or Felipe Juaristi. It is not

---

1. *Vide:* http://www.unesco.org/courier/2000_04/uk/doss14.htm): "Basque writer leaps into translation: Interview by Lucía Iglesias Kuntz, UNESCO Courier journalist". In reply to the question "You're completely bilingual: why do you always write first in Euskera?", Atxaga replied: "In literary terms, I'm used to thinking in Euskera. My stories or poems come to me in Euskera. It's my first personal language, the one I use to jot down ideas in my notebooks,

surprising, then, that the Scottish poet and novelist Christopher Whyte pointed out just a few years ago that "indeed, self-translation is a much more widespread phenomenon than one might think" (2002: 64).

After hearing the above, highly summarised, list of authors, from John Donne to Samuel Beckett and from Goldoni to Luis de León, imagine how one feels when you have to read opinions like those of Sisir Kumar Das, Professor at the University of Delhi and President of the Indian Association of Comparative Literature, who has absolutely no idea of "the state of the art", but wrote in absolutely categorical terms that "Undoubtedly he (Rabindranath Tagore) is the only major writer in the literary history of any country who has decided to translate his own works to reach a larger audience". One is tempted to ask Sisir Kumar Das: "What do the names of Thomas More, John Donne, Andrew Marvell or Joachim Du Bellay mean to you? Or Leonardo Bruni and Cardinal Bembo, as well as those previously mentioned, all of whom translated their own work into another language?

However that may be, at one time or another all self-translators come up against the special problem of transferring to another language and culture what belongs to and is sometimes exclusive to the language and culture in which their texts were first written. But there is an essential difference between them and myself or any other translator, because the stamp of identity that distinguishes them from other translators is the freedom they enjoy when working with their own texts.

Surprised by the changes the Catalan novelist Carme Riera made to her translations into Spanish, Kathleen M.Glenn (1999:47) questioned her and Riera answered: "I don´t know. If another person were translating my work, that person would have to be faithful to the original, but when I translate my own work..."

Quite possibly the answer resides in those three dots of the unfinished sentence. Of course, self-translation may or may not be translation. The author-translator works on his/her second piece of writing with an optional freedom of action not permitted to translators of work that is not their own ("something denied to versions made by other translators"), but a freedom that can be exercised without any sort of hang-ups, as Talât Sait Halman,

---

whether I'm in Stockholm or Madrid. I've become used to doing that. It's not much to do with ideology, it's just the way I work. Some writers need to go into a monastery and stay there for a few months without setting foot outside. My writing ritual involves writing first in Basque. I've come to the conclusion that it isn't very important..."

who translates his own Turkish poems into English, confesses: "With one's own poems, there is also the splendid advantage of doing new and quite different versions. After all, one is not constrained by the duty of remaining faithful to the original composed by someone else. Translating your own work provides the best kind of freedom..."[2].

The Canadian novelist Nancy Huston recalls how Air Canada asked her for an article for the airline bilingual French-English magazine. She accepted and wrote the article in French. "They told me that they loved the article and asked me if I could translate it (into English) myself... So, they paid me twice, once for the article and again for the translation. I took a lot of liberty with the translation, more than I would have allowed another (translator)" (Shread 1998: 249).

In 1952, Josep Palau i Fabre published a clandestine edition in Catalan of his book *Poemes de l'alquimista*. Over twenty years later, in the mid-seventies, the publishers Plaza and Janés asked the author for a bilingual edition of his work, in Catalan and Spanish, which meant that the poems had to be translated into this latter language. Palau i Fabre recalled (1979:13) that:

> Faced with the job of finding a translator, I spent a long time procrastinating. In whose hands would I place this offspring of mine, fruit of my innermost soul and efforts... Perhaps, perceiving the upsets and stumbling that this self-sacrificing task could cause me if it were put in the hands of another, my friend Montserrat persuaded me to take on the task myself... The problem of translation suddenly presented itself on quite different terms to what I had experienced before. Translating myself was not like translating another poet, however close I felt to him. My area of work was a lot more relaxed...*I could...allow myself to interpret—a liberty of movement—that I would never have dared take with another poet.*

This is rewriting, then, in freedom, quite different from what the translator does chained to another person's work. In 1582, Bernardino Gómez Miedes published a biography of Jaime I of Aragón in Latin (*De vita et rebus gestis Jacobi primi, regis Aragonum*). Two years later his own translation came out in Spanish with the title *Historia del muy alto e invencible rey don Iayme de Aragon, primero deste nombre,* in the prologue of which the author wrote:

---

2. "The Mad Nomad: Interview with Talât Sait Halman". Interview by Gönül Pultar. In: http://www.bilkent.edu.tr/jast/Number5/Pultar /html

...Not only did I dare to translate, but also to add and take away, to redo and improve what with greater clarity and truth was offered to me renewed by history, after the Latin edition came out. It is just as well that the actual author has more freedom (which would be denied to any other interpreter), a more than poetic licence (Mestre 1990:265-266).

And around the same time, towards the end of the 16th century, one of our most famous grammarians and teachers, Pedro Simón Abril explained the reasons for the distance that separates author and translator[3]:

> Translating what others have said is very different from translating your own words, because in your own text you can cut out words to fit the style of the sentences. But in the translation of the writing of others from one language to another, the words do not always come as readily as the interpreter would wish.

This is where the whole difference lies: whoever translates their own work "makes it their own", goes back to editing their own text "in a form and style" which, the second time round, they think is best. In effect, time has passed since the first text was done: this means that the author has a new perspective—given by time—and that there will be new readers, but above all that the cultural milieu in which the new edition appears will now be different. And he is the sole author of both texts, which he could freely alter for a second or third edition. Rabindranath Tagore, for example, clearly warns his readers that in his English versions he modified "not only the style of the original, but also the imagery and the tone of the lyric, not to mention the language register which is made to match the target-language poetics of Edwardian English" (Sengupta 1995: 57).

This method of "translation in freedom", so different and distant from that of the other type of translator, is evident in all areas of self-translation, but particularly in cultural aspects which are no longer subject to scandalized criticism regarding accuracy and are changed around with tiresome frequency, adapted or even quite simply removed by the author who is concerned about a new public and a different culture. It is not surprising then, that the text becomes "another text", after all the swaps, changes, adaptations, substitutions and omissions, in short the work of a translator in freedom. With such varied and different casuistry in this area, I take the liberty of choosing, by way of illustration, a few examples from thousands of possible ones.

---

3. "Prólogo del intérprete al lector", in the translation of the *Ethics* by Aristotle, Madrid: Real Academia de Ciencias Morales y Políticas, 1908, p. 21.

Carme Riera wrote *Contra l'amor en companya i altres relats* in Catalan and shortly after she translated the work into Spanish, *Contra el amor en compañía y otros relatos* (Barcelona: Destino 1991). Regarding the Spanish version Luisa Cotoner commented (2004:165):

> [In the Spanish translation] Catalan names and characters are transformed into those which could be their equivalents in the sphere of Spanish culture. Perhaps the most successful one would be the adaptation done in [the story] "La novel.la experimental" [The novel and the experimental], in which references to the world of Catalan literature are swapped for those of the Spanish world. In this way, the main character of the Spanish version does not refer to Espriu [as in the Catalan], but to Cervantes. "Premi Prudenci Bertrana" changes to the "[Premio] Planeta" and also "el germà de la cunyada d'en Ricard Masó" changes to "el hermano de la cuñada de la mujer de Lara", etc.

In 1997, Jordi Vintró published in Barcelona *Insuficiencia mitral*, a long poem presented in bilingual form, Catalan-Spanish, on facing pages. On the cover it states: "Translation to Spanish by the author himself". Jordi Vintró has not actually translated the poem, according to the standard concept of the term, but rather, he has quite consciously poured the Catalan version into new mould of Spanish culture, thus transforming all those elements in the original that belong to Catalan culture and might seem strange or unfamiliar to a Spanish reader. Therefore, where the Catalan original mentions towns and places which are well known in Catalonia, such as Vulpellac, Cuixà, the Bulloses or Carlit in the Eastern part of the Pyrenees, in the translated version, at the same point, the reader will find Alfaro, Burgos, Vivar and Quintanilla, Vallecas, Vigo and Valencia. Also, while in the original Catalan version there is a reference to the *sardana* called *Els degotalls*, in the Spanish translation the reference has been changed to the popular song *La Dolores*. While the first text speaks of the youth magazine *En Patufet*, the second text refers to the youth comic *Jaimito*. Similarly, *Saló del Tinell* changes to *El Escorial*, and *la Rambla* to *la callé de Alcalá*. One of the verses reads in Catalan: "i corren més que els comtes pel Mogrony", and in Spanish "y corren más que el Cid con sus sayones"; another verse: "quan passa per Canet i per Sant Pol" transforms into "cuando pasa por Pinto y Ciempozuelos"... If another translator had done that to Vintró's poem, I cannot imagine what sort of criticism and censorship would have fallen on him, including that of the shocked and angry author. But, as Carme Riera pointed out, "when I translate my own work..."

The term *paíño* is not at all common in Spanish and perhaps for that reason it does not even appear in the best known lexical compilations.

However, it is a common word in ornithological texts, where you can easily find the names of the distinct varieties of the bird: *paíño comun* (storm petrel), *paíño de Wilson*, *paíño pechialbo* (white faced storm petrel), *paíño Leach*, etc. Manuel Rivas wrote a story in Galician about emigration which he called "*A man dos paínos*" (Vigo: Xerais 2000), it was published initially in Spanish as a series of six chapters in *El País*, with the literal title *La mano de los paíños* (The hand of the storm petrels). When the Spanish version was published in 2002 as a book (Madrid: Santillana), the title chosen by the author was now slightly different: *La mano del emigrante* (The hand of the emigrant). This is probably because, as in the previous case, the use of the term "paíño" was "meaningless" for the majority of readers in the target language and culture.

In Adoración Elvira Rodríguez's excellent analysis of the self-translation into French of *Un pájaro quemado vivo / Un oiseau brûlé vif* (1984) by Agustín Gómez Arcos, there are many examples, always in context and well explained, of such transferences of a cultural type. The novel is set in Spain during the fifties and sixties, and it logically develops in the sort of socio-cultural background where the *Fiat 600*, *Anís de Chinchón*, *Lagarto soap*, the *ABC* newspaper, the *18th July Bonus Pay* or the *Social Security* all form an essential part. The public media (they were all official at the time) made continual references to the *Régime*, to the anthem *Cara al Sol* and to the *National Crusade*... What would all that mean to a Frenchman in the mid-eighties? Having eliminated, as inappropriate in a novel, the option of a forest of explanatory footnotes, the French text began to spawn obvious semantic non-equivalents inspired directly by the culture of the new reading public. Consequently, the bargain price "*seiscientos (Fiat 600)*" becomes "*sa petite voiture utilitaire*" or "*sa petite bagnole d'ocassion*", *Lagarto soap* becomes "*savon de Marseille*", the Catalan cured meat becomes "*charcuterie française*", the *Cara al Sol* changes to "*L'Hymne de la Phalange*" and *anís de Chinchón* becomes "*anisette maison*". The *Regime* and the *National Crusade* lose their sharp characteristic connotative outline and become "*les pouvoirs publics*" and in "*la guerre*". The French text also avoids making any direct allusion to the "*Seguro*" (Social Security contributions) or the "*Paga*" (Extra pay) of the 18th of July...

It is well known that the playwright Fernando Arrabal co-translates his work with his wife Luce Moreau, without defining very clearly the parts they have each worked on. In the play *Picnic* the Spanish text goes: "He hecho una tortilla de patatas que tanto te gusta" (I have made the potato omelette you like so much), a "tortilla" being quite typical of Spanish country cuisine. This would be normal in a Spanish text and perfectly understandable for a reader or audience from the Peninsula. During the process of translating the play into French, Arrabal wrote his wife a note in the margin which said: "Luce, put in a typical French dish like those they eat when they go to the countryside." And so the Spanish omelette did disappear from the French text, replaced by something more typically French (in cultural terms): "Du saucisson, des oeufs durs, tu aimes tellement ça"[4].

Sometimes ("language is part of a culture", Vermeer 2000: 222), it is the actual use of language that comes marked by particular "signs of cultural identity", signs which are less clear and explicit than the previous ones, and therefore less evident. They are hidden in the nature of language, and in it they take on a cultural identity. Geographical dialects and diatopic variations, word games and colloquial or sub-standard uses of language reveal important signs of identity which are not only linguistic, but are also cultural, buried down at the roots of the actual nature of language, so that both the translator and the self-translator are confronted by serious problems, sometimes unsolvable, and at times they may even end up in—as an inevitable final solution—the voluntary suppression of a fragment of text.

The use of diminutive suffixes, for example, is not the same, nor comparable in Galician and in Spanish, even though there is an evident linguistic proximity between both languages. Being much more common in Galician, above all in oral registers, they take on a connotative dimension which is rarely to be found in similar Spanish forms. In such cases, the Galician-Spanish self-translator wavers indecisively between different textual solutions, sometimes imitating the forms in the target language, at other times deleting them, with the inevitable loss —admittedly—that this implies. Observe, for example, Manuel Rivas's method in *A man dos paíños* (Vigo: Xerais 2000), translated into Spanish by the author with the title *La mano del emigrante* (Madrid: Santillana 2002):

— ... como se estiveses alí, con aquela *xentiña* mareada, no embarcadoiro (pp. 23-24)
— ... como si estuvieses en el lugar, con aquella *gente* mareada, en el embarcadero (p. 30)
— Viñan bretóns en bicicleta, *cargadiños* de cebolas en ristras (p. 28)
— Venían bretones en bicicleta, *cargadísimos* de ristras de cebollas (p. 35)

---

4. *Pic-nic*, Madrid: Cátedra, 1983 (6th ed.), p. 132.

— Puxéronche pezas *noviñas* no carro, incluída a chavella (p. 36)
— Te pusieron piezas *nuevas* en todo el carro, incluida la clavija del timón (p. 44)

— Pasa e senta, dixo ela, que me vou compoñer un pouco. É un *minutiño* (p. 41)
— Pasa y siéntate, dijo ella, que voy a arreglarme un poco. Es un *minuto* (p. 49)

— Atopáraa Albino na praia de Sabón, *tiradiña* na area (p. 44)
— La encontró Albino en la playa de Sabón, *tirada* por el mar (p. 53)

— O primeiro que se lle entendeu, moi *clariño*, era Tito, Tito (p. 52)
— Lo primero que se le entendió, muy *claro*, era Tito, Tito (p. 61)

These are examples that become more numerous throughout the work and that the reader will also find repeated in the versions by Conde, De Toro or Cunqueiro[5]).

Even so, this freedom in the work does not make it any easier. The self-translator is free to manipulate his text, but that does not mean that it is any easier for him to translate the elements which are culturally marked than it would be for another translator. It is not difficult to agree with the remarks made by the Puerto Rican novelist Rosario Ferré with which I began this text: *"Translating has taught me that it is ultimately impossible to transcribe one cultural identity into another"* (1991: 157). The author herself describes (there are few who do) a particular case of cultural and linguistic "difficulty" she found when translating her story *Maldito amor* into English, and the reasons why she radically changed the title in the new language to *Sweet Diamond Dust*. I cannot resist including here her actual words (ibid.: 159-160), as they are so explicit:

> As I began to translate my novel, *Maldito Amor*..., the first serious obstacle I encountered was the title. "Maldito amor" in Spanish is an idiomatic expression which is impossible to render accurately in English. It is love that is halfway between doomed and damned, and thus participates in both without being either. The fact that the adjective "maldito", furthermore, is placed before the noun "amor", gives it an exclamative nature which is very present to Spanish speakers, in spite of the fact that the exclamation point is

---

5. On Alvaro Cunqueiro, *vid* the study by Rexina Rodríguez Vega "A tendencia á hipercorrección do escritor bilingüe: O caso das autotraduccións ó castelán de Alvaro Cunqueiro", in: http://www.ctv. es/USERS/mforca/Critica/Rexina/a_tendencia_hipercorreccin_do.htm

missing. "Maldito amor" is something very different from "Amor maldito", which would clearly have the connotation of "devilish love". The title of the novel in Spanish is, in this sense, almost a benign form of swearing, or of complaining about the treacherous nature of love. In addition to all this, the title is also the title of a very famous danza written by Juan Morell Campos, Puerto Rico's most gifted composer in the nineteenth century, which describes in its verses the paradisiacal existence of the island's bourgeoisie at the time. As this complicated wordplay would have been totally lost in English, as well as the cultural reference to a musical composition which is only well known on the island, I decided to change the title altogether in my translation of the novel, substituting the much more specific *Sweet Diamond Dust*. The new title refers to the sugar produced by the De Lavalle family, but it also touches on the dangers of a sugar which, like diamond dust, poisons those who sweeten their lives with it (1991: 159-160).

As author of the two texts, the original in Spanish and the English version, "I decided—she says—to change the title altogether in my translation of the novel", certainly because the more direct and immediate Spanish title was not going to "work" adequately in the new culture and for the new public for which the English translation was destined.

This was not by a long stretch the only "obstacle" which Rosario Ferré would encounter with the English version, nor was it the only one that she had to overcome. Nor has she been the only one to have built up such experiences in the course of her writing life.

The novelist Nancy Huston, who has lived in Paris for many years, recalled her own experience in this respect in an interview with Carolyn Shread (1998: 247-248)

I wrote a very crazy text called *Limbo* where I talk about Beckett... It's filled with word play, because a lot of Beckett, much more than is usually studied, is based on expressions, manners of speaking and figures of speech. I wanted it to be totally in English: it's not a successful piece. Then I tried to translate it into French, contrary to everything I had promised myself, and it indeed did not work at all, at all, at all in French, the meaning just withered away, disappeared because I had to choose between sound and sense, whichever I chose half of it was gone, and there was nothing left, just total incoherence and chaos, and that was really frightening to me, terribly frightening.

The Brazilian writer João Ubaldo Ribeiro published his novel *Viva o povo brasileiro!* (Lagoa: Nova Fronteira) in 1984. Five years later, Harper and Row of New York published the English version of the work translated by the author with a completely different title: *An Invincible Memory*. What reasons could justify such a radical change? Luis Angélico da Costa tried to give them (1996:184), without completely succeeding, and ended up admitting a fact which is eminently cultural, for although the direct translation of the title is possible, it "would be absolutely meaningless in the English language".

> O título da versâo inglesa é longe do virtuosismo de síntesi histórica, visâo satírica e sofisticaçâo narrativa do original brasileiro, uma típica tirada de marketing editorial bem ao gosto americano. Nâo deve ter sido invençâo ou opçâo do autor-tradutor do original: ele apenas provavelmente concordou. Afinal, a traduçâo ipsis litteris, de plena correspondência formal como a do título da versâo francesa, seria absolutamente inexpressiva em língua inglesa.

Not without a certain amount of humour, Ribeiro recalled the odysseys of two of his self-translations into English, *Sargento Getúlio* and *Viva o povo brasileiro!*:

> The first novel I worked on was *Sergeant Getúlio*, which, written in dialect, is hard to understand even for Brazilians. The hapless American translator to whom this torture was assigned couldn't avoid doing a terrible job on the first thirty pages, after which he gave up. They sent it back to me, and because it was my first publication outside Brazil, because I was young and had illusions, I volunteered to do the translation. It was an ordeal I swore I would never go through again.
> But my agent arranged for me to go to New York, where he then lived, and proceeded to convince me that my new book [*Viva o povo brasileiro!*] (a bricksized monster, written in all kinds of "sub-languages") would be all but murdered by any translator other than myself. I was properly flattered, but stood my ground. Never, I said. So he ordered two bottles of Scotch, saying he had to drink to forget my foolhardy decision—and I joined him, and two hours later, reciting parts of Byron's *Don Juan* and believing myself to be the full equal of Dickens, I signed the contract that he had been hiding in an envelope under one of the bottles.
> It took me longer to translate the book than to write it: almost two years of hard labor and gnashing of teeth, during which I honestly thought I would never finish, and had suicidal fantasies. There were, first of all, problems of a cultural nature. Generally speaking, people in England and the United States know as much about Brazil as about traffic conditions in Kuala Lumpur. They are very much astonished to find out that we speak Portuguese, not Spanish, and that some of us wash, have teeth, wear clothes and live in houses. So should I suffocate the book with hundreds of footnotes, making it longer than the New York telephone directory? I decided I wouldn't. That involved a little cheating here and there —with knowledge of the publishers, I hasten to add...

The major decision made, I set out to tackle, one by one, the ever-multiplying problems of any translation, some of which caught me off-guard. Forms of address, for instance. It is impossible to duplicate the formality, even pomposity, of Portuguese forms of address. In English there is not much besides "you", as everyone knows... And what of the profanities, obscenities, curse words and assorted racial slurs with which Portuguese is so opulently endowed, making foul-mouthed English sound virginal in comparison? Again an impossible mission... And there were the popular names for fish, some of which do not even exist in English... And plants, fruits and trees entirely unknown in the Northern Hemisphere, except by specialists, who call them by tongue-twisting taxonomic nicknames... And the many poems, of all sorts, including parodies. Sometimes I managed to get the rhymes and puns, but at other times this was utterly unachievable... I did promise myself I will never do it again...

Among the many cases in which the author threw in the towel when translating his work is that of the Indian novelist Agyeya (Ajneya, Ajñeya). Initially he published his novel *Antara* (1975) in Hindi. Nine years later, in 1984, he published it again, but this time in his own English translation, with the title *Preparing the Ground* (New Delhi: Abhinav). In the prologue the author writes: "*Preparing the Ground* is not ... a complete translation of *Antara*: a number of passages had to be omitted. No principle of selection was involved: the passages were simply untranslatable..." Untranslatable for reasons concerning its cultural content.

For one reason or another, the truth is that a text translated this way becomes, as Miguel Saenz claims (1993:113), "a new work, distinct from the original, a translation which no independent translator would dare to have done, creating the phenomenon of a work which, in reality, has not been translated, but actually has two versions".

***

Self-translation, then, is and is not translation. It is, above all, translation with the freedom of an author to reconstruct a second version of the original. "The writer self-translator*"* wrote Zarema Kumakhova (1999) "is a unique phenomenon with the ultimate license most translators do not have". The Canadian writer Nicole Brossard (2001) also wrote: "Bien sûr, quand je me traduis moi-même, je peux tricher parce que c'est mon texte, et ainsi ce qui devrait être une traduction devient une sorte de transcréation, de transformation". So, rather than "transcribing", or making transferences or transcriptions from one cultural identity to another, self-translators tend to settle for a less strident arrangement, in which—the traditional concept of equivalence aside—there is no grating of the target language and culture.

That is, of course, when this can be achieved, because—as has already been seen—even they often do not bring this off.

Under the supposed rules for translation, the solutions that a self-translator adds to the transference of a specific cultural identity may or may not be correct, equivalent or acceptable. But the truth is that they are indisputable, because both texts, the original and the translation, have the same signature and the translated text is subject to the same authority and creative licence out of which the original emerged. This is precisely the difference and is what makes self-translation such an interesting phenomenon, however much it has been forgotten up till now by Translation Studies. It is not just my opinion. Years ago, Brian T. Fitch wrote: "Direct discussion or even mention of self-translation is virtually non-existent in writings on theory of translation" (1988: 21). Even in 1997, you could still read in the *Dictionary of Translation Studies*, by Mark Shuttleworth and Moira Cowie (p. 13): "Little work has been done on autotranslation". Rainier Grutman also wrote in successive editions (1998, 2000 and 2001) of the *Encyclopedia of Translation Studies*: "Translation scholars themselves have paid little attention to the phenomenon" (2001: 17).

Perhaps the time has now come to pay more attention to this, to work in this field so scarcely exploited, particularly in that area where translation and cultural identity converge and overlap. It is quite possible that the fruit of such work could help change to some extent present-day points of view on translation. And it is quite possible, moreover, as Shuttleworth and Cowie state, that an in-depth study of the phenomenon of the self-translator would allow us to investigate and ascertain "the nature of bilingualism and the relationship between language, thought and personality" (1997: 13). One hopes this will be so.

References

Balliu, Christian. 2001. "Les traducteurs: ces médecins légistes du texte". *Meta* XLVI.1: 92-102.

Berman, Antoine. 1984. *L'Épreuve de l'étranger: Culture et traduction dans l'Allemagne romantique*. Paris: Gallimard. English edition: *The Experience of the Foreign: Culture and Translation in Romantic Germany*. New York: State Univ. of New York Press. 1992 (translated by S. Hayvaert).

Brossard, Nicole. 2001. http://www.doublechange.com/issue2 /brossardfr.htm

Cotoner, Luisa. 2004. "Ética y estética de la autotraducción: Una cala en las versiones al castellano de Joseph Pla, Joan Perucho y Carme Riera". In *Panorama actual de la investigación en traducción e interpretación*. Ed. Emilio Ortega Arjonilla. Granada: Atrio. 2nd ed. III. 159-167.

Da Costa, Luiz Angélico. 1996. "João Ubaldo Ribeiro, tradutor de si mesmo". In *Anais do V Encontro Nacional de Tradutores / Proceedings of the V Brazilian Translators' Forum*. Eds. John Milton *et al.* São Paulo: Humanitas Publicações. 181-190.

Das, Sisir Kumar. 1994. *The English Writings of Rabindranath Tagore I: Poems*. New Delhi: Sahitya Akademi.

Elvira Rodríguez, Adoración. 2001. "Un caso de traducción perfecta, o cuando el traductor es el propio autor". In *Traducción literaria: Algunas experiencias*. Eds. José Antonio Sabio and José Ruiz. Granada: Comares. 47-70.

Félix Fernández, Leandro. 2002. "El papel de la cultura en el proceso traslativo y en la formación del traductor". In *Traducción y cultura: El reto de la transferencia cultural*. Eds. Isabel Cómitre Narváez and Mercedes Martín Cinto. Málaga: Libros Encasa. 51-90.

Ferré, Rosario. 1991. "On Destiny, Language and Translation; or, Orphelia [sic] Adrift in the C. and O. Canal". In *Papeles de Pandora: The Youngest Doll*. Lincoln, Nebraska: Univ. of Nebraska Press. 153-165.

Fitch, Brian T. 1988. *Beckett and Babel: An Investigation into the Status of the Bilingual Work*. Toronto: Univ. of Toronto Press.

Glenn, Kathleen M. 1999. "Conversation with Carme Riera". In *Moveable Margins: The Narrative Art of Carme Riera*. Eds. M. Glenn Kathleen *et al*. London: Associated University Presses. 39-57.

Gruen, Erich S. 1993. "Presidential Address". *Transactions of the American Philological Association* 123: 1-14.

Grutman, Rainier. 2001. "Auto-translation". In *Routledge Encyclopedia of Translation Studies*. Ed. Mona Baker. London and New York: Routledge.

Kálmán, György C. 1993. "Some Border Cases of Translation". In *Translation in the Development of Literatures: Proceedings fo the XIth Congress of the International Comparative Literature Association*. Eds. José Lambert and André Lefevere. Bern: Peter Lang/Leuven: Leuven University Press. 69-72.

Kumakhova, Zarema. 1999. http://aasteel.org/program/aasteel/1999/abstract-utf8-198.html

Mestre, José María. 1990. *El Humanismo alcañizano del siglo XVI: Textos y estudios de latín renacentista*. Cádiz: Universidad de Cádiz.

Miller, Grady. 1999. "The Author as Translator". *ATA Spanish Language Division: Selected Spanish-Related Presentations*. St. Louis, Missouri: ATA 40th Annual Conference. 11-17.

Mooney, Sinéad. 2002. Review of: Michaël Oustinoff's *Bilingualisme d'écriture et autotraduction* (2001). *Translation and Literature* [Edinburgh Univ. Press] 11.2: 288-292.
Palau i Fabre, Josep. 1979. *Poemas del alquimista*. Barcelona: Plaza y Janés.
Sáenz, Miguel. 1993. "Autor y traductor". *Senez* 14: 103-118.
Sengupta, Mahasweta. 1995. "Translation, Colonialism and Poetics: Rabindranath Tagore in Two Worlds". In *Translation, History and Culture*. Eds. Susan Bassnett and André Lefevere. London and New York: Cassell. 56-63.
Shread, Carolyn. 1998. "Interview: Nancy Huston". *Sites: The Journal of 20th-Century Contemporary French Studies* [Storrs, Connecticut: Univ. of Connecticut] 2.2: 247-248.
Shuttleworth, Mark and Moira Cowie. 1997. *Dictionary of Translation Studies*. Manchester, UK: St Jerome Publishing.
Sylvester, Richard S. Ed.. 1963. *The Complete Works of St. Thomas More. Vol. 2. The History of King Richard III*. New Haven, CT and London: Yale University Press [Introduction to Vol. 2].
Tanqueiro, Helena. 2000. "Self-Translation as an Extreme Case of the Author-Translator-Dialectic". In *Investigating Translation: Selected Papers from the 4th International Congress on Translation (Barcelona 1998)*. Eds. Beeby Allison *et al.* Amsterdam-Philadelphia: John Benjamins.
Vermeer, Hans J. 2000. "Skopos and Commission in Translational Action". In *The Translation Studies Reader*. Ed. Lawrence Venuti. London: Routledge. 221-232.
Whyte, Christopher. 2002. "Against Self-Translation". *Translation and Literature* [Edinburgh Univ. Press] 11.1 (Spring): 64-71.

CHAPTER TWO

THE LANGUAGES OF TRANSLATION
KEYS TO THE DYNAMICS OF CULTURE

JOSÉ LAMBERT

Quot capita, tot sensus...

Among the traditional difficulties in any (scholarly) discourse on "translation" in any cultural environment, one has to take into consideration the exact position and goals of the speaker. The ambiguity connected with translation is heavily influenced by the fact that (what is usually called) "translation" is always a combination of several kinds (traditions) of verbal communication. By definition, several relevant statements may apply to the object of study, but most of these statements are only partly relevant: they cannot be a sufficient basis for any fundamental explanation, certainly not in scholarly terms. At this point, the idea of multiperspectivism would seem to be particularly apt, but multiperspectivism is probably not the answer that scholars tend to accept as a global explanation since it seems to imply that the entire and the full truth can be discovered if at least the various possible perspectives are envisaged: they seem to complete each other. In the case of interdisciplinarity, this is not really sure: sociological, medical explanations may be incompatible with psychological (legal) ones, etc. Interdisciplinarity certainly tends to become a priority in research, and universities tend to stress it, at least in theory. But is it really more unproblematic than multiperspectivism?

Such difficulties are the more embarrassing when the hypothetical speaker refers to the tradition of the various scholarly disciplines that may be involved, since most of these disciplines focus on particular components of the translation phenomenon rather than on "translation" in its (linguistic, cultural...) complexity. The most obvious illustration of this—almost inevitably—reductionist perspective is the traditional dilemma of linguistic *versus* literary approaches to translation (cf. Lambert 2005). Doubts are not cast on the merits of Vinay and Darbelnet, Mounin, Catford, Nida, Neubert, Koller and so many other linguists who have started theorizing on the translation phenomenon, nor on the merits of the many scholars from the literary field(s)—and this was (and often is) the reason why so many colleagues assume more or less that all comments on translation can only belong to literary studies, or to linguistics, or to both of them, and only to them. The rich bibliography of translation through the ages demonstrates how religious, political, legal, and social insights are also needed when it comes to analyzing the dynamics of translating at any given cultural moment, in any given cultural/social situation. And the state of the art of disciplines such as linguistics or literary studies will never be the ideal or sufficient instrument for the analysis of such complexities: in linguistics as well as in literary studies, the focus is on the linguistic/literary components, not really on translation. This is even more clearly reflected in most handbooks of linguistics and literary theory: "translation" is hardly recognized as one of the central items in the introduction to the discipline. Hence only interdisciplinarity can provide Translation Studies with the open spectrum needed for the interpretation of translated verbal communication.

Even within this new discipline called "translation studies" (since around the end of the 1960's, but not everywhere[1]), the awareness of this need for interdisciplinarity has not been fully developed, to put it mildly. As Toury (and a few others, after him) has demonstrated, most translation theories refer to an ideal(istic) view of translation rather than to actual (historical) translation phenomena (Toury 1980). For many years, most books on translation were concerned with what translations should look (sound) like, which was to offer a far from realistic future for translation, and a "normative" one at that. From the point of view of research and scholarship, the issue can never be what our objects of study should look like, but rather: what they in fact look like, and how we can account for this. And such distinctions appear to be indispensable from the moment a given discipline— e.g. research on translation—claims to be conscious of its goals, its range, its priorities: training translators is one thing (and it does not make much sense to train the translators from the past), while analyzing actual translation phenomena as cultural activities or documents is a very different issue.

---

1 There is no doubt about the origins of the concept of "translation studies", which was discussed since the 1960s in the work and activities of James S. Holmes (Holmes 1972); and Gideon Toury left no doubt about the continuity between Holmes' concepts and his own—much more explicit—views on (Descriptive) Translation Studies (Toury 1980; Toury 1995; http://www.tau.ac.il/~toury/), while working out the (first) program of a new (inter)discipline. One of the key issues in the shift from the first translation theories into the definition of an academic (inter)discipline was the distinction between "training" and the various components of translation research: "translatologie" (in French) and "translatology" (in English) or even the Skopos-theory oriented "Translationswissenschaft" tend to insist much less on such distinctions (translation practices, translation training, academic research on translation from various scholarly perspectives).

How homogeneous are cultural shifts?

But it is true that due to cultural dynamics—according to many recent surveys—new challenges are facing translation scholars and translation scholarship. There are no arguments for explaining them neither in terms of language nor in terms of literature. It seems that our contemporary world makes use of translations firstly under various names and labels (this has always been the case), and/but secondly also in a more and more collective and international way, as part of the internationalization movement. Is it really true that in our modern world of translation everything is "different" nowadays—or is it rather naive to imagine that anything related to translation would suddenly change in radical terms, after so many centuries (Snell-Hornby 2006; Lambert 2007)[2]?

It was almost predictable that the internationalization of societies worldwide, which obviously started long before the 20th century and which has continued to accelerate since World War II, was going to affect the function and position of translation. This may be easy to confirm in statistical terms[3], though the comparison of statistics from different moments and ages is a delicate enterprise. In sociological terms, a few indicators do confirm, however, that translation has become part of the organizational task of international activities: almost all multinational organizations (the European Union, the United Nations, UNESCO, to mention a few), including almost all the nations on our globe, have an impressive number of translators and interpreters among their crew—and the network of "language services" has recently expanded into e.g. "community interpreting" and "localization". There can be no international communication any more, not even within the world of the so-called global English, without this institutionalization of "translation" (as we shall call it here, for pragmatic reasons): but in this case institutionalization often happens to be worked out behind the curtain. What's in a name? More is at

---

2 The chapter on Globalization in Snell-Hornby 2006 has been discussed several times before the book was published. In one of the debates, Peter Newmark wonders why, after all, after so many centuries, translation would happen to change at all...(See http://zif.spz.tu-darmstadt.de/jg-08-2-3/beitrag/Newmark1.htm).
3 One of the interesting developments in Translation Studies from the last 10 years was the expansion of a sociology-oriented approach, partly under the impact of a team around Pierre Bourdieu (G. Shapiro, P. Casanova, J. Heilbron, etc.). They systematically make use of bibliographical statistics, which until say 2000 was an underdeveloped area of the discipline. On the other hand, they tend to ignore linguistic, discursive and textual trends that were central in TS since the mid-70s.

stake than the question of names (translation, dubbing, voice over, localization, language services, technical writing, etc.) or the question of recognition. Does translation continue to be the same thing for ever? The public organization of modern societies provides us with explicit answers that are very different from previous ages (Cronin 2003; Snell-Hornby 2006; Pym 2004; Lambert 2007).

The very basic rules of translation activities and translated communication seem to move rapidly into new "paradigms". Or maybe these rules have never stopped changing, they have never been (fully) static—and nowadays they are submitted to new waves of changes, which may have technology and globalization as a common denominator (Lambert 2007): translations are less and less in the hands of individual translators, they are more and more planned as part of international networking by individuals or groups of people (or enterprises and other institutions) as part of the ongoing international/multinational/global circulation of discourses. And they are part of this uninterrupted and hard-to-identify international discourse—as on the Internet—either as fragments or as fully imported and transferred discourses to the extent that it is more and more difficult to establish which texts/utterances have NOT been translated, the most fundamental change being the shift from the more bilateral mobility of communication into the multilateral mobility of communication: a large percentage of our contemporary translations are the result of parallel operations between more than two languages, whereas most (but not all) translations from the past happened to take place between two languages. At least as far as we know. If this is a correct theoretical assumption about communication(s) worldwide, the consequences for languages and for the language(s) of translation are supposed to be considerable.

Whatever our feelings may be about internationalization or globalization, it would be quite mistaken to envisage it as an exclusively contemporary phenomenon. In fact it is due to the (rather recent) impact of the nation-state model (since say romanticism) that we have been struck with blindness: business communities and religious communities extended their ramifications through the ages and countries centuries before any "national" communities were in view. The cultural changes are not exclusively in the object, they may also be in the eye; they teach us as much about the observer as about the observed.

Trends underlying shifts

According to Walter Ong's well-known book (Ong 1982), the question of communities ("What kind of communities? What kind of rules do they obey, e.g. in terms of communication? And to what extent is this a matter of technology?") has a lot to do with technology. And so does the question of languages. But how this set of questions and concepts really applies to translated language, or rather: to translated discourse—was not part of his discussion.

In both ancient and in contemporary societies, it may be assumed that the more communication becomes collective, and the more it becomes long distance communication (since the age of print, since the age of telephones and media, then since societies can be virtual), the more it depends on organization, or planning—or management, as we would call it nowadays. Organization Theory and Management Theory have recently developed into new disciplines, somewhere in between (social) psychology, economics, sociology, etc. For very understandable reasons, most of these disciplines ("for social research"?) focus on contemporary situations, on questions related to "How to do things?" rather than on "the past". The use of "actual data" in view of solutions to be formulated is, generally speaking, linked with the analysis of "actual phenomena and situations", but the historical/historiographical perspectives are certainly not the central focus of these disciplines. Which implies that the connections between say linguistics or translation studies, and certainly literary studies, are not simple at all. The fact is that the more a translated communication/discourse is a collective and organized—or institutionalized—activity, the more insights about "management" are needed and relevant, whether concerning past or present or future situations.

In our contemporary international societies, the international circulation of discourse(s) comes within the competence of managers (general managers, or more specifically, communication managers; translation managers are still largely unknown). They (have to) decide about the use of one (or more) languages, about the necessity to translate or about the use of a given *lingua franca*, about the budgets that will (not) be spent, about the possible enrolment of interpreters and about the necessity to use in-house translating rather than external teams: it is not the simplest aspect of their job, hence they often abandon it to lower level colleagues (and decisions). And in fact it is not one of the privileges of contemporary managers, since "multilingual communication"—like multilateral communication—is not new at all in the history of mankind. But it is only in recent years that "management", "business studies" etc. have been professionalized, which implies that the discovery of new fields of competence, of research and training belong—only—to the recent history of Higher Education. But since a few basic questions from management and organization competence may be applied very well to situations within cultures at any moment, including the past—and since they may provide us with relevant methodological and theoretical tools for our understanding of communication, languages, discourse(s), translation, etc.—the idea of management and organization enriches our scholarly programs, whether in relation to ancient or modern times.

Communication and people: translations don't drop down from Heaven

One of the assumptions underlying this discussion is the idea that, due to given views on the language phenomenon, or rather, due to the fact that translation has mainly been envisaged as a language phenomenon of a particular kind, basic components of the translation phenomenon have been underestimated or even ignored. One of the shortcomings of the widespread view on language(s)—among intellectuals and even among scholars, including many linguists—is linked with the idea that languages are territory based, if not nation-based. Not many linguists have explicitly supported such (static) ideas about language, not even that many translation theoreticians. But their institutional power, their infrastructure depend on other structures and people where the geographical and the nation-state oriented concepts, partly because of money and power reasons, stress the links between territory and culture. Many subareas of linguistics are affected by such priorities, and the survival of the language pair based research on translation indicates how strong the confidence is still put on the idea of "neighbors" and how the mobility of languages as well as the interplay between languages, or the interlinguistic dominance of particular languages within large cultural frameworks have been influential through the ages.

It is the mobility of languages and communication through the ages, across linguistic, cultural and political borderlines, that has been sacrificed to a nation-state oriented view on linguistic communities, even when applied to the middle ages and much older cultures. Two one-sided and contradictory—and anachronistic—views on culture and society are at stake: the Western nation-state idea of societies, cultural identity, language, etc. (Hobsbawm 1990, 1996) which has projected modern concepts on prenational centuries from the past; and on the other hand the influence of the modern idea of mobility, which is booming in the age of electronic communication. It would be naive to overemphasize the birth of 20th century views on communication while accepting that languages and communication have been mobile through the ages, that communication has always transcended geographical and political frontiers, but it would also be disastrous to ignore them and to overlook their consequences for the continuous redefinitions of cultures and societies (as has happened in historiographical panoramas and debates on periodization etc.).

In recent years scholarly debates have tended to reschedule time and space through the ages in relation with the dynamics of languages, translation, communication (Hobsbawm 1990; Ong 1982; Lambert 1997; Pym 1997; Kittel 2004). The difficulty has partly been solved already by some simple historiographical revisions: the development of language families (Romance languages, Germanic Languages, etc. etc.), i.e. the substratum of language families through the ages and territories, often in complex combinations, leaves no doubt about the, more or less limited, mobility of languages—which is also confirmed by the phenomenon of the *lingua(e) franca(e)*. There can be no doubt, on the other hand, about the role of people in the mobility of languages and communication: languages don't influence nor invade other languages without the intervention of people, individuals or collectivities (Hobsbawm 1990; Ong 1982; Pym 1998).

Whatever may have happened since the so-called cultural turn, some of the most crucial social questions in the area of research on translation appear to have been more or less ignored so far (see Resch *et al.* 2005; Steyaert *et al.* 2006; Hjorth *et al.* 2009). Such as:

— Who exactly decides (has decided) to make use of translation, or not to do so, in a given situation—whether past or present, in Western or other societies?

— Will this kind of discourse be given a particular name, will translated discourse be treated differently from "normal" (everyday) discourse in similar circumstances, e.g. by indicating that it is the result of "translation" (as is often the case with books), or will the identification of this different technique and organization be kept for insiders?

— And what will be the consequences of the overall decision process underlying the entire planning and execution of this communication/ message?

It is not strange at all that there should be shifts in communication, in societies, in language and in the use of languages, hence in translation and in the use of translations. Translation is supposed to be dependent on current trends in the use of languages, and (or) on current trends in translation norms and standards; it is worth mentioning also that languages—as discourse— are also submitted to trends, they are not static. And the borderlines between linguistic trends and trends in translation tend not to be clear at all, as any text distributed by the European Union (or on the Internet) may show: which texts are NOT the result of translation?

It is not beyond the bounds of possibility that at given moments translation (translated sentences, technical terms or even mistakes) may be the origin rather than the result of shifts in the "surrounding" areas. Many legal documents tend to sound like "foreign" texts... In terms of research, the ambiguity may be that priorities are not given once and for all: revolutions in language may be brought about by political processes (such as revolutions) or by social ones (such as migration). Changes, shifts, evolution and revision are important issues in scholarly debates, and they often lead into very divergent explanations. The truth about such matters, when formulated by scholarly disciplines, may be heavily dependent on institutional positions within academia—and much less on empirical research: the revision of religious texts, or children's literature, in various cultures and at various moments may have been conditioned by authors or great theoreticians (such as...Martin Luther!). In fact it is easy to assume that besides a few exceptional ones (Luther, German romanticism, the French *Belles Infidèles*...) such situations have hardly ever been studied, simply because the question of translation has hardly ever been recognized as a worthwhile topic for research in say theology, in children's literature, in literary studies, in law studies, in politics, etc. etc. In other words: the scholarly discourse on translation is as much dependent on norms and power as translation discourse as such. It is also a matter of norms and their institutionalization.

Almost half a century ago, Jiří Levý discussed translation as a "decision process" (Levý 1967). He was focusing on very specific components of the decision process, not on the component of the social/institutional organization. There can be no doubt however about the relevance of reconsidering decision processes in translation activities in a holistic way nor about the relevance of integrating the entire decision process into decision and management and organization—or into "social research".

Until say the 1970s (and often far beyond the 1980s), translation theories tended to use linguistics as an obvious framework, while locating the dynamics of translation between language pairs. Such a representation of translation has not fully disappeared, but it is far from being an obvious model any more. This is why a few translation scholars feel the need to support "a linguistic turn", after the "cultural turn" and after so many other turns listed e.g. in Snell-Hornby 2006[4]. The problem is whether these various approaches and turns exclude or rather strengthen and complete each other.

And this is why the goal of this essay is to revive dialogues between various scholarly traditions to propitiate a new and better interaction between disciplines. Recent and basic changes in our contemporary cultural landscapes have made urgent such programs for interaction. Not only is the responsibility of particular disciplines at stake, but also the responsibility of research institutions such as universities and research foundations, be they national or international.

One of the obvious reasons why it has become possible to re-examine the relationships between language(s) and translation(s) is the birth of computer linguistics, which is of course heavily indebted to new technological knowledge and resources. It has now become possible to indicate where, when, how (the use of) language in translation(s) is particular and/or different from non-translated discourse. Let us not say (yet) that it is simple, especially since the relevant technological programs for the interrogation of (translated) discourse depend most heavily on programs of questions to be worked out (and/or improved) by scholars. Hence time and efforts will be needed—and not just theories: it is a task for (Descriptive) Translation Studies, though corpus linguistics and its applications to translation, which have popped up at a later stage, need to be integrated. And interdisciplinary research is becoming more necessary than ever, as our discussion is supposed to illustrate.

Does the development of computer linguistics as well as corpus linguistics and their application to translated language/discourse mean that from now on questions and discussions on "the language of translation" have become superfluous?—Ay, there's the rub!—First of all because the answers given so far are not, and cannot be presented as final and global ones.—But also because there is probably not just ONE language of translation, there are always several possible ones, and some of the linguistic options tend to be(come) more successful than others. Why exactly a given option happens to be more successful than another one is also an open question that can be approached in several ways.

---

4   See Vandepitte *et al.* 2007.

Long before computer linguistics indicated how the exact relationships between translations and languages could be made transparent and even measurable in concrete cultural and linguistic situations, the conceptual formulations from the fifties and sixties had been re(de)fined in various subareas of translation studies. It is true that general translation theories and general theories of language, sociology, sociolinguistics, semiotics have not yet updated all their panoramas: the language of translation is a neglected area of study, in theoretical as well as in historical-cultural terms, for translation in general as well as for the unlimited number of subareas (business worlds, legislation, media, tourism, literature…)[5].

In the 1950s and 1960s—and (sometimes) until this very day—experts have assumed that translation is simply part of language: translating was supposed to be first of all an operation between (two) languages, which implied that translation was simply and unavoidably part of given language pairs. If the syllabi for translation training are anything to go by, our collective representation of translation has not radically changed: translation training is still heavily language-pair oriented.

In the meantime however, lots of developments in the field have shown that not all translations are simply formulated in the same kind of language, and certainly not in the same kind of discourse, be it written or spoken. Within Descriptive Translation Studies as defined by Toury (and probably far beyond), all translations appear to be the result of selections and options (priorities) on the basis of norms and models, hence also of exclusions: translation is never the result of static operations between pre-existing linguistic systems, it is rather the result of dynamic operations. And the selection/exclusion/priority patterns are by no means reduced to the so-called target language (English, French, Spanish or whatever): first of all because translators and their teams (and networks) often prefer NOT TO TRANSLATE and prefer "loan words" or NON-TRANSLATION to actual translation as such (Lambert 1995).

Since its very beginning in the *stylistique comparée* until today, translation theory has tried to deconstruct the translator's operations (devices) in microscopic terms with the aid of concepts such as—in French—*modulation, transformation, adaptation*, etc., while generally excluding the interplay between microscopic and macroscopic levels (e.g.

---

5   Legal translation has been recognized from the beginning as one of the subareas in Translation Studies, but it has been mainly integrated into translation training. In Olsen *et al.* 2009, however, legal translation is approached as an area of academic research.

as in the case of the particular vocabulary or register associated with given text genres, in TV discourse as well as in popular literature) and while generally reducing the translator's activity to its relation with "the original". In fact the best basis for the observation of the translator's language is not simply the linguistic operations, it can be captured much better in terms of rhetoric (*repetition, deletion, inversion, addition*, etc.), as was shown years ago (Van Gorp 1978). And on the microscopic level it is clear that any translation introduces items and models and hence languages from various angles into the newly constructed combination of linguistic and textual resources. On the basis of such concepts, Frederic Rener has analyzed several centuries of translation culture as a chapter in the European history of rhetoric (Rener 1989): it is hard to deny, since Rener's demonstration, that several languages may be heavily affected by parallel rhetorical options and that such options (which we may call traditional, in this case) are visible in translated discourse, but not exclusively at all in translated discourse. It is not made clear, so far—and it will never be easy to make clear—if and to what extent translations really influence the state of language, or whether they simply reflect it.

Due to historical discussions of large intercultural panoramas such as Rener's, the question of the relationships between languages and translation(s) could be approached with the aid of the following questions:

(1) What kind of linguistic options and priorities within a given language can be identified, or: what kind of a discourse is being produced by a given translator or by groups (generations?) of translators within a given (national) language?

(2) What kind of interlinguistic options and priorities can be identified, i.e. in the relationships between two or more languages, especially in the case of large (geographical, multicultural) translation movements, including indirect translation phenomena via a given *lingua franca* (e.g. the distribution of an international lexical jargon; the establishment of new colloquial styles as in the case of film dialogues or detective stories; the development of new stylistic repertoires as in email or sms correspondence)?

(3) Are such (normative) tendencies specific to translated discourse (within particular text genres, or within larger genre categories), or do they simply illustrate how translated discourse is subject to the same basic rules as everyday discourse in the same language? Diachronic tests might indicate the opposite, i.e. how everyday discourse is directly influenced by translations (and/or the *lingua*

franca), as in the case of legal terminology or electronic terminology (where international trends are manifest in many languages).

All these questions are part of both synchronic and diachronic frameworks and investigation, though (3) refers more explicitly to "the position" of translations within language(s) (as suggested years ago in Even-Zohar 1978). In none of these distinctions is it assumed that the historical-descriptive answers will/should be homogeneous or explicit within one given language or, even less, in several languages, but "the (more/less peripheral) position of translations" is an important cultural issue—not a strictly linguistic one. As has often been demonstrated in large historical projects[6], there are good chances that dominant linguistic options are structured in a particular way for different text genres or disciplines: academic or literary text genres might be very open to a given *lingua franca* (since quite a few years) whereas popular literature and media discourse might be permeated by another *lingua franca*. The distinction between more popular text genres and the more elite ones tends to refer to sociological parameters (as in the high vs. low distinction).

Are translators and their language that individual?

In the introduction to his remarkable book *Die literarische Übersetzung* (1969), Jiří Levý wrote that one of the common features of linguistic approaches to translation happened to be—at that moment – a certain blindness to the individual contribution of translators to the translation process (Levý 1969: 13-17). During the last fifty years, insights about the individual and the collective have certainly made quite some progress, e.g. due to the use of the *norms* concept, but many crucial areas between the individual, the collective and the institutional remain to be identified. In theoretical terms, but also and mainly in historical terms: how are various models and traditions competing at a given moment, not just in the Shakespeare or in the Dante translations, but also in the tradition of legislation, religions or in the media?

---

6   Let us refer to three particular projects, in a reverse chronological order, while also moving from larger into smaller space-and-time frameworks: the Göttinger Sonderforschungsbereich (Germany, 18th-19th century); the Leuven project (France, 1800-1850) and Gideon Toury's PhD thesis (Israel, 1976) —see our bibliographical references to work by Kittel (and the Göttinger Beiträge zur Internationalen Übersetzungsforschung), Lambert, D'hulst, Delabastita, etc. and by Toury.

Within every individual translation, the battle for the best formulation is going on from the beginning to the end, it is also part of the linguistic options, e.g. in terms of register or in terms of loan words (as in computer manuals, where the use of technical terms in English is a matter of diplomatic behavior, from the first to the last page). But also in terms of diachrony, especially in the case of canonized texts such as the Bible, the "Great Books" in world literature, or legal documents. And such battles are not reduced to particular subareas of the history of translation, they are also part of the dynamics of languages: no translations without language—but— no translations can be reduced to language(s)!

Notwithstanding the impact of computers on our contemporary intellectual activities, we are not yet able to identify—in scholarly terms— the individual author of a given text. Translators working in teamwork environments such as the media world tend to identify with simple reading techniques the name of their colleague who has subtitled a given movie on the TV screen[7]. In certain countries—and among many translators—the texts distributed by the European Union tend to be envisaged as the illustration of a collective "style": beyond the individual language of a large number of translators, a given collective "model" in the target language takes on a collective identity. And since such European Union texts are known as the products of translation, they are taken for prototypes of *translationese*[8], though it is difficult to explain their features as—indeed— (proto)typical of translations. Hence the following paradox: while the language of translation tends to respect the sensibility of experienced readers of the target language/discourse (it tends to be an *acceptable*, a conservative kind of discourse)—on the other hand it has a good chance of becoming the new standardized discourse in the same area (in case of success, it can become fashionable discourse due to *innovative* features). In environments open to international messages and languages, the language of translation has a good chance of becoming "the language" without being

---

7   In the case of subtitling, translators tend to be convinced that they can identify the translations produced by their partners. In Desmet 1989, it has been demonstrated how in a particular case of subtitling, linguistic (and/or discursive) categories allow for the identification of two different translators.
8   Among translators, "Translationese" (translatese, translatorese) is a well-known neologism that refers to strongly source-oriented translations, i.e. translations in which the source language remains very visible; it has been used since the origins of translation training handbooks; it has been considered to be "bad translation", since one of the rules was supposed to be: "A translation should not read like a translation".

further labeled as "translated" (computer manuals as well as legal translations are good examples, given their penetration into real life situations).

Let us distinguish between the synchronic and the diachronic perspective, and between the linguistic and the textual perception on the one hand vs. the socio-cultural perspective on the other hand: the translation techniques as well as the layout will have their impact on the reader's eye, but the same eye may become familiarized—a few months or years later?—with imported terminology and unidiomatic expressions, and gradually find them acceptable. They may become the norm. But only diachrony and usage (or power and success) will favor the final decision.

Just like good readers of literary works, experts familiar with a given individual translator may be able to provide a repertoire of idiosyncratic options in the work of their favorite translators. And it may not be utopian to expect that corpus linguistics will soon provide us with a few spectacular cases of individual styles selected from among the best-known translators. The fact is that disciplines that focus on linguistic, textual, and discursive questions (from linguistics and literary studies to sociology and communication studies) tend to swing between the very individual (and microscopic) and the very general options (on the level of "language"), while leaving entirely open the field of collective behaviors and traditions (such as "slang" or typical genre features).

The translator's language(s)

Between 1950 and say 1975, most translation theories displayed translation schemes as a binary kind of communication between (mainly) two languages and cultures in which the individual translator and his habits were hardly taken into consideration. And the two (?) languages at stake were in most cases (except e.g. in Catford 1965 and in Levý 1969) taken as obvious—and rather static—phenomena. During the last three decades this view on "language" has been systematically refined, but not always in a theoretically explicit way. It is probably due to the "cultural turn" that (1) other components than (just) language (first of all: "norms") have been taken into consideration and that (2) the idea of "language" has been submitted to new distinctions and differentiations. In these new and less mechanical concepts, the idea that individual translators may have a few distinctive features and options in their texts is simply one of the most explicit hypotheses about the fact that translations are never just (merely) "translations into a given target language", they are the result of selections, priorities and combinations between (more) individual and (more) collective options within a given language and sometimes also between more than one language—often also between more than one preexistent textual example ("model").

It is (more and more) assumed that translations are also produced between texts and discourses, in networks of intertextual relations which become stronger due to networking processes, even long before computers were at work—and of course also due to the profile of individuals and groups. This is why the question whether translations produced by female translators can be identified makes sense. It will be a much more delicate enterprise to establish to what extent individual translators share particular components of their style—in their vocabulary, or in their terminology—with their colleagues.

It is not difficult to recognize among these questions several well-known *topoi* from the history of (linguistic) stylistics such as: "How can we analyze an impressionist's style?" There can be no doubt about the possibility of testing out such questions and hypotheses. One of the difficulties in the analysis of the translator's language with the aid of corpus linguistics is the distance between oral and written, or between dialect and language. The analysis with the aid of computers of messages/texts, be they oral or written, does not simply involve the object of study—the corpus—on the one hand, and the "language" on the other hand—it depends on the tools worked out by experts in order to "interrogate" the corpus on the basis of a list of parameters which can be called "a program" or "a model". Individual speakers and writers as well as translators tend to be aware of the individual features of their own speech (discourse); they know more or less that their "words" or "speech" (their "parole", as Saussure would call it) has quite a few (very?) individual features. And linguists who need to interrogate texts realize in principle that the "parole" which they analyze can never coincide with the "langue", hence they depend on their intermediary model that is supposed to position the corpus within larger textual frameworks.

Translators themselves are supposed to be more or less (!) aware of the paradoxes underlying their own devices and priorities: their text is supposed to replace another text, in another language, which they generally simulate to ignore, except in bilingual editions, subtitles, etc. (*the translator's paradox*); and their translation contains a proliferation of similar paradoxes from the beginning to the end, e.g. when rewriting

Shakespeare in alexandrine verse, or when representing a Frenchman in colloquial English dialogues. Notwithstanding their confidence in their own mastery of languages, notwithstanding their confidence in computers and their electronic dictionaries, translators realize how many roads are open to them in their own translations. They are aware of the translators' paradoxes and their variations when moving from French texts on cricket games into English academic dialogues, into American business or into computer guides. They realize that in specific domains the "jargon" of translators (and international journalists)—in touristic reports about contemporary China—or about New York—is easier to tolerate than in the case of political speeches. The traditional name given by experts to the translator's jargon is familiar among (experienced) translators, who try to avoid it as much as possible: it is called "translationese", sometimes also *macaronic language*.

One of the confirmations of the conflictive and—even—functional signification of "translationese" is linked to the selection of translators and to the source/target conflict in many cultures: in standard situations, native speakers are supposed to be the best translators. They ought to know about the target audience and their discursive habits. They are less needed, less unavoidable, however, from the moment technical and (exotic) cultural expertise are highly needed, as in the case of opera texts, arts exhibitions, tourism or scientific matters. The tolerance towards "foreign translators" happens indeed to be much higher in technical subareas (computer language, sports, etc.) than in the everyday newspaper. The translation concept always tends to be treacherous. "Translating" never appears to be "translating—simply—into a national and standard language", it always implies specific options within the various corners of the standard (national) language in which lawyers, priests, professors, soccer players, novelists recognize their partners and their expertise. Mistakes against the conventional rules which keep changing together with the canon are much worse than grammatical mistakes: in stock market operations grammar is not the issue, nor even language; terminological mistakes, however, tend to fully compromise the intended communication (e.g. in contracts), often also the translator.

The traditional formulation "Translating from Language 1 into Language 2" offers a superficial and mechanical idea of translating: professional translators realise that they need to establish how exactly in the given circumstances Language 1 and Language 2 are made use of, they know it is a matter of *discourse* (or usage), a matter of routines and even predictability. This is exactly where the various kinds of computer supported translation (whatever the terminology may be) have redefined translation: in their vocabulary, in their idiomatic expressions and in their metaphors or even in their use of text genres, experienced translators go for consistent options in which previous translations or previous texts in the same language may function as examples (or models); they try to select from historical options in canonical texts, translated or "original" ones (quoted as examples in dictionaries, or in computers which are used as repertoires) and when feeling the need to innovate, they select their solutions in harmony with these repertoires.

In many situations it may be a matter of meeting the standards of specific audiences, whose discursive traditions might also be the object of computer analysis: not only may translated discourse have specific features, but the language may also be used by particular subgroups within the target languages. Legal texts translated into Dutch or into French may be meant either for Dutch or Flemish audiences—in the first case—or for audiences in Switzerland, in France, in Canada—in the second case. Just like religious texts, which often also happen to be translations, they have become part of the people's memory, and it is a delicate enterprise to revise people's memory.

"Translating from Language 1 into Language 2" reflects a mechanical view on discourse, not only because many options are open within the two languages under consideration, including neologisms—but also because the options are not limited to two languages: a given *lingua franca* may provide solutions (they tend to be visible), and a third language is often used either as an occasional support or as the real "original" which has been preferred to the official references in Language 1 and Language 2 (as can be illustrated by business life, by the EU, by international bestsellers). Just like the European tradition of rhetoric has provided translators with international ready-made models, the *Übersetzungen aus zweiter Hand* (*Second Hand Translations*) have supported (German and other) translators in their exploration of foreign cultures, quite often on the basis of French translations[9]. Translation manuals and translation training often exclude third language options as well as innovations from their concept of translation. It is often assumed that they belong to past centuries, and that our contemporary age works with honest and even scientific concepts, but

---

9   As has been demonstrated e.g. in the work around Jürgen von Stackelberg (Wilhelm Gräber, Geneviève Roche), and in the history of European Shakespeare translations.

it is not difficult to demonstrate that localization and the Internet actually intensify the use of international languages and text models.

Our traditional views on "Language 1" and "Language 2" also happen to produce difficulties in relation with more/less regional cultures and their linguistic identities. Flemish translators of French texts happen to be in trouble with French concepts and idiomatics when addressing Dutch target groups since Holland has adopted/ integrated many French words and expressions, but not at all the same ones as Flanders; and the same applies to English in these contacts between neighbor languages (interferences between English and Dutch in Dutch translations from French produced by Flemish translators). Due to pronunciation habits, Flemish interpreters working for Dutch audiences (or Austrian ones working for German audiences) are even more in trouble than Flemish translators of written texts, especially in the case of French words or in the case of "non-translation" (Lambert 1995). Flemish speakers who want to sell computer programs to French and French-Belgian audiences have experienced how strange "le logiciel" sounds for their French speaking countrymen, who are less scared by "le franglais" than French citizens and who simply correct their partners: "*Ah bon! le software vous voulez dire!*" One single word may betray the "foreign" roots of the speaker/writer, even in cases where his linguistic repertoire is superior to the repertoire of his audience: his discourse simply reveals that he does not belong to the same group. Francophone readers outside of France (e.g. Flemish francophones) often happen to dislike translators who write "too well", who go for the academic (and *hypercorrect)* discourse: they all know very well that "septante" is equivalent to "soixante-dix", but their partners are not supposed to use one instead of the other at the wrong moment.

What is at stake here is the use of intermediary languages that interfere with the source and target language: local (regional) ones, or very international ones, or even their combination. Indirect translation has always been part of translation history, in almost all cultures: French has often been used as the model for the formulation of international texts, as Shakespeare translations as well as legal texts or gastronomic terminology may confirm; nowadays, English tends to fulfill the same function. Translating legal texts from German into Dutch, for a Belgian audience, will almost certainly imply the systematic use of a terminology whose French origins would never suit readers from Holland: excellent translators with an excellent mastery of the Dutch language, when crossing cross the Dutch-Belgian border in one direction or in the other, will face problems with their audience from the moment they need French or English loan words.

In the world of translators, dialects have traditionally been supposed to be a technical problem. They are also a new problem of modern societies, since the impact of standard languages has become clear only in recent times; moreover, they are being supported by the power of governments. The truth is that linguists and linguistics are in trouble with their definition of language as soon as the idea of dialect pops up: are languages supposed to be those dialects that have become "langue"? Or are they those dialects that happened to have an army as well as canons? For the entire history of mankind previous to the nation-state the idea of a monolingual culture as well as the idea of dialects made no sense. The very idea of language as a national institution is a rather recent—and very Western—phenomenon (Anderson 1993; Hobsbawm 1990). And sociolinguistics also makes it obvious that in our contemporary societies monolingualism is an academic (or nationalistic) idea.

Between communities

One of the most manifest symptoms of the flexibility of the translator's languages has indeed a lot to do with the "nationalization" of languages: centuries after the vernacularization of language(s) in Europe (in the transition between the dominance of Latin and the new European languages), most nation-states have developed and institutionalized their national languages, which explains that the United Nations recognize more or less 200 languages whereas linguists list around 7000 ones (De Swaan 2001). Notwithstanding the impact of nations around the world on the development of languages, political borderlines are and have always been a treacherous key to linguistic borders: the heroes and advocates of the French Revolution had to translate the *Déclaration des Droits de l'Homme* into many dialects because a large percentage of the new French citizens did not really understand the French language; in modern times the romantic idea of "One Population, One Language" is fully irrelevant in Africa and even largely irrelevant in Asia. Notwithstanding the impressive contemporary mobility of communication, translation is often complicated by linguistic barriers: the interplay between Holland and Flanders has been examined in previous paragraphs, and it is not an isolated case; the Portuguese and the Spanish translation market function separately from the Latin-American one; and even English is an issue for division; notwithstanding its prestige as the international *lingua franca*, English translations have no chance to be successful when the source culture and the target culture belong to different corners of our planet.

The differentiation of geographical-cultural maps that might render the world of translations more transparent looks like a utopian task, except in limited and specific areas, because there are no common rules for one and the same "linguistic territory": on the Internet, English may justify more or less its global claims, as long as it has been produced by British or North-American (?) citizens; but texts about soccer ("football"?) or about cricket, newspaper reports and almost all screen based (translated) communication are limited in their global flexibility. Media translation, notwithstanding its key role in globalization, has only a limited range on the world map, except for those channels that have conquered a position in the daily world news. And it is almost utopian to transfer translations and translation services from one country to the other as soon as legal matters are involved: in an environment where bilingual and multilingual speakers are ubiquitous, the EU systematically avoids interferences between citizenships and languages while reducing the activities of its translators to the country that they represent (including the Russian spoken by citizens from the Baltic states).

It has been established recently, at least in explicit theoretical terms, that "the language(s) of literature" never simply coincide(s) with a given language as such, that there are—inevitably—various options / models in the construction of literary worlds by individuals and by collectivities (Boyden *et al.* 2007). In a recent thesis about the Belgian francophone tradition, one of the central insights is that a given literary-cultural program claimed to construct literary values as a set of linguistic and cultural values with the aid of translations borrowed from their Flemish-Belgian neighbors (Meylaerts 2004): translated discourse was intended to become the model of the French language to be used in Belgium. And this could only be worked out by having recourse to a particular type of French: translated French was supposed to become a/the new language. This model itself has not been successful (it has even been rejected, and not many francophone Belgian citizens have any awareness of it), except for a limited period and in a particular environment: it has been rejected by the dominant groups within the environment where it was generated. Which implies that, at least in this case, both translation and literary production are the output of collective (even political) combinations of selections and exclusions, hence of models in the use of language (as discourse). But in the same time-and-space conditions, Belgian translators of the national Constitution adopted quite different principles, and disseminated (?) francophone lexical and syntactic structures as the only possible canon of the Flemish constitutional counterpart.

In very different circumstances, intellectuals from 20th century Burundi have accepted their Constitution in the translation from Belgian-French models (produced by Belgian missionaries) into their own Kirundi language as the basis for their everyday legislation: this occurred exactly around 1960, in the years of their decolonization. Notwithstanding the very exotic features of their national legislation, which was not really accessible to the literate elite, they have got used to the translated legislation and have recognized it as their own legal discourse (Bigirimana 2009). The idiosyncratic language of translation has become the language of their Constitution; hence it has become part of their canonized national language.

Due to translation, languages may change, even in the middle of the 20th century. In a given cultural, political and even linguistic environment, translation can make use of very different languages or linguistic models: such solutions happen to be rejected (as in the literary French-Belgian case) or accepted (as in the legal Burundi case).

The kind of translations we need

The mobility of communication may have become impressive in recent decades and the mobility of *messages* is obviously much more remarkable than the mobility of *languages*. Anyway, the mobility of translations as well as the mobility of the language of translation is more complex and more limited than the mobility of multilingual communication. Through the ages, mobility has been one of the determining factors of translation since the Tower of Babel. Through the ages, given communities have borrowed their canonical texts and messages and discourses and stylistic conventions from external traditions, with the aid of translations or other procedures. External traditions do not necessarily come from neighboring territories, they may come from far away (as in the case with English nowadays, for so many populations) or even inside the country (as in the case of Russian in Israel at a given moment). Messages, texts and entire text traditions have migrated, but the stability of languages has not really been disturbed. What exactly may account for the selection and decision processes is a matter of power and organization, though not necessarily of political power in its traditional meaning. It happens however that, through the ages and cultures, certain societies have little by little assimilated a neighbor language, due to a long period of cohabitation: during the 19th and 20th centuries, until say 1970, the Flemish part of Belgium did not always need the translation of French texts, except for political reasons and little by little, whereas the French population was not able to understand the textual traditions coming from Flanders; one of the results of the Belgian language and translation policy is that, nowadays, translation has become compulsory, but also necessary. Translation has been a factor in the linguistic separation of different linguistic communities (Meylaerts 2004).

Academic / international communities:

Universities are among the most complex areas in the mobility of communication, simply because their linguistic borderlines have not (really) coincided with the political ones. One of the strange confirmations of this irregularity deserves to be investigated by translation studies. The incredible paradox is that universities have no clear memory of their translations, nor do they keep record of their translation activities. The link with the *lingua franca* solution to communication may be an interesting answer to the lack of academic translations: in various cultural situations, *lingua franca* and translation happen to be complementary, hence they follow different roads into intercultural communication. Universities and scholarly worlds are indeed indicative of the linguistic stratification that conditions translation as intercultural communication.

The contemporary academic world, in particular, is indeed a privileged area for investigation about language and discourse priorities, including translation and interpreting. It is the more remarkable since it represents traditional structures (the universities of Bologna, Sorbonne, Cambridge, Leuven, Prague are centuries old) that have been woven into modern networks. Their international communication policy, under the impact of American and British institutions as well as part of the international search for excellence, has opted in a spectacular way for English as the international language, whatever the various language policies may be in the different home countries. In order to get recognition within the Internet and the Google or Wikipedia eLearning networks, universities worldwide adopt English as their international language, and they even organize translation services into (good) English in order to improve their international ranking.

Academic publications translated into the English *lingua franca* are another remarkable illustration of the strategic use of translations as a road into national and international canonization. The planning, the people involved and the language policy underlying these activities have hardly anything to do with the various national language policies in the countries involved. In many cases an international (more or less English speaking) population is in charge of these activities. And the translation of publications organized by universities is parallel to the production of the Internet websites where English is the almost unavoidable language next to the national language and other widely spoken languages. The general motif, anyway, is that the language of translation promotes multilingualism of a new kind, i.e. as part of globalization.

Getting access to new worlds is also one of the underlying principles in international advertising. In Western Europe, posters can be offered in several languages, but English is one of the very common options. In such cases, the chances are very high that non-translation is the key. But advertising in English as well as advertising in the local language(s)—for foreign companies—may be largely relying on translation. And in both options the organizational power is linked with internationalization.

Precisely, one of the motor forces in the contemporary multilayeredness of translation is internationalization: it is one of the channels into new worlds. Long before universities and academic worlds were invaded by the waves of internationalization, the media world made use of translations—not in a very traditional way, but largely through a combination of techniques—and languages—that were embedded in promotional strategies. The development of dubbing (Danan 1994) and subtitling (Gambier 1996) is one of the symptomatic moments in the dynamics of translation, but also in the dynamics of languages. So far, historians of languages have not really explored the ways in which both have functioned, in different languages, as one of the laboratories of the new discourse; politicians and linguists have rather considered them as— and reduced them to (?)—one of the safeguards of standardization. Because it has always been obvious that film was a privileged channel in the (international) innovation of discourse, and internationalization is interpreted as a threat to national values.

In the movie world of the 1930s, a political and economic struggle took place between the French "dubbing" and the American model of the "film en versions multiples" (Danan 1994); smaller countries (Israel, Belgium, Czecoslovakia, Scandinavian countries) opted for subtitling, i.e. for bilingual translation, whereas most bigger (and stronger) countries adopted dubbing. There is no doubt about the nationalistic and protectionistic strategy in France (Danan 1994), but modern historiography has not yet started investigating the ideological backgrounds of the European media languages. The development of the television and video empires has generated several other new techniques, such as *voice over*, etc. (Franco 2000). One of the interesting explanations of the distinction between the various options is the dilemma between the so-called *overt* and *covert* translations (i.e. more/less visible translations: more or less "translationese" oriented translations), or between *domestication* and *foreignization* (Venuti): many cultures want to have access to both the original speech and to the translation into their own language; others prefer being kept in the illusion that the imported movie really "talks" their own languages (the illusionistic option).

The proliferation of new translation techniques via film and television screens maintained a more or less visible frontier between imported (foreign) and local (national) communication. One of the symptomatic changes in the general approach to translated discourse, in the age of the Internet, is the more and more pervasive option for a systematic infiltration of the local media channels with the aid of international (and imported) discourse: in the thousands and thousands of Internet pages, or in the documents distributed by the EU, it is hard to establish which has NOT been translated. What kind of a language do these (translated?) channels provide?

A major function of contemporary media is indeed the integration of translated discourse into the everyday menu: be it through dubbing, subtitling, voice over, or via other techniques (such as the systematic integration of quotations—in translation—in the newspapers and other news reports). The overall offer of written and audiovisual media reflects the international world of *globalization* to the extent that we have the feeling that we are reading the same world news in various languages. The various games around the terminology applied to localization, dubbing, technical writing, etc. all are submitted to general commercial strategies of the illusionistic kind in which the idea of globalization is made more or less invisible but pervasive. Newspapers, television and video may still indicate the borderlines between translated and "original" speech. But on the Internet, nothing is less clear than the answer to the question: "What has NOT been translated?"

And this is where the languages of translation show their real power. Within the European Union, all public messages are made available in two dozens of languages: the public discourse of the European Union coincides in fact with the total amount of translated messages. In this case, the languages of translation are (almost) the only language. Such situations may appear to be typical of our times. However, one may also wonder which (limited) part of our national Constitutions, which part of our canonical religious texts is NOT the result of translation: the pervasiveness of translation within our languages has started long ago, but it was limited to particular areas and social groups. And the same applies to the transfer of legal and religious texts down through the ages, in various layers and in different styles. If language is really one of the substrates of power, translation cannot be ignored as one of the building blocks of societies. Experts in management are entitled to insist on the question: who are the owners, who are the architects, the workers, the inhabitants? Which languages do they speak or write? Which modes of translation do they use or promote?

And while the idea is quite relevant that translation plays a key role in the development of languages and literatures down through the ages, scholars may wonder why their own discourse on translation has so systematically ignored translation at work in the construction, not just of languages and literatures, but of societies.

Bibliography

Anderson, Benedict. 1993 (1983). *Imagined Communities*. London and New York: Verso.
Bigirimana, Jean-Baptiste. 2009. "Translation as a Dynamic Model in the Development of the Burundi Constitution(s)." In *Translation Issues in Language and Law*. Eds. Frances Olsen, Alexander Lorz and Dieter Stein. London and New York: Palgrave Macmillan. 193-212.
Boyden, Michael, José Lambert and Reine Meylaerts. 2007. "La Langue de la littérature: l'institutionalisation des lettres par le biais du discours." In *Plus Oultre. Mélanges offerts à Daniel-Henri Pageaux*. Ed. Sobhi Habchi. Paris: L'Harmattan. 455-470.
Catford, J.C. 1965. *A Linguistic Theory of Translation*. London: Oxford University Press.
Cronin, Michael. 2003. *Translation and Globalization*. London and New York: Routledge.
Danan, Martine. 1994. *From nationalism to globalization. France's challenges to Hollywood's hegemony*. PhD thesis Michigan Technology University.
Delabastita, Dirk, and Lieven D'hulst. Eds. 1993. *European Shakespeares. Shakespeare Translations in the Romantic Age*. Amsterdam and Philadelphia: John Benjamins.

Delabastita, Dirk, and Lieven D'hulst and Reine Meylaerts. Eds. 2006. *Functional Approaches to Culture and Translation. Selected Papers by José Lambert.* (Benjamins Translation Library 69). Amsterdam and Philadelphia: Benjamins.
Desmet, Marleen. 1989. *Le sous-titrage comme probleme de traduction: Ganz unten (J. Gfrörer et G. Wallraff) et ses sous-titres néerlandais et français.* MA. KULeuven, Romance Philology.
Franco, Eliana Paes Cardoso. 2000. *Revoicing the alien in documentaries: cultural agency, norms and the translation of audiovisual reality.* PhD thesis. KU Leuven.
Gambier, Yves. Ed. 1996. *Les Transferts linguistiques dans les médias audiovisuels.* Villeneuve d'Ascq: Presses Universitaires de Septentrion.
Hjorth, Daniel and Chris Steyaert. Eds. 2009. *The Politics and Aesthetics of Entrepreneurship: a Fourth Movements in Entrepreneurship Book.* Cheltenham UK: Edward Elgar Publishing Ltd.
Hobsbawm, Eric J. 1990. *Nations and Nationalism since 1780: Programme, Myth, Reality.* Cambridge and New York: Cambridge University Press.
Holmes, James S. 1972. "The Name and Nature of Translation Studies" (Preprint). Amsterdam: University of Amsterdam, Department of General Literary Studies.
— José Lambert and Raymond van den Broeck. Eds. 1978. *Literature and Translation. New Perspectives in Literary Studies.* Leuven: Acco.
Kittel, Harald, Armin Paul Frank, Norbert Greiner, Theo Hermans, Werner Koller, José Lambert and Fritz Paul. Eds. 2004. *Übersetzung— Translation—Traduction. Ein Internationales Handbuch zur Übersetzungsforschung. An International Encyclopedia of Translation Studies. Encyclopédie internationale de la recherche sur la traduction.* (Handbücher zur Sprach- und Kommunikationswissenschaft). Berlin and New York: de Gruyter.
Lambert, José. 1995. "Van de nul-vertaling tot het niet-vertalen. Nog eens een andere kijk op vertaalbaarheid en op de vertaalproblematiek." In *Letterlijkheid, woordelijkheid. Literary Verbality.* Ed. Henri Bloemen *et al.* Antwerpen and Hermelen: Fantom. 167-177.
— 1996. "Language and Translation as Management Problems: A New Task for Education." In *Teaching Translation and Interpreting 3.* Ed. Cay Dollerup and Vibeke Appel. Amsterdam and Philadelphia: John Benjamins. 271-293.
— 2004. *"La Traduction dans les société monolingues."* Kittel *et al.* I. 69-85.
— 2005. "Is Translation Studies too Literary?" *Génesis. Revista cientifica do ISAI. Tradução e Interpretação* 5-20.

Lambert, José. 2007a. "Translation and Globalization." Kittel *et al.* II. 1680-1700.
— 2007b. "The Language of University and the Idea of Language Management: Before and Beyond National Languages. A Position Paper". In *European Networking and Learning for the Future. The EuroPace Approach*. Eds. Annemie Boonen and Wim Van Petegem. Antwerpen and Apeldoorn: Garant. 198-215.
— 2009. "The Status and Position of Legal Translation: a Chapter in the Discursive Construction of Societies." In *Language and Law: Key Perspectives*. Eds. Frances Olsen, Alexander Lorz and Dieter Stein. New York: Palgrave/Macmillan. 76-95.
Levý, Jiří, 1967. "Translation as a decision process." In *To Honor Roman Jakobson*. The Hague: Mouton. II. 1171-1182.
— 1969. *Die literarische übersetzung. Theorie einer Kunstgattung.* Frankfurt a.M.: Athenäum.
Meylaerts, Reine. 2004. *L'aventure flamande de la Revue belge: langues, littératures et cultures dans l'entre-deux-guerres*. Bruxelles: Archives et Musée de la Littérature/Peter Lang.
Olsen, Frances, Alexander Lorz, and Dieter Stein. Eds. 2009. *Translation Issues in Language and Law.* London and New York: Palgrave/MacMillan.
Ong, Walter. 1982. *Orality and Literacy. The Technologizing of the Word.* London and New York: Routledge.
Pym, Anthony, 1992. *Translation and Text Transfer. An Essay on the Principles of Intercultural Communication*. Frankfurt/Main: Peter Lang.
— 2004a. "The Use of Translation in international organizations." In Kittel *et al*. 69-85.
— 2004b. *The Moving Text: Localization, Translation and Distribution.* (Benjamins Translation Library 49). Amsterdam and Philadelphia: Benjamins.
Rener, Frederick, 1989. *Interpretatio: Language and Translation from Cicero to Tytler.* Amsterdam: Rodopi.
Resch, Doerte, Pascal Dey, Annette Kluge, and Chris Steyaert. Eds. 2005. *Organisationspsychologie als Dialog*. Lengerich: Pabst Publishers.
Sapiro, Gisèle. Ed. 2008. *Translatio. Le Marché de la traduction en France à l'heure de la mondialisation*. Paris: CNRS.
Snell-Hornby, Mary, 2006. *The Turns of Translation Studies*. (Benjamins Translation Library 66). Amsterdam and Philadelphia: Benjamins.
Stackelberg, Jürgen von, 1984. *Übersetzungen aus zweiter Hand. Rezeptionsvorgänge in der europäischen Literatur vom 14. Bis zum 18. Jahrhundert*. Berlin: de Gruyter.

Toury, Gideon, 1980. *In Search of A Theory of Translation*. Tel Aviv: Porter Institute for Semiotics and Poetics.
— 1995. *Descriptive Translation Studies and Beyond*. (Benjamins Translation Library 4). Amsterdam and Philadelphia: Benjamins.
Vandeweghe, Willy, Sonja Vandepitte, and Marc Van de Velde. Eds. 2007. *The Study of Language and Translation, BJL, Belgian Journal of Linguistics*. Amsterdam: John Benjamins Publishing Company.
Van Gorp, Hendrik. 1978. "La traduction littéraire parmi les autres métatextes." In *Literature and Translation. New Perspectives in Literary Studies*. Eds. James S. Holmes, José Lambert and Raymond van den Broeck. Leuven: Acco. 101-116.

Websites
- http://www.tau.ac.il/~toury/ (Gideon Toury).
- http://www.tinet.cat/~apym/ (Anthony Pym).
- http://www.tau.ac.il/~itamarez/ (Itamar Even-Zohar).

CHAPTER THREE

LINGUISTIC PREFERENCES IN TRANSLATION FROM ENGLISH INTO SPANISH: A CASE OF "MISSING IDENTITY"?[1]

ROSA RABADÁN

Introduction

The idea that identity is inscribed in language practices and that linguistic preferences reflect identity issues in discourse is far from new. Recent scholarship hosts concepts such as domestication, foreignization, cannibalism, visibility, the status of translation etc. and focuses on the processes suffered by texts in their encounter with the target language readership (among others Venuti 1995 and 1998, Simon 1996, Von Flotow 1997, Bassnett and Trivedi 1999, Cronin 2006, Gentzler 2008 and Nikolau and Kyritsi 2008). However, the question of how these processes are related to language roles and linguistic choices has received much less attention (Sidiropoulou 2004).

Rather than focusing on one single perspective, I will use translational concepts and the (socio)linguistic toolkit to explore (1) the awareness of the target language as a marker of identity (or otherwise), (2) how identities are built through language, and (3) the use of translation to create/reinforce identities either real or fictitious. The aim of this paper is twofold, to discover whether linguistically-marked source identiti(es) are reflected in Spanish target texts, and to examine whether grammatical choices in target texts reflect identity appreciation or, on the contrary, reveal an unconcerned unawareness of the identity issue. In short, to either corroborate or refute the working hypothesis of the "missing identity" referred to in the title in translated Spanish. To this end, I will review different perspectives about

---

[1] Research for this paper has been funded by the Spanish Ministry of Science and Education and ERDF through project *Contrastive Analysis and Translation English-Spanish. Applications. (ACTRES)*. [Ref. HUM2005-01215].

language and identity that are relevant to the purpose of this article, namely the use of language as a marker of identity, the creation of identities through language and the role translation plays. The second part of this article will be devoted to two corpus-based empirical studies that will provide evidence of the status of Spanish as a target language in relation to identity issues. And finally, the conclusion will present the translation strategies and linguistic preferences in translated Spanish for identity marking or otherwise.

Identities in language

The possession of a language of one's own is generally considered a necessary condition for claiming—at least—a group identity. The relationships between the possessors of one or more languages and their particular uses give rise to different sociological roles of language. Gobard (1976: 34) proposes a tetralinguistic model of the sociological roles of language:
— A vernacular language, which is the language of the community, the one used spontaneously to mark ethnic or nation membership and the one which is considered by his/her possessor as his/her mother tongue or, in Gaston Miron's terms "*la langue natale*" (the native language) (quoted by Brisset 1990: 278)
— A vehicular language, learned or acquired and used for communication outside the native group;
— A referential language, which operates through intertextuality and ties users to a textual and cultural tradition, and
— A mythic language, which is involved in the transmission of spiritual and religious beliefs.

Most of the studies to which this model has been applied so far are devoted to the multilingual societies that emerged and/or developed in English speaking contexts (Gentzler 2008), and efforts to understand the relationship between identity and language preferences have focused on the real or perceived relationships across language borders in the same setting. This situation also applies to other milieux, involving languages other than English.

The usefulness of Gobard's taxonomy was put to the test by Deleuze and Guattari in their study of Kafka's work (1996:23). They explain that these roles or language functions differ in terms of spatiotemporal location:

"vernacular is here; vehicular language is everywhere; referential language is over there; mythic language is beyond" (23). In Kafka's case the authors face a plurilingual subject whose identity is a composite of different languages with different uses: Czech is assessed to fulfill the role of vernacular language, Hebrew is the mythic language, whereas Yiddish and German are Kafka's vehicular languages in the narrow ethnic sense. Yiddish helps to de-territorialize while German becomes his major vehicular language (Deleuze and Guattari 1996: 24-26). This multicultural environment becomes the territory of the multilingual self where translation happens beneath the surface across language boundaries.

A second milieu is post-Quiet Revolution Québec, one in which language is made to appear as proof of rights and becomes a near-synonym for the territory (Brisset 1990 and 2000). Here, the affirmation of "québécois" as a native language is an attempt to integrate "all in one" the vernacular, the referential, the mythic and the vehicular language.[2]

As a global language Spanish takes on different roles on both sides of the Atlantic. Like English, Spanish is a *lingua franca,* a vehicular language. For many it is also the vernacular, the referential and the mythic language. While Chicano writers such as Rolando Hinojosa create their fiction in Spanish, recreate (self-translate) it in English and then back into Spanish in a two-way reflection of an identitarian "third code" created through translation (Frawley 1984:168; Øverås 1998), in Spain perceptions about the function(s) and status of Spanish are tied to historical and territorial issues. The rationale for the study of contemporary European Spanish as an identity marker needs to take into account the historical (and linguistic) isolation during Franco's regime (1939-1975) following the Spanish Civil War (1936-39); the language map that emerged after democracy was reinstated (1978); the present-day reality of migration and Spanish as a world language.

Cultural isolation was accompanied by a brutal enforcement of the use of Spanish as the sole official language. The result was the promotion of Castilian Spanish as a symbol of a national identity, a status which is nowadays a matter of contention. Arturo Pérez-Reverte, the best selling

---

[2] Quebec's traditional and very influential Roman Catholicism was transmitted in French with a special aside for profanity in the vernacular. Francophone religion-based curses and expletives are known as *sacres*, and are similar to blasphemy in Italian or Spanish. However this practice is not reported in the case of English. See Sheila Fischman's English translation of *La Guerre, Yes Sir!* by Roch Carrier where many of these expressions are left in the original Québécois (Carrier 1970).

autor of the *Capitán Alatriste* series (Santillana Ediciones Generales S.L.), a member of the *Real Academia de la Lengua Española* and a former war correspondent and journalist, maintains that "el español no es una lengua nacionalista, porque no es una seña de identidad para nadie; es plurinacional y multilingüe". (EFE 2007). [Spanish is not a nationalist language because it is nobody's mark of identity; it is plurinational and multilingual]. According to this view this plurifunctional monolingualism is not a choice, but a state, part of an unmarked identity.

A further scenario is provided by those regions that boast a language of their own alongside Spanish; the most prominent being Catalonia, the Basque Country and Galicia (Milián Massana 1984). In these areas translation into the native language has been pivotal in the promotion of their language planning programs which include successful schooling in the native language and interventionist measures in audiovisual translation (García Ripoll 2001). Despite frequent declarations of allegiance of political parties and citizen groups to the vernacular and against Spanish, any overt enforcement of a monolingual (vernacular) language policy in these regions tends to find some resistance and in practice Spanish still functions as the superposed *lingua franca* across language borders.

Migration into Spain is also affecting the reality of Spanish. While it might be excessive to talk about the emergence of a multilingual community as most Castilian-speaking Spaniards remain unapologetically monolingual, it is true that the influx of immigrants will necessarily have an effect on the resources of European Spanish. It is interesting that according to figures released by the National Statistics Agency (Instituto Nacional de Estadística 2008) nearly 1.5 of the 4.5 million foreign nationals living and working in Spain have Spanish as their first language. As most of this contact happens orally (spoken forms and multimodal texts), this interaction is accountable for a timid modification of linguistic preferences, mainly lexical, which are at the core of intralinguistic innovation in European Spanish.

In addition to this timid attempt at internationalization and its increasing role as a global language, Spanish is being superseded by English in certain professional groups, among them scientists, academics and top-level executives. As reported by Gimeno Menéndez and Gimeno Menéndez in their study of newspaper language (2003), in addition to this professional diglossia, there is evidence of a second effect of the dominant position of English in the global market—the displacement of the lexical resources of Spanish and the acceleration of the process of lexical transference as calques, adapted loanwords and the lexical hybridization of the language in a number of fields. In this sense, perhaps Gentzler's "border spaces" (2008:145) are applicable here: areas where the distinction between original and foreign is not significant any more, because words tend to belong to both categories simultaneously.

Building identities through language

In addition to the external (possessed) sociological roles of languages reviewed above, language identity may also be construed through the negotiation of the users' relationships with the social groups to which they belong (Trudgill 2002:473). These variable relationships are at work in different domains in which identity-marking linguistic behaviour corroborates Pérez-Reverte's notion of Spanish as a "multilingual language".

In this perspective, identity is understood as "an individual and collective-level process of semiosis" (Mendoza-Denton 2002: 475) which may benefit from a linguistic variation approach. Variationist research by Potter (2000:22) defends the use of "situated practices" rather than traditional formal categories in the analysis. For the purposes of Case Study I in this paper both stratified sociodemographic categories and situated, practice-based expectations will be used as organizing devices. Sociodemographic categorization (Labov 1994:58) works on the assumption that the deployment of linguistic resources correlates with systematic and stable identity profiles, e. g. (in Case Study I below) teenage peer group language in pairs C and D, foreignness as in E, etc. Situated practices acknowledge the multiplicity of profiles associated with socially controlled use of linguistic (and other semiotic) resources (Eckert 1999). Illustrations of these are the language choices according to the rank hierarchy of the participants, as in pairs B or G below. Practice-based expectations of linguistic choice are also linked to the notion of "community of practice". As quoted by Meyerhoff (2002:527-30), to be regarded as such, a given group must comply with at least three necessary conditions: first, there must be conscious, mutual engagement of the members in their shared practice, second, members need to share some enterprise, and third, members have a shared repertoire, i.e., "...resources (linguistic or otherwise) that are the cumulative result of internal negotiations" (Meyerhoff 2002:528). A good example is provided by the fine-pen linguistic identity differentiation of characters in the film *Working*

Class/Armas de mujer, geographical dialects (New Jersey and Boston accents) co-exist in the same characters with the repertoire of two differentiated communities of practice: the secretaries' pool and the executive boardroom respectively (Bravo 2002:209). The main character, Tess, is taking diction classes in an attempt to "change" her language (and social) identity as part of her particular program of upward mobility. Her untrained English speech is the result of both conscious and unconscious preferences that betray her geographical, social and professional group membership.

Up to this point, the discussion has been confined to language and identity issues with little attention being paid to the role of translation in the construction of identities.

Identiti(es) through translation

I will now briefly review two phenomena involved in the (re)creation of fictional identities through translation processes. The first has been dubbed "fictitious translations" (Toury 1995 and 2001) or "pseudotranslation" (Rabadán 2000; Merino and Rabadán 2002), the second is known as "retranslation" (Chapdelaine 1994).

Pseudotranslation is a semiotic process involving the presentation of a non-translated text as a translation. In other words, a text composed originally in the (supposed) target language dealing with topics and situations typical of the (supposed) source culture and frequently displaying linguistic choices that users readily associate with translations (Santoyo 1996: 155-65). Common reasons for pseudotranslating are the introduction of new genres in the target society, the prestige or popularity—and therefore market interest—of the products in the "source language" or, in censored contexts, the additional protection it may offer for certain authors and products (Rabadán 2000:257).

A core feature of pseudotranslating is the "cloning" of textual models and the transfer of grammatical and lexical uses, a practice which necessarily presupposes the existence of "real" translations of similar products in the target society. It could be said that pseudotranslating rests on intertextual relations at various levels that underlie both the creation and the acceptance of these fake translations. Spanish pseudotranslations of subgenres such as spies or horror stories in the 1950s and 60s constitute a prototypical illustration. Dubbed US films had popularized these stories, and made the heroes and their "third code" jargons a familiar component of modern fashionable entertainment. These were characterized by massive direct transfer at all levels, lexical, grammatical and textual, resulting in the creation of new transferred associations between form and meaning in Spanish that made their way to the printed page. This intersemiotic transfer (Jakobson 1959) proved productive exclusively in cloned narrative, but never went beyond that to become part of the regular native Spanish inventory of resources.

Retranslation consists in either "repatriating" or "sanitizing" the text which had been made available earlier in "the same" target language. The Quebecization of translated foreign texts by Michel Tremblay, among others, in the late 1960s is a prototypical example of "the search for a native language" (Brisset 2000:364). Very often retranslation means a second process that happens entirely within the boundaries of different varieties of the same target language. The text is then a vehicle to promote the literary and cultural adequacy of the native variety of the language and remove it from its non-standard status.

Making the text more acceptable to final users is another reason for retranslating. This type of "sanitation" involves downtoning distinctly alien characteristics of speech so as to make the text less "foreign" to the recipient audience. Occasionally patterns of American varieties of Spanish in translated products have been fully retranslated or "sanitized" to different degrees of adaptation to Castilian Spanish. Eric Segal's bestselling *Love Story* was first translated in Buenos Aires (1970) and a very small number of copies of this unmodified Argentinean text was distributed in Spain in 1971. A few months later, a new edition of the same text offered readers a "sanitized", re-translated version into Castilian Spanish. Changes affected mainly lexical selections of colloquial language, which play an important role in recreating the fictional identities of the characters in the target language (Gómez Castro 2005: 67-74).

Likewise, contemporary Spanish history has provided fertile ground for retranslations motivated by the need to clean up censorship distortion after Franco's control apparatus was dismantled (Gubern and Font 1975; Gutiérrez-Lanza 2000). Spanish retranslating affects all sorts of creative texts, but it is more frequently associated with audiovisual products, arguably because of their wider audience as compared to the printed page. Adaptation to Spanish ears suggests market and economic interests more than any agenda about the promotion and/or preservation of identity through language use. Alternatively, a conscious "identity erasing" practice was (and still is to some extent) dubbing foreign language products into a non-existent, artificial "international Spanish" variety, which is overtly disapproved by users, but saves the movie companies considerable expense (Bravo 2005:130). On the contrary, retranslation to reinstate films to their non-censored textual selves, restoring the notorious footage cuts (*cortes*) and cleaning up language manipulation was part of a program of information transparency and political visibility. In the early 1980s both were valued as defining properties of democracy in the collective imagination. Since the greater volume of footage cutting and dialogue tampering had taken place during the 1950s and 60s, the cleansing operation also involved linguistic updating and gradually de-euphemizing the texts (Gutiérrez-Lanza 1999).

Pseudotranslation would thus be an important procedure for fixing fictional identities in the Spanish context. Translated language—"a third code" according to Frawley (1984:168)—, embodies the linguistic marks of the popular hero and promotes *translationese* (Tirkkonen-Condit 2002) to the status of Gobard's referential language. By contrast retranslation, in whichever variety, has the effect of promoting and asserting the value and status of Spanish as both vernacular and referential language. Linguistic sanitation or updating of the kind referred to above may be taken as proof of the target context willingness and need to preserve and endorse Spanish as a bearer of identity.

Once the roles and relative status(es) of Spanish and their relation to identity issues have been established, I will offer corpus evidence of how identities are reflected in translated as opposed to non-translated Spanish. Case Study I focuses on whether and how linguistically-marked fictional source identities are handled in the target text; Case Study II explores whether grammatical choices in target texts can be said to reinforce the target language or whether, on the contrary, direct transfer is accepted and even prioritized.

Identities in translation: The "empirical zone"

Case Study I: Source language identiti(es) in translated Spanish

Translation data are sourced from the Parallel English-Spanish Contrastive Analysis and Translation corpus (P-ACTRES)[3] (P-ACTRES

---

3 A small demo is currently available at: http://actres.unileon.es.

2000-2008). It features over 2,400,000 words distributed among "fiction", "non-fiction", "newspapers", "magazines" and "miscellaneous" (see Table 1). The English-Spanish parallel texts have been aligned with a new upgraded version of the *Corpus Translation Aligner* (Hofland and Johansson 1998) and tagged using *TreeTagger* (Institut für Maschinelle Sprachverarbeitung). It can be searched with the Corpus Work Bench browser (CWB) (Institut für Maschinelle Sprachverarbeitung)[4].

P-ACTRES is an open corpus and its copyrighted materials cover the period 2000-2008[5] Legal restrictions are the reason P-ACTRES includes chunks of 15,000-20,000 words each rather than complete texts. This is also the reason why it is a restricted access corpus.

P-ACTRES	English	Spanish	Total
Books – Fiction	396,462	421,065	817,527
Books – Non-Fiction	494,358	553,067	1,047,425
Newspapers	115,502	137,202	252,704
Magazines	119,604	126,989	246,593
Miscellaneous	40,178	49,026	89,204
TOTAL	1,166,104	1,287,349	2,453,453

Table 1: Contents of the English-Spanish Parallel Corpus: number of words (June 2007)

Since identity marking can be detected more easily in creative texts as they generally display dialogue, the P-ACTRES "fiction" subcorpus was queried for suitable aligned pairs. The search strategy has been to use as key items the personal names of those characters in the narrative texts included in P-ACTRES that were thought likely to deploy linguistic identity markers. Thus, the query yielded 710 pairs and the statistical sample to be analyzed, 256 diagnostic pairs. The source texts make a motivated use (as opposed to the regular neutral one) of various language resources for identity inscription in at least the following situations: Marking ethnic

---

[4] We are grateful to Knut Hofland for his co-operation in the setting up of the P–ACTRES parallel corpus.
[5] There are two exceptions dated 1995 and 1998 respectively. All the translated materials are reviewed for "threshold quality" before becoming part of the corpus. The "threshold quality test" reviews two aspects: overall intelligibility in Spanish and degree of semantic match between original and translation.

group, age group, foreignness, social class, monolingual vs. multilingual condition, and geographical provenance. Real language usage is messy, and some of these identity markers overlap in one and the same speech. These markers are typically foreignness, monolingual vs. multilingual condition and geographical provenance. The P-ACTRES pairs below illustrate identity inscription practices:

i) Grammatical misuse consisting of using 3rd person present tense forms with other speech roles is employed as a marker of Elf language, a type of "ethnic group" speech as in A

A	I says to Dobby, I says, go find yourself a nice family and settle down, Dobby. (FRJK2E.s59)	Le he dicho a Dobby, se lo he dicho, ve a buscar una buena familia y asiéntate, Dobby. (FRJK2S.s65)

B	My name is Winky, sir—and you, sir—"her dark brown eyes widened to the size of side plates as they rested upon Harry's scar, 'you is surely Harry Potter!' " (FRJK2 E.s42)	Me llamo Winky, señor... y usted, señor... (FRJK2S.s44) —En ese momento reconoció la cicatriz de Harry, y los ojos se le abrieron hasta adquirir el tamaño de dos platos pequeños—. (FRJK2S.s45) ¡Usted es, sin duda, Harry Potter! (FRJK2S.s46)

ii) Teenage, age group speech is recreated by particular lexical selections and by "restricted code" (Bernstein 2003) formulations, as in

C	"Slimy gits", Ron muttered, as he, Harry and Hermione turned to face the pitch again. (FRJK2E.s120)	—Asquerosos— murmuró Ron cuando él, Harry y Hermione se volvieron de nuevo hacia el campo de juego. (FRJK2S.s132)

D	"No, listen—get back and get Ron —grab brooms from the flying-key room, they'll get you out of the trapdoor and past Fluffy—go straight to the owlery and send Hedwig to Dumbledore, we need him". (FRJK3E.s559)	No: vuelve, busca a Ron y coge las escobas del cuarto de las llaves voladoras. (FRJK3S.s578) Con ellas podréis salir por la trampilla sin que os vea Fluffy. (FRJK3S.s579) Id directamente a la lechucería y enviad a Hedwig a Dumbledore, la necesitamos. (FRJK3S.s580)

iii) A foreign accent is conveyed by means of graphic representation of transferred phonetic use, as in

| E | "Vell, ve fought bravely", said a gloomy voice behind Harry. (FRJK2E.s348) | —" Vueno", hemos luchado "vrravamente" — dijo detrás de Harry una voz lúgubre. (FRJK2S.s380) |

iv) Whereas social underclass membership and poor education is marked by reduced forms of verbal endings and function words, as in

| F | "Dunno", said Hagrid casually, "he wouldn' take his cloak off." (FRJK3E.s61) | —No lo sé —dijo Hagrid sin darle importancia—. (FRJK3S.s64) No se quitó la capa. (FRJK3S.s65) |

A higher social position is signalled by more elaborate syntax and more formal lexical choices, as in

| G | Ryder said to Luke: "Can you produce this... waitress?" (FFK1E.s318) He pronounced "waitress" with distaste, as if he were saying "prostitute". (FFK1E.s319) | —¿Podría hacer venir a esa... camarera? —preguntó a Luke, pronunciando "camarera" con la misma repugnancia que si hubiera dicho "prostituta". (FFK1S.s329 |

v) Bi-/multilingual characters are occasionally individualized and set apart by making them use a language other than English, a feature which also functions as a marker of geographical provenance, as in

| H | "C'est ennuyeux" Sophie grumbled. (FBD1E.s473) | —Qué aburrido —protestó Sophie sin dejar de avanzar. (FBD1S.s450) |

| I | "Bonjour, vous êtes bien chez Sophie Neveu", the recording announced. (FBD1E.s977) | "Bonjour vous êtes bien chez Sophie Neveu" —decía—. (FBD1S.s914 |

The Spanish solutions show the following translation practices: i) correction and standardization of grammatical misuses, as in A and B; ii) changes in formality scale which negatively affect lexical and syntactic selections, as in C and D; iii) reproduction of foreign phonetic characteristics in English; iv) standardization and normalization of speech peculiarities, as in F; v) transferred expressions and structures from English into Spanish, as in G; vi) use of standard Spanish to represent a foreign language other than English and vii) transcription of the foreign language expression into the Spanish text.

Technically, the first three solutions obey the general trend of translated language towards normalization and standardization (Toury's law of growing standardization 1995: 267ff), but also reveal a common translational practice in Spanish consisting in producing semantic translations of the text without paying due attention to identity inscription by means of language features. The pragmatics of the teenager characterization in C and D have been radically changed, as the Spanish language choices are not necessarily associated with this age group. "Asquerosos" (< disgusting) certainly translates the core meaning of "slimy gits", but it is very unlikely that a school-age Spanish teenager would ever select it to express unworthiness and offence. A more likely choice would have been "cerdos gilipollas" (<foolish and dirty). Also the target text verbal selections in D are too formal and correct for somebody this age.

Social characterization, which is clearly marked in the source text (example F), has totally disappeared in the Spanish. Reduced forms do happen in Spanish (e.g. in past participles, "llegado = llegao" < arrived) but their distribution is more restricted than it is in English, as are the possibilities of conveying social meanings in this way.

Representation of foreign identities by phonetic traits has been completely mishandled in our example. In the English text, the substitution of graph "w" for "v" is a way of identifying a speaker of either German or some Eastern European language (Bulgarian in this case), in Spanish however, the only hint that this may not sound as normal speech is the double r in "vrravamente". In terms of spelling using graph "v" instead of "b" might be understood as a sign of poor schooling, but not as a marker of defective pronunciation as "b" and "v" in Spanish constitute an archiphoneme and show no difference in pronunciation.

Evidence about the handling of geographical provenance features in translation is not conclusive, as documented by pairs H and I. In H the marks have been ignored in the translation whereas in I the translator has preferred to mirror the source author's strategy and risk unintelligibility by maintaining the identity markers of the character.

Case Study II: grammatical anchor *poder* (lexical equivalent of *can, may*)[6]

My second case study will address the question of whether translation practices play a role in the promotion of Spanish, or whether "the missing

---

6   "Anchors" are those grammatical resources that are perceived as being cross-linguistically equivalent in any two languages but that tend to and/or do convey partially divergent meanings. Language-specific associations between grammatical meaning and formal resource can be used as indicators of the degree of success in cross-linguistic transfer (Rabadán 2008: 107).

identity hypothesis" is gaining ground. The grammatical anchor chosen for this case study is *poder* (lexical equivalent of *can, may*), a producer of unnecessary translationese and redundancy in Spanish (Rabadán and Ramón 2008). This translational behaviour may be taken as a disregard for the expressive capabilities of Spanish and therefore of its status as a target language.

Spanish does not have one central formal resource specialising in the expression of modality as obvious as that of the English modal verbs. Modal meanings are encoded by means of a variety of resources indicating non factuality including choice of verbal mood, tense or aspect and a number of lexical constructions (Jiménez Julià 1989). This results in the fact that users do not readily associate any particular form with modal notions (Hoye 1997:76). Still, Spanish offers a closed set of constructions normally referred to as modal periphrases (Gómez Torrego 1999: 3347-3364), which tend to be regarded as the formal equivalents of English modals. In this view, the equivalent of modal verbs *can* and *may* in Spanish is *poder* + *infinitive*.

Corpus-based contrastive work has been carried out using cross-linguistic labels as *tertium comparationis* (Krzeszowski 1990:15) on both comparable and translation corpora English-Spanish, i.e., C-ACTRES and P-ACTRES respectively. The non-translated empirical data for the "grammatical anchor" have been sourced from two different corpora: The BoE (Bank of English, HarperCollins Publishers Ltd) for English and the CREA (Corpus de Referencia del Español Actual, Real Academia Española de la Lengua) for Spanish. Both function as source corpora for building a custom-made comparable corpus. "Source" means that both monolingual corpora are used as a starting point to build phenomenon-specific comparable corpora according to needs.[7] For both non-translated language corpora the "general language" subcorpora have been selected. These are "books", "newspapers", "magazines", and "ephemera/miscellaneous". This means that, in quantitative terms, both online source corpora have been trimmed down to some 30 million words. Translation materials come from P-ACTRES, which performs the role of "diagnostic corpus".

---

7   The key feature that allows for these ready-made corpora is the possibility offered by CREA of selecting the chronology of the materials. The BoE does not offer the chronological restriction feature and so searches of English language materials are always done by default. The usual corpus building strategy is then to search the English corpus first and use the chronological selection feature in CREA so as to obtain a statistically comparable volume of materials in Spanish.

The role of the comparable corpus is to contribute empirical data concerning the correct grammatical usage both in English and in Spanish of each anchor phenomenon. That of the diagnostic corpus is to provide evidence to be contrasted with that obtained from the comparable corpus. In addition, CREA plays an all-important role in verifying the "target language fit" (Chesterman 2004:6). This three-tier procedure is employed to reveal possible discrepancies in grammatical usage between original and translated texts which will provide some insight into the role of translation and status of Spanish as identity marking tools.

In addition, some contrastive tool is needed to collate profitably the empirical information obtained from the corpora. This is known as *tertium comparationis* and, as mentioned above, in this analysis it is a set of cross-linguistic labels used to discriminate uses in both English and Spanish. Labels have been borrowed from previous work in the field, (Fernández de Castro 1990; Gómez Torrego 1999), otherwise new ones have been assigned to particular functions, such as "aspectual" (see Table 6). Coates (1983: 90-91) considers it as a minor subgroup of CAN-*ability* referring to either sensorial or intellectual capability contexts generally signalled by a perception verb (see, understand, hear, etc.). Yet corpus-based contrast of non-translated English and Spanish identifies this "transferred" function as a useful grammatical anchor (Rabadán 2006: 273-75 and 282-85). The reason being that it usually underlies overtranslation and introduces surplus materials into Spanish. This tendency can also trigger the transfer of unnecessary roles, alien to conventionally accepted non-translated Spanish.

Representativeness of the corpus materials to be analyzed was secured by means of statistics (table 2). In the Spanish monolingual reference corpus CREA, the 2000-onwards fiction section (novel) including texts only in European Spanish contains 2,157,056 words. The fiction section in P-ACTRES contains 421,065 words.

POPULATION (N)	CREA SAMPLE (n)	POPULATION (N)	P-ACTRES SAMPLE (n)
2,395	331	538	224

Table 2. Sampling anchor *poder*

The size of the samples (331 examples from CREA and 224 from P-ACTRES) has been calculated by means of simple random sampling, which means that it replicates the actual distribution of occurrences in both the

Spanish and the translation corpora.[8] The analysis of the various functions of *poder* + *infinitive* in non-translated and in translated Spanish has yielded the following results:

CREA % RAW CASES		PODER	P-ACTRES RAW CASES %	
44.1	146	*POSSIBILITY*	88	39.28
28.4	94	*ABILITY*	47	21
7.85	26	*PERMISSION*	31	13.83
—	—	*ASPECTUAL*	24	10.71
0.9	3	*PREDICTION*	4	1.78
18.73	62	*OBLIGATION/ADVISABILITY*	30	13.39
100	331	**TOTALS**	224	**100**

Table 3. Quantitative and qualitative data for *poder*

Possibility and ability are the most obvious and prototypical functions of *can/poder*, followed by obligation/advisability. The main difference between translated and non-translated language is the aspectual function. Although a normal use in English (Rabadán 2006:274), there is no evidence of it in non-translated Spanish. Corpus data show, however, that this transferred use exists in translated Spanish.

The verification stage (i.e. the "target language fit" step) aims at making sure that divergent usage between translated and non-translated language is relevant. The test of statistical significance known as z-score has been used to ensure stringency of results and provide a reliable transition from quantitative to qualitative information. Additionally, a team of ten informants has provided semantic/pragmatic assessment about the empirical data whenever necessary. By applying statistical analyses, it was found that just two functions were significantly different, as shown in Table 4:

PODER	z-score
POSSIBILITY	1.13
ABILITY	1.97
PERMISSION	*-2.28*
ASPECTUAL	*-6.09*
PREDICTION	-0.91
OBLIGATION/ ADVISABILITY	1.66

Table 4. Statistical significance of *poder* values

---

[8] This was solved by means of the formula: $n = N / ((N-1)E2 + 1$ where 'n' is the sample to be analysed and 'N' the population, i.e., the total number of occurrences yielded by our searches and 'E' the estimative error (0.05) (Lowry 1999-2007).

Only "permission" and particularly "aspectual" show statistical significance concerning their use in translated and non-translated Spanish, which means they are good candidates to be used as anchors for the assessment of identity reinforcement or promotion. The very significant transfer of the "aspectual" function points at a poor "policing" of translation practices that allows for a free flow of direct transfer into Spanish thus detracting from its status as an identity symbol. An alternative and equally plausible explanation is that there is no need to reinforce or promote any identity marks in the language because the acceptance of these uses is constrained and restricted to "third code" situations.

Conclusion

Identities and their linguistic reflexes are the result of a multiplicity of choices, many of which do not "travel well" across language borders. Spanish makes a strong case for Pérez-Reverte's statement of a non-nationalist multilingual language, where notions of reinforcement of identity are not an issue.

Empirical data point to unawareness of roles other than the vehicular function of language. Translation practices into Spanish show a noticeable unconcern for the preservation of cross-linguistic fictional identities and a disregard (or absence of need) for the reinforcement of Spanish as a target language. It would seem that cross-linguistic behaviour is regulated by a vehicular view of language, in which aspects of "foreignness" or "nativeness" do not take center stage. Spanish prioritizes instrumentality and intelligibility over the creative aspects involved in the search for appropriate markers suggestive of the identity represented in the source text. Moreover, there are no identity drawbacks arising from the "foreignnizing" use of certain grammatical traits (here termed anchors). These, rather than enriching the resource pool, diminish and clutter the expressive capabilities of Spanish.

Corpus-based evidence confirms that neither identity marking nor the promotion of a target identity is a priority in translation practices into Spanish. Whereas non-translated English deploys effective identity builders as shown by Case Study I, translated Spanish shows a preference for standardization and normalization, and attempts at reconstructing fictional identities in the target language are not particularly successful. Concerning the reinforcement of a Spanish identity through language use and translation, empirical data reveal that this ambition is partisan to a number of political views that largely ignore real practices. Case Study II has contributed evidence that shows the permeability of Spanish to grammatical translationese and the absence of any identity monitoring or language reinforcement in translated texts.

At this point, it seems reasonable to conclude that these findings corroborate "the missing identity hypothesis" put forward in the title of this paper and endorse the view of Spanish as a non-identitarian, plurinational and multilingual language.

References

Bassnett, Susan and Harish Trivedi. 1999, *Post-Colonial Translation: Theory and Practice*. London and New York: Routledge.
Bravo, José M. 2002. "Translating the Film Dialect of Hollywood for Dubbing". In *Nuevas Perspectivas de los Estudios de Traducción*. Ed. J. M. Bravo. Valladolid: Universidad de Valladolid. 187-224.
— 2005. "La investigación en traducción cinematográfica en España: el doblaje (inglés-español)". In *Trasvases culturales: Literatura, cine, traducción*. Eds. R. Merino, J. M. Santamaría and E. Pajares. Vitoria-Gasteiz: Universidad del País Vasco. 123-144.
Brisset, Annie. 1990. *Sociocritique de la traduction. Théâtre et altérité au Québec (1968-1988)*. Québec: Éditions du Préambule.
— 2000. "The Search for a Native Language: Translation and Cultural Identity". In *The Translation Studies Reader*. Ed. L. Venuti. London and New York: Routledge. 343-375.
Carrier, Roch. 1968. (1981). *La Guerre, Yes Sir!* Montreal: Stanké.
— 1970. *La Guerre, Yes Sir!* Toronto: Anansi.
Chapdelaine, Annick. 1994. "Transparence et retraduction des sociolectes dans *The Hamlet* de Faulkner". *TTR: Traduction, Terminologie, Redaction: Etudes Sur le Texte et Ses Transformations* 7.2: 11-33.
Chesterman, Andrew. 2004. "Hypotheses about translation universal". In *Claims, Changes and Challenges in Translation Studies*. Eds. G. Hansen, K. Malmkjær and D. Gile. Amsterdam and Philadelphia: Benjamins. 1-14.
Cronin, Michael. 2006. *Translation and Identity*. London and New York: Routledge.
Deleuze, Gilles and Felix Guattari. 1975. *Kafka: Pour une littérature mineure*. Paris: Les Éditions de Minuit.
— 1996. *Kafka: Toward a Minor Literature*. Trans. By D. Polan. Foreword by Réda Bensmaïa. Minneapolis and London: University of Minnesota Press

Eckert, Penelope. 1999. *Linguistic Variation as Social Practice*. Oxford: Blackwell.
EFE – Madrid/Barcelona – 11/05/2007. "Gregorio Salvador asegura que el castellano sufre discriminación" http://www.elpais.com/articulo /cultura/Gregorio/Salvador/asegura/castellano/sufre/discriminacion/el pepucul/20070511elpepicul_5/Tes Accessed 12/05/2008.
English-Norwegian Parallel Corpus (ENPC). http://www.hf.uio.no/ilos/ forskning/ forskningsprosjekter/enpc/ Accessed July 2007.
Fernández de Castro, Félix. 1999. *Las perífrasis verbales en español actual*. Madrid: Gredos.
Frawley, William. Ed. 1984. *Translation: Literary, Linguistic, and Philosophical Perspectives*. Newark: University of Delaware Press.
García Ripoll, Martí. 2001. "L'intervenció lingüística en versions doblades i subtitulades. El cas català". In *La traducción en los medios audiovisuales*. Eds. F. Chaume and R. Agost. Castelló: Universitat Jaume I. 123-28.
Gentzler, Edwin. 2008. *Translation and Identity in the Americas. New Directions in Translation Theory*. London and New York: Routledge.
Gimeno Menéndez, Francisco and M. Victoria Gimeno Menéndez. 2003. *El desplazamiento lingüístico del español por el inglés*. Madrid: Cátedra.
Gobard, Henri. 1976. *L'alienation linguistique: Analyse tetraglossique*. Paris: Flammarion.
Gómez Castro, Cristina. 2005. "*Love Story:* La traducción (inglés/ español) de una historia de amor y desamor con la censura franquista". In *Trasvases culturales: Literatura, cine, traducción*. Eds. R. Merino, J. M. Santamaría and E. Pajares. Vitoria-Gasteiz: Universidad del País Vasco. 65-76.
Gómez Torrego, Leonardo. 1999. "Los verbos auxiliaries. Las perífrasis verbales de infinitivo". In *Gramática descriptiva de la lengua española*. Eds. I. Bosque and V. Demonte. Madrid: Espasa. II. 3323-3390.
Gubern, Román and Domènec Font. 1975. *Un cine para el cadalso, Cuarenta años de censura cinematográfica en España*. Barcelona: Euros.
Gutiérrez-Lanza, Camino. 1999. *Traducción y censura de textos cinematográficos en la España de Franco: Doblaje y subtitulado inglés-español (1951-1975)*. León: Universidad de León.
— 2000. "Proteccionismo y censura durante la etapa franquista: Cine nacional, cine traducido y control estatal". In *Traducción y censura inglés-español: 1939-1985. Estudio preliminar*. Ed. R. Rabadán. León: Universidad de León. 23-61.
HarperCollins Publishers Ltd. 2004. Bank of English. http://www.collins. co.uk/ books.aspx?group=153 Accesed March 2007.

Hofland, Knut and Stig Johansson. 1998. "The Translation Corpus Aligner: A Program for Automatic Alignment of Parallel Texts". In *Corpora and Cross-linguistic Research: Theory, Method, and Case Studies.* Eds. S. Johansson and S. Oksefjell. Amsterdam: Rodopi. 87-100. Also at http://khnt.hd.uib.no/ files/align3.pdf Visited December 2006.

Institut für Maschinelle Sprachverarbeitung (IMS). http://www.ims.uni-stuttgart.de/projekte/corplex/TreeTagger/ Accessed July 2007.

— http://www.ims.uni-stuttgart.de/projekte/CorpusWorkbench/ Accessed July 2007.

Instituto Nacional de Estadística (INE). http://www.ine.es/ Accessed April 2008.

Jakobson, Roman. 1959. "On Linguistic Aspects of Translation". In *On Translation.* Ed. R. A. Brower. Cambridge, MA: Harvard University Press. 232-39.

Krzeszowski, Tomasz P. 1990. *Contrasting Languages. The Scope of Contrastive Linguistics.* Berlin and New York: Mouton de Gruyter.

Labov, William. 1994. *Principles of Linguistic Change: Internal Factors.* London: Blackwell.

Lowry, Richard. 1999-2007. *Concepts and Applications of Inferential Statistics.* http://faculty.vassar.edu/lowry/webtext.html/ Accessed November 2006.

Mendoza-Denton, Norma. 2002. "Language and Identity". In *The Handbook of Language Variation and Change.* Eds. J. K. Chambers, P. Trudgill and N. Schilling-Estes. Oxford: Blackwell. 475-499

Merino, Raquel and Rosa Rabadán. 2002. "Censored translations in Franco's Spain: The TRACE project—theatre and fiction (English-Spanish)". *TTR* 15.2: 125-152.

Meyerhoff, Miriam. 2002. "Communities of Practice". In *The Handbook of Language Variation and Change.* Eds. J. K. Chambers, P. Trudgill and N. Schilling-Estes. Oxford: Blackwell. 526-548.

Milián Massana, Antoni. 1984. "La regulación constitucional del multilingüismo". *Revista Española de Derecho Constitucional* 4.10: 123-54.

Nikolaou, Paschalis and Maria-Venetia Kyritsi. Eds. 2008. *Translating Selves. Experience and Identity Between Languages and Literatures.* London: Continuum.

Øverås, Linn. 1998. "In Search of the Third Code: An Investigation of Norms in Literary Translation". *Meta* 43.4: 557-570. Also http://id.erudit.org/ iderudit/003775ar.

Parallel English-Spanish Contrastive Analysis and Translation Corpus (P-ACTRES). 2000-2008. http://actres.unileon.es/corpussearch/ (Password-restricted access). Accessed June 2008.

Potter, Jonathan. 2000. "Realism and Sociolinguistics". *Journal of Sociolinguistics* 4.1: 21-24.
Rabadán, Rosa. 2000. "Modelos importados, modelos adaptados: Pseudotra-ducciones de narrativa popular inglés-español 1955-1981". In *Traducción y censura inglés-español: 1939-1985. Estudio preliminar*. Ed. by R. Rabadán. León: Universidad de León. 255-277.
Rabadán, Rosa. 2001. "Las cadenas intertextuales inglés-español: Traducciones y otras transferencias (inter)semióticas". In *Trasvases culturales 3: Literatura, cine y traducción*. Eds. E. Pajares, R. Merino and J. M. Santamaría. Bilbao: EHU/UPV. 29-42.
— 2006. "Modality and Modal Verbs in Contrast. Mapping out a Translation (ally) Relevant Approach English-Spanish". *Languages in Contrast* 6.2: 261-306.
— 2008. "Refining the Idea of 'Applied Extension'". In *Beyond Descriptive Translation Studies*. Eds. M. Shlesinger, A. Pym and D. Simeoni. Amsterdam and Philadelphia: Benjamins. 103-118.
— and Noelia Ramón. 2008. "Corpus Linguistics for English-Spanish Translation Quality Assessment (TQA): A Case of Applied Corpus Research (ACTRES)". Paper presented at the *IV Inter-Varietal Applied Corpus Studies (IVACS 4)*, June 13-14, in Limerick, Ireland.
Real Academia Española. Banco de datos (CREA). Corpus de Referencia del Español Actual. http://corpus.rae.es/creanet.html Accesed July 2007.
Santillana Ediciones Generales S.L. "El Capitán Alatriste", Santillana Ediciones– Alfaguara,http://www.capitanalatriste.com/aventuras.html. Accessed May 2008.
Santoyo, Julio César. 1996. *El delito de traducir*. León: Universidad de León.
Sidiropoulou, Maria. 2004. *Linguistic Identities through Translation*. Amsterdam and New York: Rodopi.
Simon, Sherry. 1996. *Gender In Translation: Cultural Identity and the Politics of Transmission*. London and New York: Routledge.
Tirkkonen-Condit, Sonja. 2002. "Translationese – a Myth or an Empirical Fact? A study into the linguistic identifiability of translated language". *Target* 14.2: 207-220.
Toury, Gideon. 1995. *Descriptive Translation Studies and Beyond*. Amsterdam and Philadelphia: Benjamins.
— 2004. *Los Estudios Descriptivos de Traducción y más allá. Metodología de la investigación en Estudios de Traducción*. Translation, introduction and notes by R. Rabadán and R. Merino. Madrid: Cátedra.
— 2001. "Enhancing Cultural Changes by Means of Fictitious Translations". http://www.tau.ac.il/~toury/works/fict.htm Accesed

May 2008. Spanish version in *Trasvases culturales 3*. Eds. E. Pajares, R. Merino and J. M. Santamaría. Bilbao: EHU/UPV. 43-58

Trudgill, Peter. 2002. "Domains. Introduction". In *The Handbook of Language Variation and Change*. Eds. J. K. Chambers, P. Trudgill and N. Schilling-Estes. Oxford: Blackwell. 473-74.

Venuti, Lawrence. 1995. *The Translator's Invisibility: A History of Translation*. London and New York: Routledge

— 1998. *The Scandals of Translation. Towards an Ethics of Difference*. London and New York: Routledge.

Von Flotow, Luise. 1997. *Translation and Gender: Translating in the "Era of Feminism"*. Manchester, UK: St. Jerome.

CHAPTER FOUR

A MAP AND A COMPASS FOR NAVIGATING THROUGH TRANSLATION

PATRICK ZABALBEASCOA

Introduction

In this paper I am going to bring together several strands of theoretical thinking that I have been engaged in over the past two decades. In short, the point is to provide conceptual tools for finding and defining translation problems, and then trying to establish criteria by which to find justifiable solutions to these problems. My research actually began by addressing the latter of these two tasks, and more recently addressed the former. The order of presentation here is to start with an exploration of problems and possible solutions; and then to move on and provide, "a sense of direction", a model (of priorities and restrictions) for establishing translational criteria (for purposes such as description, analysis, or even for providing consistency in actual translating processes). The metaphors I have chosen are those of a map and a compass. The map is an attempt to convey the full range of all possible solutions to a given translation problem, in the context of the translating task, to raise awareness of how the translation solutions account for a problem as perceived either by the translator or the translation scholar, (and they may agree in their perception). Thus, one can see translational solutions in the light of a given interpretation of the source text and in relation to potential solutions that are discarded.

Points of departure for the mapping model include an interest in finding: (i) a way out of the maze of so many variables that come into play; (ii) a common ground for dealing with the enormous diversity of problems encountered during the translating process; (iii) a basis for translational criteria; (iv) translation as a problem-solving activity, involving identifying problems and finding solutions for them; (v) a search for a simple model that does not oversimplify the complexity of translation. My motivation is to offer an alternative to ill-defined "theoretical" terminology, while providing a new reading of proposals from other authors, such as: Nida's idea (1964) of translation as a matter of priorities; translation strategies as proposed and explained by Vinay and Darbelnet (1957) and Newmark (1988), among others; Toury's (1995) study of metaphor translation; Delabastita's study of pun translation (1993).

Following Toury's (1995: 14-19) suggestion that fruitful proposals can come out of speculative approaches (as well as descriptive and prescriptive studies), I will not be looking at the issue from an entirely descriptive or entirely prescriptive point of view. In the speculative approach, one looks into many possible solutions (actual and hypothetical), and this, in turn, contributes to a greater understanding of solutions found in descriptive studies and those suggested by prescriptive models. The hope is that many translational problems will benefit from this proposal for binary-tree mapping, especially for the case of non-segmental features of texts, when they need to be dealt with or rendered somehow in the target text (translation).

2 Let's start by mapping metaphor translation

From Toury (1995: 82-83) I quote the following "replacing + replaced segments" as a sort of map for solving the problem of rendering metaphors in translations: (i) metaphor *into* "same" metaphor; (ii) metaphor *into* "different" metaphor; (iii) metaphor *into* non-metaphor; (iv) metaphor *into* ø (i.e. complete omission, leaving no trace in the target text); (v) non-metaphor *into* metaphor; (vi) ø *into* metaphor (i.e. addition, pure and simple, with no linguistic motivation in the source text). Each one of Toury's first four possibilities shows a corresponding segment in the translation for metaphor-segments of the source text, including the possibility of ø (no segment). His last two options, however, deal with metaphor exclusively as a segment of the TT (target text, translation) when it is related to a non-metaphorical segment of the ST (source text, the text to be translated).

Options where metaphor is not the starting point are discarded, here, so as to be consistent with a metaphor-as-problem approach, unlike one which might involve studying all the problems for which metaphor is the TT solution or part of it. The point of interest here is to find out: (a) What possibilities are there for translating source-text metaphors? (b) What kinds of relationships and classifications might be established for the solutions to the metaphor-as-translation-problem, along with the (methodological or theoretical) advantages of certain typologies over others? (c) Ultimately, what conditions will favour a given type of solution in the everyday practice of translation?

Possibly the biggest problem posed by a metaphor-as-unit approach is that of finding other units in the text that can be "added" to the metaphor-units to give us the whole text. Moreover, authors like White (1996: 58) point out that even counting the metaphors in a text is no straightforward matter. You cannot compare metaphors to linguistic units (phoneme, morpheme, lexeme, clause, sentence) because they are of a different order. The same would be the case for textual units (e.g. title, introduction, conclusion). [Metaphor *into* ø] is, of course, possible but segment ø has not yet been proven to be a non-metaphor in all cases; metaphorical value might be assigned to a pause, a silent moment, an ellipsis, a blank space, a reluctance or inability to respond, etc. However, in terms of units, it does make perfect sense to speak of ø to mean the absence of a unit. So, to delete a metaphor in the translating process is not exactly the same as deleting the segment where it appears; it has more to do with destroying by whatever means available the triangular relationship between the constituents of a metaphor, i.e. Topic, Vehicle and Ground (Goatly, 1997).

The category of segment ø should not enter the discussion at an early abstract stage of binary branching although it might appear more meaningfully later on (i.e. not on the main branches, but on the third, fourth or fifth binary split). In a binary-tree approach, a given segment ø solution might be an instance of metaphor or non-metaphor, or, rhyme or non-rhyme, (or, as I shall argue below, whatever the source-text problem may be).

To retain the same ST metaphor in the TT may not inevitably entail interlinguistic rendering (see below discussion on the L2 / not L2 dichotomy). By "same metaphor" I am not referring to mathematical or objective sameness but to subjective sameness, i.e. what is the same according to the translator or researcher. In any case, it seems counterproductive to take for granted that all solutions that are not L2 renderings, such as L1 borrowings, or the use of L3 (presence of items from any number of languages different to the main ST and TT languages) and non-verbal textual elements cannot express the same metaphor.

Likewise, literal translation (interlinguistic lexical equivalence) does not entail that the same metaphor be retained in all cases, since it can only guarantee that one part of the metaphorical relationship is kept (the Vehicle or expression), and even that guarantee is questionable. Thus, literal translation does not guarantee that the same metaphor is rendered if two cultures use a given word or expression with different metaphorical (idiomatic) meanings even though they may be equivalents for their non-metaphorical meanings. For example, there is a clear difference in the metaphorical image of a dragon depending on whether we are using it within a Christian tradition or a Chinese one. Another example, from English and Spanish, can be found in the metaphorical idioms or similes that are used to describe a person as being busy and hardworking; in such a case, one would expect *bee* and *hormig(uit)a* (*ant* or *little ant*), respectively.

From the translator's point of view, it is important to note in this particular example that the choice of *bee* is motivated not only by the Ground of the metaphor, but also because of other factors, like alliteration, as a popular cohesive device, sound symbolism associated with bees buzzing, and possibly a certain bias towards monosyllables for such idioms. When these other factors are not present there is often a greater coincidence between Spanish and English. A further example can be found in the passage below from *The Bonfire of the Vanities*. *Claw* as it is used in the English text is meant to conjure up an image of a bloodthirsty predator or vulture, whereas the Spanish version uses a translation of *claw* (*zarpas*) which overlaps somewhat in its meaning with *paw*; this, added to the fact that *zarpas* is a noun, makes the most plausible interpretation of the translated metaphor an image of a clumsy bear fumbling with the newspaper while trying to open it. *Zarpas* is quite a common Spanish metaphor for clumsiness in handling things.

Toury also considers the possibility that a metaphor (M) may not constitute a whole unit, and be a part of a unit, either [M+X] or [X+M]. However, if we do not consider a metaphor as a unit or segment, then we might wish to regard a metaphor (M) and whatever it might be coupled to (X) not as units but as features. This leads us to consider that a textual metaphor will either have no accompanying feature, or will be coupled to some other feature(s) or component(s), regardless of where they appear in the text. So, for metaphor as a relevant textual feature we might wish to discriminate between a "bare" metaphor (M=M°) and a "coupled" metaphor (M=M°+X). For more on *bare* v. *compound*, see Section 3 (β-split 3).

The conclusion that I have reached at this point is that in establishing binary divisions for the purpose of mapping we must be very careful not to mix up different planes of reference. Since metaphor does not entail verbal expression, since metaphor does not necessarily exclude ellipsis or empty-unit, since metaphor does not entail a given language to the exclusion of all others, then we will have to discard binary divisions such as: (i) metaphor *versus* nothing; (ii) metaphor *versus* picture; (iii) metaphor *versus* borrowing. First, we need to know what the solutions (S) mean in metaphorical terms if our goal is to understand what happens to source text metaphors in translation. Second, we cannot impose a single typology of metaphors as the one that will always be best.

3 Binary-tree mapping and type-within-type categorization

We are now in a position to outline criteria for mapping all possible solutions for the translation of a given metaphor. First of all, there is the subjectivity of identifying metaphors (including the treatment of certain expressions as being metaphorical). This subjectivity affects both the translator and the scholar as analyst or critic. The scholar will have the additional task of distinguishing between those metaphorical interpretations which he/she shares with the translator and those which he/she does not.

Second, the aim is to understand how metaphors are translated on metaphorical grounds, first and foremost. In other words, what does a given solution entail in terms of metaphoricalness, metaphor type and any metaphor-related factors? To propose a model of analysis with this in mind forces us to discard metaphor *into* ø in an abstract tree-diagram, not because it cannot happen but because first we need to know what ø means on a metaphorical plane. If it means an omission of a segment, a physical nothing, then it seems rash to discard the possibility that segment ø might turn out to be meaningful (i.e. something), metaphorically or otherwise. Moreover, since binary-branching is meant to prove its usefulness beyond the case of metaphor translation analysis, the formal and functional implications of an ø-branch (option) would become more and more unpredictable. For *figures 1* and *2*, the empty segment ø could *a priori* appear anywhere.

Third, the present proposal is a relation of the set of possible TT solutions and solution-types (S-set) for a given feature or item of the ST which is perceived as posing a translation problem (ρ). Solutions are distributed according to no other criterion than how they relate to the ST feature as defined in the problem. So, once ρ is established as being a metaphor, we must look at the solutions in terms of metaphor membership and type (subsets), or, on a more general plane (supersets), categories of which metaphor could be regarded as a member (a superset for metaphor could be figures of speech, see examples below). In our binary tree analysis, the first split points at either [1], a subset of solutions that might be regarded by the translator and/or scholar as "the same" metaphor, or at NO, for all other solutions that do not belong to subset [1], and further splits are for subsets of broader categories. The higher the number the broader the category. NO is shorthand for a subset of solutions within the S-set that includes all the subsets of all the splits that come after it; for the first split, NO covers [2] to [n+1], the second NO includes [3] to [n+1], and so on. [n+1] is the subset of solutions not belonging even to the largest category of the typology, which would be [n]. In *figure 1*(a) and *example 1* [n+1] = 5.

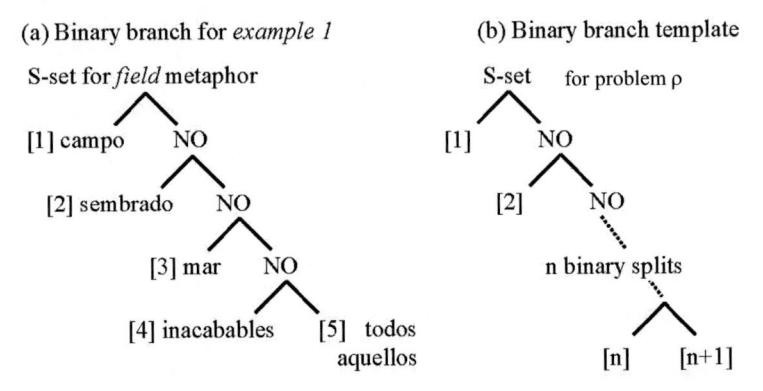

(a) Binary branch for *example 1*

S-set for *field* metaphor

[1] campo   NO

  [2] sembrado   NO

    [3] mar   NO

      [4] inacabables   [5] todos aquellos

(b) Binary branch template

S-set   for problem ρ

[1]   NO

  [2]   NO

    n binary splits

      [n]   [n+1]

Figure 1. Binary tree diagrams for type-within-type set of solutions in translation

This is illustrated in *figure 1*(b) where [1]+[2]+(...)+[n+1] covers the set of all theoretically possible solutions and each number in square brackets indicates a subset of a certain type, which, in turn, is a subset of the type which defines the next number as we move along the branches of the tree. The actual amount and definition of types and sub-types will depend on the typology chosen, the only limitation being that as the numbers get higher the categories they represent get broader.

Let us look at the case of ρ (metaphor) and a five-node tree for an S-set like the one in *figure 1*(a), which illustrates *example 1*(a ... e), below. Different instances of what is regarded as "the same metaphor" are all included in [1]; all metaphors "of the same type" as [1] are to be found in [1] and [2]; [1], [2] and [3] cover all metaphors; [1], [2], [3] and [4] account for "all rhetorical devices" as long as [4] is meant to include "all rhetorical devices except metaphor"; sets [1], [2], [3], [4] and [5] include all types of expressions. There are instances of all five solution-types in *examples 1* and

2 below. A cline defined by [1] and [n+1] at either end might be useful as a measure of "equivalence" since each category has a weaker condition for type-membership as one moves towards [n+1]. We must not forget, however, that a greater or lesser degree of equivalence according to one typology or tree analysis says nothing about similarity according to other criteria, which would require a separate tree (see below, simple vs. complex analyses). It now becomes apparent that binarism presents each category or type in opposition to all others, e.g. category [3] is the complementary of [1], [2], [4], and [5] put together. This type of analysis probably has a number of limitations but it might be productive for certain case studies or theoretical models so it is worth exploring.

The following dichotomies can be used as binary splits that may occur within any of the solution-types, i.e. they would branch off from [1], [2]...[n+1], as for β in *figure 2*.

β-split 1 (fig. 2, first split): Is the solution verbal or non-verbal? Not all solutions will necessarily be purely verbal. In this respect "non-verbal" does not only imply "purely non-verbal" but a broader category of "not verbal only" (see Hammond Hughes, 1978, for non-verbal metaphor and punning). The *rose* metaphor can be expressed in words or images, as in the film *American Beauty*.

β-split 2 (second split): Is the solution L2 or not? L2 is the main language of the TT (Spanish, in the examples provided here), but because texts can resort to various languages as well as a range of dialects and sociolects, e.g. Shakespeare's *Henry V*, L2 would probably be more accurately defined as all the linguistic signs that convey meaning to a given TT readership, and likewise for L1 and ST. If L2 is the language of the translation, then "not L2" includes both borrowings from L1 and any third-language solutions. If L2 is further restricted to cover only a certain variety (e.g. official or standard) then "not L2" will also have to include all other varieties. L2 could split again (if deemed interesting) to express the literal translation/non-literal translation dichotomy.

β-split 3: Solution S may be *bare* (S^o) or *compound* (S^o+X). S could be an idiom, a rhetorical question, a noun clause, a line of verse, a proper noun, a culture-specific word, etc. A *compound* solution involving a metaphor is [S^o+X] where +X stands for anything before, within or after the metaphor (S^o) and is an integral part of the solution. So, *compound* solutions include some instances of what Newmark (1988: 32) calls couplets (or triplets), the combined effort of two (or three) translation strategies. Here are four examples of what X might be for S^o(*rose* metaphor): (a) X before S°, *a beautiful rose*; (b) X after S°, *a rose standing alone*; (c) X somewhere else, e.g. a translator's footnote; (d) X as an additional trait within S°, such as *rose* rhyming with *grows*, especially relevant if rhyming is used to highlight the presence of the metaphor.

β-split 4: Segmental/non-segmental. Non-segmental solutions include certain types of compensation that involve the use of intonation patterns, or typographical conventions, or the addition of features to existing segments (e.g. irony, understatement, intertextuality).

β-split 5: Something/nothing (ø). It is essential to clarify whether we are using these terms as units (*nothing* stands for empty segment) or features (whereby *nothing* entails the absence of any features).

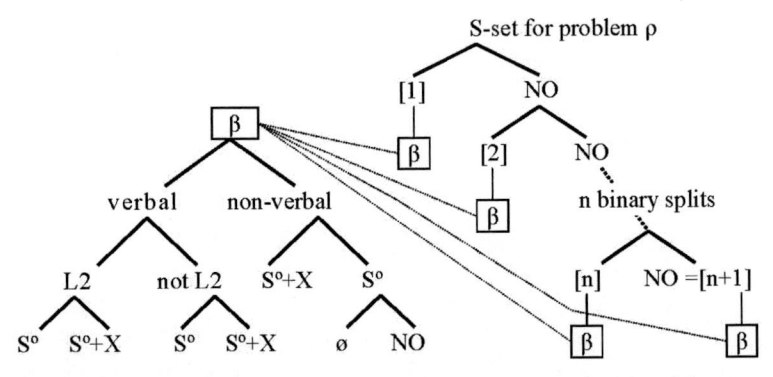

Figure 2. β is for binary branching stemming from each subset [1] to [n+1]

This mapping of possible solutions in translation for a given source text metaphor could be adapted to many other problems. Mapping in this way involves the analysis of each feature or element on a single plane of reference, the one that characterises it as a translation problem ρ. If I wished to analyse many instances of jokes as problems ρ, then each subset of solutions could be analysed as belonging to one of the following categories: [1] solutions regarded as versions of the *same* joke; [1] and [2] cover all instances of the *same type of* joke; [1], [2], and [3] cover *any* joke; [4] *something that is not a* joke *but belongs to a broader category that* jokes *also belong to* (e.g. phaticism or attention-getter); [5] *solutions that do not relevantly belong to any type of* jokes *or any broader category that* jokes *also could belong to*. The same could be done for translations of examples, insults, rhymes, acrostics, parodies, dialectal traits, etc. as well as more traditional linguistic, literary and semiotic units like nouns, sonnets, and cultural elements. The resulting number of categories or types is meant to be variable [n], depending mostly on the number of subtypes of jokes, for instance. In each case, it is up to the researcher, the critic or the translator to decide on the most convenient number of categories and their definitions.

Simple analyses would involve a single binary tree structure. Complex analyses would involve applying more than one tree to a given source-text element, when it is interpreted as posing two or more significant problems. For example, I might choose to analyse *dragon* as a ρ-metaphor, ρ-insult, ρ-idiom, ρ-lexical unit, etc., or, as we have seen in the previous section, *claw* can either be analysed as ρ-metaphor or ρ-verb. Of course, for certain analyses, a subtype of metaphor could be a grammatical category such as verb (and vice versa). This is illustrated in example 3, below, where metaphor is a subtype of irony for that particular analysis.

The same binary-branching idea can be represented differently (*figure 3*), as areas that include all possible solutions of a given type or sub-type in accordance with the typology of solutions for a given problem as defined by the scholar or translator. An important point to remember is that β splits may appear in any area.

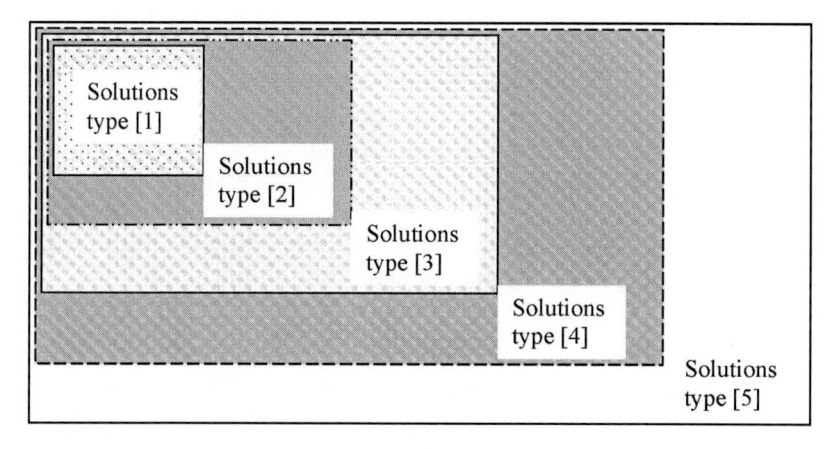

Figure 3. Areas of the "map" covered by each subset of solutions

4 Three examples of analysis

This section provides three examples taken from the following passage of *The Bonfire of the Vanities* (Tom Wolfe 1987: 169).

Fallow took advantage of this *hiatus* to make his way across the room toward his cubicle. Out in the middle of the *field* of computer terminals, he stopped and (...) picked up a copy of the second edition, (...) Just think of the *fine sense of gutter syntax* that inspired them to create a headline that was all verbs and objects, with the subject missing, the better to make you *claw* your way inside these smeary black pages to find out what children of evil were fiendish enough to complete the sentence!

Two problems ρ are analysed as metaphors and one as an instance of irony. All of the solutions provided in Spanish are plausible, depending on the aims of the translation (see priorities below). Solutions from Murillo's (1988: 169) published translation are marked TT. I provide a ranking order of preference, from most to least preferable, merely as an aid for readers who are not proficient in Spanish. It is based largely on a criterion of naturalness and idiom; there is no particular preference for retaining the same metaphor or for literal translation. Precisely, a model of how to organise criteria for preferences is presented below in the discussion of the P-R model.

Example 1 is "field" as ρ-metaphor, with the newspaper office as Topic of the metaphor, *field* as Vehicle, the Ground being large open space. Rank: c, d, a, e, b.

(1)   a.   *Campo* → "field"
      b.   *sembrado* (TT) → "sown field"
      c.   *mar* → "sea"
      d.   *inacabables* → "never-ending"
      e.   *todos aquellos* → "all those [terminals]"

The numbers in square brackets below correspond to binary branching as illustrated in Figures 1, 2, and 3. *Figure 1*(a) illustrates the following analysis of *example 1*.

[1]   Same metaphor, in Spanish, e.g. 1a (literal translation).
[2]   Same—rural—type of metaphor, e.g. 1b.
[3]   Other—not rural—types of metaphor, e.g. 1c.
[4]   Other—not metaphorical—rhetorical, e.g. hyperbole, as in 1d.
[5]   Non-rhetorical solutions; e.g. a literal description, as in 1e.

Example 2 is the hiatus ρ-metaphor. The Topic is coffee break, *hiatus* is the Vehicle, the brevity of the pause is the Ground. Rank: c, h, a, e, f, b, g, d.

(2)   a.   *hiato* → "hiatus"
      b.   *cesura* → "caesura"
      c.   *paréntesis* → "parenthesis"

d. *freno* → "brake"
e. *alto en el camino* → "stop on the way"
f. *interrupción (tan) breve como un hiato*
   "interruption (as) brief as a hiatus"
g. *interrupción* → "interruption"
h. *descanso* (TT) → "rest"

[1] Same metaphor, e.g. 2a (by means of literal translation into L2 Spanish).
[2] Same —metalinguistic— type of metaphor, e.g. 2b and 2c.
[3] Other metaphors (i.e. not metalinguistic), e.g. 2d and 2e.
[4] Other rhetorical devices (i.e. not metaphorical), e.g. a simile, as in 2f.
[5] Non-rhetorical solutions, e.g. literal language, as in 2g and 2h.

Murillo finds his solution for *hiatus* at [5] but for *field* at [2]. This may be due to a certain inconsistency in his solutions. It may, however, be due to my particular analysis in establishing items *hiatus* and *field* as ρ-metaphor, and semantic field of the Vehicle (metalinguistic and rural) as the requirement for subtype membership.

Example 3 is the ironic expression *fine sense of gutter syntax*. Rank: b, a, d, g, c, f, e.

(3) a. *magnífica sintaxis del arroyo* → "magnificent gutter syntax"
   b. *magnífica sintaxis de cloaca* → "magnificent syntax of the sewer"
   c. *cuánta sensibilidad sintáctica por el morbo más cruel* → "all that syntactic sensitivity at the service of a most cruel morbid pleasure"
   d. *fina sensibilidad sintáctica* → "sophisticated feel for syntax"
   e. *Qué magnífica capacidad de síntesis* (TT) → "What a magnificent ability to synthesize"
   f. *horrible estilo* → "horrible style"
   g. *sintaxis inmoral* → "immoral syntax"

[1] Same irony; e.g. 3a.
[2] Same type of (metaphorical antithetical) irony; e.g. 3b.
[3] Non-metaphorical antithetical irony; e.g. 3c.
[4] Non-antithetical irony; e.g. 3d and 3e.
[5] No irony; e.g. 3f and 3g.

5 The compass: a model of Priorities and Restrictions

Priorities and Restrictions is a "performance model" of translation[1]. The word "priority" is rescued from Nida (1964). From this revival of the term priority, within a didactic/evaluative paradigm, I can then provide a personal account of subjectivity, scope, ambition, and difficulty, proposing them as evaluative criteria. I deal with equivalence as a (variable) characteristic of priorities, although I am fully aware that this is not the only possible account of equivalence, even within this paradigm[2]. I assume that the objects that translators work with and produce are texts and the constituent elements of texts are verbal and nonverbal signs.

Levý, (1969: chapter 1), an exact contemporary of Nida, proposed a "functional hierarchy" that would determine the relative ranking of importance of various aspects of word meaning for the translator to use as a criterion[3].

I think the idea can be interesting if we regard the priorities of translation not as universal, or constant (as in "to be established by Nida"), but as variable and context-sensitive, to be re-established for each new assignment (by those who are responsible for the translation). Priorities are goals and objectives that are intended for the target text, as established by the translator[4]. For Chesterman (1997: 68), "different translation tasks may require balancing acts between different priorities, a point that I overlook here". Here, the point is picked up and given centre-stage.

In broad terms, *restrictions* constitute the constraining nature of the translator's circumstances or conditions[5]. Thus, factors such as deadline for

---

1 From the translator's point of view, it is a tool for justification (hopefully, a contribution towards the justification procedures as proposed by Toury, 1995: 37); for the critic and reviewer it can be seen as an evaluation aid (unlike Toury's two-way path which couples justification procedures with discovery procedures, addressing himself first and foremost to researchers and theorists rather than critics).
2 For example, in Chesterman, 1997: 69, "One kind of relation might of course be "equivalence" [...] of some sort. One translation task might require a translation which gave priority to a close formal similarity to the original [...] Another might prioritize stylistic similarity [...] yet another might highlight the importance of semantic closeness [...] yet another might value similarity of effect above all [...]".
3 For a full discussion of Levý's hierarchical model, see Gutt, 1991.
4 Regardless of whether s/he is (more or less reluctantly) taking on board the priorities of others.
5 I refer the reader to Chesterman, 1997: 54, for a distinction between conditions and norms, the important point being that conditions are a component of a definition of norms according to Bartsch, 1987: 76.

the translation, choice of translator, (insufficient) revision and copy-editing, structural differences between ST and TT languages —and other systemic differences— as well as technological limitations and some forms of censorship are restrictions that cannot be regarded as *priorities*. It is interesting to note that even such a norm theorist of the stature of Toury (1995, Chapter Ten, especially in Section 3 "Using revisions to uncover constraints") resorts just as often to the notion and term "constraints"— restrictions— as to norms. He frequently refers to the translator as "restricting himself to [certain characteristics intended for the target text that can be conceived of as hierarchically structured]"[6]. This is what I would prefer to call the translator's *priorities*, to be able to distinguish between priority-oriented restrictions and situations such as restricting oneself to such things as not asking anybody else for help, typing with one hand, or finishing the job in 320 minutes, for instance. He actually writes of "A certain aspiration for adequacy should [...] be added to our list of constraints. This [...] would rank hierarchically *lower*[7] than most of the constraints listed" (p. 204). Chesterman (1997: 78), like Toury, also refers to restrictions in his account of norms, "Lefevere (1992) distinguishes five constraints which determine the way translators [...] manipulate texts".[8]

From a text producer's (writer's, speaker's, translator's) angle, *priorities* are the intended formal and functional characteristics of a text. What makes a translation stand out from other forms of text production (that might also be considered as priority-driven) is that *its* priorities will necessarily reflect the way in which one text is to be regarded as a version[9] of another text, referred to as the source text.

A set of *priorities* will not necessarily include all of those factors that norm theorists would call norms, only those that the translator establishes as intended characteristics for the text. For example, a norm that "forbids" footnotes is not considered a *priority* because the inclusion of footnotes is a resource, or tactic, the X in [S+X] type solutions as stated above, but not a priority in the sense of a goal or objective *per se* for the target text. In this example, the non-inclusion of footnotes due to banning would be a *restriction* rather than a *priority*. Any "priorities" the translator may have in

---

6 e.g. "the text was translated under a rigid prosodic constraint, which Shlonsky had already subjected himself to before he ever set out to translate this particular monologue", p. 196.
7 Italics as in original.
8 i.e. patronage, poetics, the universe of discourse, the source and target languages, the translator's ideology.
9 The relation norm, in Chesterman, 1997: 69.

the larger context of his/her life (such as responsibilities and ambitions other than the translation at hand) are not *priorities* in the sense used here; they are *restrictions* if they prove to be in the way of achieving the best possible result for the TT by the best possible means.

In this scheme of things, a translation is the result —although a single "ideal" result is not envisaged— of an interaction of a hierarchical set of goals for the target text (*priorities* or P-set). Each *priority* is conditioned by restrictive circumstances. The success of a translator, TR, (human, machine, or assisted; individual or team) for a given task can be measured according to the number of conditioning factors that were[10] identified and taken into consideration; and according to how each individual factor was dealt with and accounted for within a global pattern, i.e. a specific set of priorities for each new translation.

When no solution can be found that will simultaneously account for all of the goals initially established for the TT, the translator can decide which characteristics have priority over others. In other words, *priority sets* are organized as hierarchies, as an operational principle, in order to justify and account for what is lost, gained, omitted, added, substituted, and compensated for.

Each *priority* implies the potential existence of its opposite (e.g. both "hilarious effect" and "dead serious effect" are potential priorities). No two opposing priorities can appear (*globally*, at least) in the same set, although they may appear in different sets (i.e. for different TTs, even if the ST is the same), or as *local priorities,* in different parts of the text. Even "be informative" is not universal (it is certainly not universally *high*) as a priority. For example, when translating nonsense poetry, or certain kinds of advertising jingles (where the *top priority* is "get the public to buy the product") or jokes (where the *top priority* is "laughter-eliciting"), the translator may not be interested in the ST information content at all, but will aim at conveying other aspects which respond to why the ST is being translated (to convey effects and impressions rather than information).

As a theoretical principle (momentarily considering translation outside of its social reality), translators are free to decide what priorities to include and their hierarchical arrangement. But in the real world many of a translator's

---

10 Assumptions and questions with the verb in the past tense apply for evaluation or discovery of a rationale behind the solutions as they appear in an existing target text. The past verb tenses can be switched to present and future tense—or even modalities expressing hypothesis or prescription—if the model is to be used by a translator during the process.

decisions are predefined, coming from various sources of prescription (editors, censors, laws, academic institutions, etc). From the point of view of evaluation or criticism, translators cannot be held entirely responsible for an unjustifiable *priority set* if it was imposed by someone in authority.

TT priorities do not always mirror ST priorities. There may be differences in their nature (they may not be the same ones), number (there may be more or less), or *rank*. *Scope* and *subjectivity* (see *evaluative criteria* below) are two concepts which derive from this observation. Variation in translation can be accounted for by using, among other means, the concepts of priorities and restrictions. The acceptance of variation does not compromise standards of excellence (which are in fact fixed sets of priorities and restrictions). Different strategies and solution-types[11]—that may be used to fulfil the priorities and overcome the restrictions—also help to account for different renderings. From this standpoint, unforeseen solutions might be fully justifiable. Decisions are made as to how and why the ST and the TT will be different as well as similar. Full awareness of this kind of decision-making[12] is also a means of understanding, often controlling, what is lost and/or gained according to the direction the translation takes.

Before looking into *how*—and *how well*—a given text was translated it is important to know *why* it was translated (e.g. as opposed to writing a piece of original work, translating a different text, using the ST for something other than translation), *what* was translated (as opposed to what was *not* translated), *what for*, *who for* and a number of questions to do with the viability conditions of the project.

Variables such as deadline, financing, technical or material limitations, as well as ST-TT differences at a number of levels (e.g. language structures, assumed knowledge and moral values of text users, and intertextuality) are *restrictions* and they cannot be adequately classified as *priorities*. For example, a *priority* for a translation may be to make money; presumably there will be evidence of this in the text. But if the client's intention is simply to pay the lowest possible price for the job, it is a restriction that may explain why certain priorities are not satisfactorily reflected in the TT.

---

11 I prefer to use strategies to refer to behavioural patterns that are not renderings, such as reading strategies, documentation strategies, etc.; solution-types, rather than techniques, refers to the common features of a specific set of solutions; solutions is a non-evaluative term for renderings, the actual textual makeup of the translation, and it stresses the problem-solving, decision-making, nature of translation from the translator's perspective.
12 As stated in Toury, p. 86, "DECISION-MAKING and the factors which may have CONSTRAINED it".

Different norms will produce different results. Standards of acceptability for text production in the TT environment also change, including the possibility that translations might be judged by different standards from "original" texts. A TR works under prescriptive pressure from various sources, and these may be more or less obvious.

5.1 The parameters of restrictions

If there were no restrictions there could be an absolute, universal, constant type of relationship between the ST and its TT, but because there are so many contingencies this is merely wishful (or prescriptive) thinking. The nature of the restrictions actually operative for a given translation has a limiting effect on the number and the nature of the priorities; in turn, the priorities determine the relevance of the restrictions, thus creating a tension between the two. Restrictions may be characterised according to the following parameters: source, force, level, and range.

The parameter of **Source** refers to the origin and explanation of the presence of the restrictions. They may come from textual features of the ST and the TT (textual restrictions), or from their contexts or the conditions of the translating process (contextual restrictions).

Not all restrictions are necessarily of equal **Force**. This parameter, unlike source, is one of degree, e.g. on a scale of restrictive force we might speak of three degree labels: *strong*, *weak*, and *nil*. A restriction is branded as *irrelevant* when it hardly matters whether it is present or not since it does not affect the priorities; in this sense sexual taboos are usually irrelevant when translating operating instructions for a coffee grinder. It is important to point out that each *priority* is competing with the other ones. If their structure is hierarchical then we can say that a *priority* is restricted by, among other circumstances, the *force* of higher-ranking priorities.

Level & range specifications are useful since not all of the segments and features of the text are necessarily affected by the restriction. Restrictions may appear as some form of systemic or textual differences on various *levels* that might be labelled (depending on the practical needs of the moment and the sophistication of the translator or scholar) as lexical, morphological, metaphorical, lip-synchrony (in the case of dubbing), rhyming structures, etc. *Range* specifies which parts of the text—if not all of it, globally—are affected locally by each restriction.

The absence or noticeable *weakening* of a given restriction during the translating process cancels out its effect (towards *nil* on the *force* scale), which brings about a series of "favourable circumstances" to be exploited by the translator. I call this phenomenon *restrictions reversed*.

5.2 Establishing the priorities of a translation

Many, if not all, of the language- and culture-specific features of the ST usually disappear or need to be changed. Are translators aware at all times of exactly which features are going to disappear and why? Do they act consistently and coherently when applying techniques for retaining those features that (according to the acceptability norms of the moment) cannot afford to be left out of the TT? The aim here is to show the importance of being able to establish context-sensitive priorities for the simple reason that they are not necessarily the same from one translation to the next. An alternative to resorting to a specific intuition (or knack) for translation is an awareness of one's decisions (or rather, of the grounds on which they are made), and their consequences, in order to be in a position to justify what one has done. Ploughing through a mental checklist and working hard on textual analysis and word-hunting is a useful, though tiring, fallback strategy for those times when inspiration is not forthcoming. This is even the preferred method during the learning process and training period when the translator's automatisms are still to be developed.

From the translator's position, *priorities* are established partly on the basis of understanding and interpreting the ST. This approach stresses the benefits of setting clear, coherent, realistic *targets* for the TT. The *targets* are the priorities and their final arrangement once the restrictions have been identified and taken into account. It is important to stress that certain priorities will only be feasible if certain restrictions are absent or very weak; further, each priority is *restricted* by any other priorities of higher *rank*[13]. An experienced translator gets through this (P&R establishing) stage very quickly in nonchallenging assignments that have a lot in common with previous work.

ST analysis and interpretation, often called the decoding stage of the translating process, may include (especially if it is translation-oriented) a twofold process of: (1) interpreting the text and identifying its priorities; (2) assessing the quality, communicative effectiveness and authority of the ST (e.g. measuring the ST writer's success in achieving intended goals to

---

13 A concept presented and defined below in the next section, appearing in references (above) to Toury and Levý.

consider the relative importance of the textual elements actually used). Answers to questions regarding the need(s), purpose(s) and goal(s) of a translation constitute *global priorities*, *global* indicating that these priorities apply throughout the text as a whole.

5.3 The parameters of priorities

TT priorities can be characterized according to the following parameters: source, rank, range, function, form, and equivalence. **Source** is the same as for the restrictions, but in particular the question is, who decides that the priority is such (e.g. translator, client, someone else)? To what extent are these direct sources—roleplayers in the translating process—agents or stake-holders of more distant or less tangible sources (academic, political, religious institutions, business interests and so on)?

Rank[14] is the importance of each priority with respect to the others: e.g. a hierarchical set scaling down from *top* to *nil* passing first through *high* and *low*, such that *top* and *high* are mandatory, *low* is desirable, not mandatory, and *nil* means a potential priority does not belong to the P set for the TT in question. *High* Ps (strong requirements/prohibitions) are either "aspects/items that must appear in the TT", or "aspects/items that must not appear or must be avoided". A given priority may sometimes stand out as the *top* P. *Low* Ps (weak requirements/prohibitions) are "aspects that should appear in the TT whenever possible", or "aspects that should be avoided as much as possible", for negative Ps. "Possible" here means "as long as all *higher* Ps are accounted for as well".

The parameters of **level & range** are essentially the same as for the restrictions, except that "level" is broken down here into function, form and equivalence. *Range*: priorities and restrictions can be seen as either *global* or *local*, depending on whether or not they hold their *rank* (or *force*) throughout the text. *Global* priorities are operative throughout the text. Typical *global* priorities will have to do with questions of text-types, discourse and overall intention. *Local* priorities are of limited *range*, operative only over a given segment of text; there is a temporary re-shuffling of the priority hierarchy, in answer to a specific restriction that is equally limited (*local*) in its *range*.

The **functional** level of a priority (informative, aesthetic, expressive, didactic, humoristic, etc.) accounts for any aspect or item in terms of its

---

14 Rank shows how priorities are "competing" forces, whereas the forces of the restrictions have an accumulative effect.

internal textual function (cohesive, exemplifying, concluding, etc.) or its contextual function (interpersonal, pragmatic, social, etc.). The level of **form** considers formal textual elements (such as repetitions, nonverbal constituents, layout, and delivery in recited texts) as motivated in certain places, usually subordinated to some function or other, which must then be identified.

Equivalence can be seen as a label that further qualifies priorities. The concepts of *intended equivalence, intended difference* (non-equivalence), and *indifference to equivalence* are potential characteristics of a priority. Once it has been decided that a feature (e.g. comic effect) is a priority, it is then labelled *yes, no* or *indifferent* for equivalence: thus, *yes* means that equivalence is *intended* (degree of similarity would then have to be specified), i.e. the feature is a priority for the TT precisely because it was a salient feature of the ST as well; *no = intended difference*, meaning that the feature is a priority for the TT even though it was not for the ST; *indifferent* (equivalence not considered), meaning that the feature is a priority for the TT regardless of whether it was or was not a priority for the ST. As for the actual solutions or solution-types (more or less accurate representations of the priorities), TT renderings can be classified as instances of *intentional* equivalence (or difference), *casual* equivalence (for *indifferent*), or *unjustifiable* equivalence for unaccountable or inexplicable solutions, or ones contrary to the established set of priorities.

5.4 Examples of areas for establishing priorities

1) **Information load**. (i) Information items: quantity and type of information. (ii) The proportion of explicit and implicit information. (iii) The relative importance of information with regard to other aspects of the text, i.e. its *rank*. (iv) Relevance of the information to the intended text user.
2) **Decoding and text-processing**. How important is it that the text be immediately understandable, and unambiguous in its intention and/or in its meaning (e.g. road signs v. metaphysical poetry)?
3) **Text-user response**. Is there an intended single specific response or a "free" personal one? Is the response meant to be immediate or delayed? What is the degree of coaxing and hoaxing[15] on the part of the text-producer?

---

15 Please forgive me giving priority to rhyme over terminological orthodoxy.

4) **Aesthetic elements** (related to text-user response). Is the text, or any part of it, fundamentally artistic, or are the aesthetic elements mostly instrumental in achieving other *priorities*?
5) **Formal aspects**, genre, discourse, register, text-type membership traits. What kind of formal aspects are involved and how are they related to the text's functions (rhyme, repetitions, total number of words, letter size, use of colours, etc.)?

5.5 Evaluative criteria

Ps and Rs help to justify or account for: (a) the various *strategies* resorted to in the process and the *solutions* (renderings) used in the resulting version; (b) TTs as texts that respond to a variety of needs and goals dependent on the circumstances of their production and reception.

Hatim and Mason (1990: 160) say that translators may not intrude arbitrarily or inadvertently. I would like to interpret Hatim and Mason's use of *arbitrarily* as meaning *unjustifiably*, which is usually what happens when the translator is not fully aware of all of the factors involved. We will thus rephrase this statement by saying that there is a difference between *unjustified* manipulation and *priority-oriented* manipulation. *Ambition* counts the number of *priorities* for a given translation, regardless of equivalence. An example of *limited ambition* might be the characteristic priorities of *summary* or *gist* translation. On the other end of the "ambition scale" we find TTs that are rich in their expressiveness and show many-layered meanings and effects. A TT is more *ambitious* the higher the number and *rank* of its priorities. The s*cope* of a TT results from the *fulfilment of the ambition* (i.e. the degree to which the *priorities* are clearly rendered and accounted for in the TT solutions). *Ambition* can be used as a measure of *difficulty*, although it need not always be a yardstick for quality, since a TT may be considered unjustifiably, or too, ambitious.

Subjectivity measures mismatches in the hierarchical orders of the priorities of the ST and TT. A TT becomes *more subjective* as the number and importance of the mismatches grow (importance of mismatches can be seen by looking at differences on the *rank* scale), becoming more "objective" the greater the coincidence, giving rise to more *priorities* and renderings ticking off "yes" for equivalence. A TT is more subjective the greater its differences *vis-à-vis* its ST, both in the respective *ranking position* of each *priority* and the solutions used, regardless of whether the differences were intentional or unintentional (*casual*). A TR's intention(s) may be quite different from the ST author's. This can be made to surface, on the scale of *subjectivity*, by identifying priorities in the TT that were absent in the ST (and *vice versa*), and/or differences in the *rank* of shared priorities. As in the case of ambition there is no (non-prescriptive) automatic relation between subjectivity and quality.

The greater the number of *priorities*, the smaller the number of potential solutions that can do justice to all of them to the same degree, especially if the priorities are very diverse. A translation becomes more difficult as the priorities increase in number, especially those of higher *rank*, in other words, the more *ambitious* the TT is. The greater the number and force of the restrictions, the more difficult it will be for the translator to fully satisfy expectations and fulfill priorities.

The better a translation fits the criteria of its evaluation, which are variable, the better it will be. It all depends on the kind of TT that we want (or are able) to produce. Evaluative criteria may (or may not) include *ambition, scope,* and *subjectivity*; we can even evaluate the translator's choice of *priorities*. In comparing two versions of the same ST, we might say that one is better than the other because it has greater *scope*, or, from a different angle, that it has more satisfactorily fulfilled all or most of its objectives regardless of whether the other translation had set itself more priorities (was more *ambitious*). A TT may be regarded as worse than another if it has a higher number of *unjustifiable* solutions.

Ambition and *subjectivity* scales are proposed as an alternative to evaluating translations on a scale with "literal" at one end, and "free" at the other. I think it is important to realise that *ambition* and *subjectivity* are non-evaluative as concepts. One becomes normative only when one fixes what degree of ambition one expects, or how much subjectivity one is willing to tolerate. Other than that, the most normative aspect of my proposal is that it demands that a translator be able to justify his or her solutions in terms of intended goals and objectives in a given set of circumstances. Hopefully, this means that *subjectivity* and *ambition* can be applied to descriptions (e.g. for comparative purposes) as well as evaluations.

6 Conclusions

I hope this type-within-type binary-branch model of analysis, together with the proposal for looking at translation in terms of variable priorities and restrictions can be used to show up translational norms that might otherwise be difficult to account for or even identify. The model involves trying out different "trees" to find the most suitable one for each analysis, not only of individual problems but also of large numbers of instances of the same problem, in search of elusive regularities. A single segment of text might require more than one "tree" analysis for a full account of what is going on or what is at stake. Non-prescriptive tree diagrams can easily be adapted to prescriptive flowchart diagrams, whereby solution-type [2] is allowed only if none can be found for [1], for instance. A binary-tree analysis can be more meaningful if it has a justifiable structure. The present proposal has found its justification in a type-within-type structure that allows for a variable number of subtypes, according to the typology used. The complexity of the translator's job is shown by the fact that a given segment might present several phenomena or problems that require separate tree analyses. This could also be a limitation of the model. For example, translations of *dragon* might have to be analysed separately as metaphor, insult, joke, allusion, etc., according to a different typology each time.

The basic binary branch, based on type-within-type, can be further completed by incorporating other binary divisions such as: verbal/non-verbal; "bare"/compound; and L2/not-L2 splits. Finally, I could not find sufficient grounds to assign a definitive location for empty segment, and am thus forced to regard it as having the potential to belong anywhere.

References

Chesterman, Andrew. 1997. *Memes of Translation*. Amsterdam: John Benjamins.
Delabastita, Dirk. 1993. *There's a Double Tongue*. Amsterdam: Rodopi.
Goatly, Andrew. 1997. *The Language of Metaphors*. London: Routledge.
Hammond, Paul and Patrick Hughes. 1978. *Upon the Pun. Dual Meaning in Words and Pictures*. London: W.H. Allen.
Hatim, Basil and Ian Mason. 1990. *Discourse and the Translator*. Harlow, England: Longman.
Hewson, Lance and Jacky Martin. 1991. *Redefining Translation. The Variational Approach*. London: Routledge.
Holmes, James. 1988. "The Name and Nature of Translation Studies". In *Translated! Papers on Literary Translation and Translation Studies*. Ed. James S. Holmes. Amsterdam: Rodopi.
Lakoff, George and Mark Johnson. 1980. *Metaphors We Live By*. Chicago: University of Chicago.
Lefevere, André. 1992. *Translation, Rewriting and the Manipulation of Literary Fame*. London: Routledge.

Levý, Jirí. 1969. *Die literarishce Übersetzung: Theorie einer Kunstgattung.* Frankfurt: Athenäum.
Newmark, Peter. 1988. *Approaches to Translation.* New York: Prentice-Hall.
Nida, Eugene. 1964. *Towards a Science of Translating.* Leyden: E. J. Brill.
— and Charles Taber. 1982 (1969). *The Theory and Practice of Translation.* Leiden: E. J. Brill.
Nord, Christianne. 1991. *Text Analysis in Translation.* Amsterdam: Rodopi.
Toury, Gideon. 1995. *Descriptive Translation Studies and Beyond.* Amsterdam: John Benjamins.
White, Roger. 1996. *The Structure of Metaphor.* Oxford: Blackwell.
Wolfe, Tom. 1987. *The Bonfire of the Vanities.* New York: Bantam Books, Farrar. Spanish version by E. Murillo. 1988. *La hoguera de la vanidades.* Barcelona: Anagrama.
Zabalbeascoa, Patrick. 1995. "Levels of Prescriptiveness in Translation". In *Cross-Words.* Eds. Ian Mason and Christine Pagnoulle. Liège: University Liège.
— 1999. "Priorities and Restrictions in Translation". In *Translation and the (Re)location of Meaning.* Ed. Jeroen Vandaele. CETRA publications No. 4.
— 1996. "Translating Jokes for Dubbed Television Situation Comedies". In *The Translator* 2.2. Ed. Dirk Delabastita. Manchester: St. Jerome.
— 1997. "Dubbing and the Nonverbal Dimension of Translation". In *Nonverbal Communication in Translation: New Perspectives and Challenges in Literature, Interpretation and the Media.* Ed. Fernando Poyatos. Amsterdam: John Benjamins.

CHAPTER FIVE

CROSSCULTURAL TRANSLATION AND CONFLICTING IDEOLOGIES

CHRISTINA SCHÄFFNER

Introduction

Translation has frequently been defined as intercultural, or cross-cultural communication (e.g. Vermeer 1986). Such a view is based on an understanding that translation enables members of different cultures who speak different languages to understand each other. A text, initially written in a source language L1 for an audience in the L1-culture is translated into an L2 and thus made available to an audience in the L2-culture. That is, thanks to translation, a new readership is included "in a communicative act which was originally restricted to the source language community" (Reiss 1989: 107).

Describing translation as enabling communication and communicative interaction reflects a positive view. However, research, as conducted in particular within the framework of Descriptive Translation Studies and post-modern theories, has revealed that translation is also used to promote dominant ideologies, to silence minorities, or to subject messages to censorship (e.g. Venuti 1998, Baker 2006). Translation methods are applied strategically to make target texts conform to or to challenge dominant world views. The very choice of texts to be translated or not to be translated, as the case may be, is often an ideologically motivated decision. Ideology is understood here with van Dijk (1998) and Lu (1999) as socially shared belief systems of (members of) groups, as patterns of ideas, assumptions, beliefs, values or interpretations of the world by which a group operates. That is, ideologies operate in our daily lives, they can be described as "common sense", as "implicit social knowledge that group members take for granted in their everyday practices" (van Dik 1998: 102). Since translation itself is a social practice, ideologies play an important role in the production and reception of translations as products.

Although by no means limited to the field of politics, ideology is nevertheless of particular relevance for politics. Translation plays a role in political communication as well, since, for example, speeches by politicians are translated and made available on embassy websites. Some government websites are multilingual, and the language versions of bi- or multilateral treaties between governments or political parties are equally valid and authoritative. For mediating politics to the general public, mass media play a significant role, including the reporting of politics in other countries. In the case of mass media, however, translation is mostly implicit and invisible. In this chapter, I will explore translation policies and strategies for two media institutions: the German *Spiegel International*, and the UK's *BBC Monitoring Service*. I will address issues of text selection for translation, addressees and clients, the role of the translators, and ideological aspects as represented in the texts. The focus will be on texts which reflect conflicting ideologies between social groups in the source culture and in the target culture(s), with particular reference to media representations of global terror. In the concluding section, I will comment on the relationship between translation, communication, and conflict.

Case Study 1: *Spiegel International*

In its regular section "What the papers say", the weekly paper *European Voice* briefly summarises comments from selected national newspapers, including direct quotes. In its issue of October 2005, there is a reference to the German weekly news magazine *Der Spiegel*:

Der Spiegel runs an interview with the incoming chancellor, Angela Merkel, that features in this grabber headline "I am immune to the seduction of power" (European Voice, 20-26 October 2005)

The article also provides some extracts from the original 4-pages-long interview:

Sample interchange:
> Spiegel: "Some elements of the public see you as having a cool persona, perhaps all the more so because women are generally considered to be more emotional."
> Merkel: "I am not sure what you mean by female emotionality. Maybe you adhere to the prejudice that women talk too much. Indeed, that's one bias I can't say I live up to."[1]

---

1   German original: Spiegel: Sie werden von Teilen der Öffentlichkeit als kühl wahrgenommen, vielleicht auch deshalb, weil Frauen gemeinhin als emotionaler gelten.
   Merkel: Ich kenne Ihre Vorstellungen von weiblicher Emotionalität nicht. Vielleicht hängen Sie dem Vorurteil nach, dass Frauen besonders viel sprechen. Damit kann ich in der Tat nicht immer dienen.

The original interview was conducted in German and published in German in the print version of the weekly news magazine *Der Spiegel* (17 October 2005, pp. 42-46), but there is no explicit indication of translation in the *European Voice*. However, research reveals that these extracts which appeared in the *European Voice*, were taken *verbatim* from *Spiegel International* (http://www.spiegel. de/international/spiegel/0,1518,380168, 00.html).

Spiegel International (http://www.spiegel.de/international) was launched in October 2004 and is the official English version of *Spiegel Online*, which was founded in 1994. On its welcome page (http://service.spiegel.de/cache/ international/0,1518,321949,00.html), the editors comment as follows:

> [...] With the launch of our international site, SPIEGEL finally brings its unique voice to English readers. [...]

Spiegel International provides English translations of cover stories or other important articles from the print magazine, English translations of texts that were published on the German site of *Spiegel Online*, and also summaries of other texts on a variety of topics, in addition to politics e.g. culture, sports, technology. That is, news here is understood in the widest sense of the term. The English texts are produced and translated by a small team based in Berlin, consisting of journalists who are native speakers of English. In addition to their "normal" journalistic work (i.e. original reporting, conducting interviews), they also produce English texts on the basis of information extracted from a variety of German texts as well as on the basis of foreign language wire services (especially the news agencies Reuters and AP). That is, translation, including summary translation, is a regular part of the daily work of these journalists. Full texts from the print magazine are normally sent for translation to team members who are professional translators and native speakers of English (most regularly Christopher Sultan, who is based in Washington). Only the full-text translations are normally presented explicitly as translations (indicated at the very end as "Translated from the German by", followed by the name of the translator). In all the other cases, however, the translator is invisible. Moreover, the journalists in the Berlin office of *Spiegel International* do not think of themselves as translators, but as journalists.

As research into global news and translation has shown, it is a widespread phenomenon that journalists in fact do translations but do not refer to this work as translation (see the information on the project "The politics and economics of translation in global media" on http://www.warwick.ac.uk/fac/arts/BCCS/research /AHRB.html', Bassnett 2004, Bielsa 2007). As Bielsa (2007: 136) argues, "translation is not conceived as separate from other journalistic tasks of writing up and editing [...] Translation is thus an important part of journalistic work and is subject to the same requirements of genre and style that govern journalistic production in general." The work done by journalists is governed by journalistic norms and values, above all speed and good writing.

The quality of "good writing" applies to the translations as well. The institutional policy expects all English texts that are published on *Spiegel International* to be written in accurate and fluent English. In other words, the aim is to provide fluent, transparent texts that conform to the expectations and reading habits of the English-speaking addressees. In Venuti's terms, a domesticating translation method is what is being practised (Venuti 1995). This overall approach of domestication can be seen in the following translation strategies at the textual micro-level, which were identified on the basis of an analysis of a corpus of 15 full-text translations from January till June 2005 (Schäffner 2005):

(1) Explicitation and/or addition in the case of source-culture specific referents, especially politicians and place names. In the German source texts, politicians are frequently just mentioned by name, and, if necessary, their political role and/or their political party affiliation are added. In the English translations, political role and party affiliation are normally provided, with the full name of the political party instead of the abbreviation only. This can be seen in the following examples (ST stands for source text, and TT stands for target text):

> ST: Otto Schily (SPD)
> TT: Social Democratic Interior Minister Otto Schily
>
> ST: der bayrische Innenminister Günther Beckstein (CSU)
> TT: Bavarian Interior Minister Günther Beckstein, a member of the conservative Christian Social Union, or CSU,
> (Both *Der Spiegel*, 24 January 2005, p. 62 and (http://www.spiegel.de /international/ spiegel/0,1518,338766,00.html)
>
> ST: Rechtsanwalt in Breslau
> TT: a lawyer in Breslau (Wroclaw, Poland)
> (*Der Spiegel*, 24 January 2005, p. 71 and http://www.spiegel.de /international/spiegel/0,1518,338597,00.html)

The nationality of politicians is frequently added, even in the case of well known people. In the case of place names, the country is usually added for clarification, e.g.:

ST: Premier Tony Blair
TT: British Prime Minister Tony Blair
ST: vor dem Militärgericht in Osnabrück
TT: before a military court in the German city of Osnabrueck
(Both *Der Spiegel,* 24 January 2005, p. 117 and http://www.spiegel. de/international/ spiegel/0,1518,338766,00.html)

(2) Omissions, additions and/or generalisations, e.g.:

ST: in den Hamburger Kammerspielen (literally: in the Hamburg Kammerspiele theatre)
TT: in Hamburg
(*Der Spiegel*, 24 January 2005, p. 62 and
http://www.spiegel.de/international/ spiegel/0,1518,338766,00.html)

ST: Die Bin-Ladin-Story: Sie wirkt mit ihren dramatischen Wendungen fast wie eine arabische Variante der "Buddenbrooks".
TT: The bin Laden story, with its dramatic twists and turns, almost comes across as an Arab version of Thomas Mann's novel "Buddenbrooks". (i.e., addition of literary genre and author's name – CS)
(*Der Spiegel*, 6 June 2005, p. 67 and
http://www.spiegel.de/international/spiegel /0,1518,359690,00.html)

What we see in these examples, is that the translator has taken into account the lack of background knowledge of English-speaking readers. In other cases, especially if the source text has a reference to the United States of America, omissions were applied as translation strategies, as in the following examples:

ST: Lexington im US-Bundesstaat Kentucky (literally: Lexington in the US federal state of Kentucky)
TT: from Lexington, Kentucky,

ST: [...] wofür ihm das "Purple Heart", eine Verwundetenauszeichnung der US-Armee, verliehen wurde (literally: the "Purple Heart", the medal the US-Army awards to its wounded soldiers)
TT: He [...] was awarded the Purple Heart and allowed [...]
(Both *Der Spiegel*, 17 January 2005, p. 90ff and http://service. spiegel.de/cache/international/spiegel/0,1518,337091,00.html)

(3) Specifications, especially if more informal characterisations (of people or places) are used in the German text, e.g.:

ST: Die Kritik am Pentagonchef nimmt zu [...] Pentagonchef [...] (literally: the chief of the Pentagon)
TT: Defense Secretary Donald Rumsfeld particularly faces growing criticism. [...] Rumsfeld [...]
(*Der Spiegel*, 17 January 2005, p. 90ff and
http://service.spiegel.de/cache /international/spiegel/0,1518,337091,00.html)

The phrase "die Insel" ("the island"), used three times in one text to refer to Great Britain, was translated once by "Great Britain" and twice by "the British" (*Der Spiegel,* 24 January 2005, p. 117 and http://www.spiegel.de/international/ spiegel/0,1518,338766,00.html).

Main titles too, are very often changed, with one reason being that the inclusion of important keywords in the headline will allow the story to be given priority by the algorithms of search engines. For example, the main title "Angeknackste Moral" (literally: Weakened morals) in the source text was replaced by "Torture in Iraq" (*Der Spiegel,* 4/2005, 24 January 2005, p. 117 and http://www.spiegel.de/international /spiegel/0,1518,338766, 00.html). In the case of the Merkel interview mentioned above, the original title of the German text was "Ich bin nicht ängstlich" (literally: I am not afraid), which has become "I Am Immune to the Seduction of Power". Both quotes actually constitute the very last answer by Merkel in the interview:

> Spiegel: Have you felt trepidation creeping in these past few days?
> Merkel: No. I'm not afraid, I am alert and excited, but not in the slightest bit anxious. I am immune to the seduction of power; at least I think I am.[2]

The fact that this interview was conducted just a few days before Merkel officially took up the position of German Chancellor, explains the hedging in her answer ("at least I think I am"). The title of the published English version makes her come across as cool and strong (cf. the reference to "grabber headline" in the *European Voice*).

Another aspect concerning translation policies and practices is the very selection of texts for translation into English. The topics selected by the journalists in the Berlin office are primarily those that are of general interest worldwide, and particularly in the USA, at the time of publication. The texts therefore come predominantly from the international section ("Ausland") of the print magazine. Among texts selected are particularly those that deal with the topic of "the war on terror" in general, and in the last few years with the Iraq war in particular. The attitude of vast groups of the German public towards the US policy in Iraq is highly critical. The magazine *Der Spiegel* too, which is known for its investigative journalism,

---

[2] German original: Spiegel: Spüren Sie in diesen Tagen machmal ein Gefühl von Beklommenheit?
Merkel: Nein, ich bin nicht ängstlich, ich bin aufmerksam-gespannt, aber überhaupt nicht beklommen. Gegen die Verführungen der Macht bin ich, glaube ich jedenfalls, immunisiert.

takes a rather critical position towards the US administration's policy. That is, such texts represent conflicting ideologies, i.e. different beliefs, opinions and values held by social groups. As I have argued elsewhere (Schäffner 2005), it is precisely as a result of this text selection process, that English-speaking readers can get access to a point of view and an evaluation of political affairs which is different to the one they normally get from their home media. For example, with reference to English versions of texts on *Spiegel Online* (some of which were also published in *The New York Times*, as a result of a cooperative agreement), Matthias Spielkamp reported, that it had become possible in this way for readers of the *New York Times* to read a very critical article from *Der Spiegel* in which the American CIA had been accused of breaking the laws of other countries. US mainstream media had hardly been critical of their own government institutions before the Iraq War (cf. http://www.onlinejournalismus.de/webwatch/kooperation_sponnyt.html).

I will return to the issue of text selection for translation and a translation strategy of domestication in respect of conflicting ideologies below.

Case study 2: *BBC Monitoring Service*

In commenting on the inconclusive results of Germany's parliamentary elections in September 2005, the *European Voice*, again in its regular section "What the media say", quotes from Czech paper *Právo*:

> The Czech Republic's *Právo* thinks the EU should remain calm, according to the BBC translation service. "Nothing will change on Germany's striving for European integration, deeper democracy or the protection of human or minority rights," it reassures. (*European Voice*, 22 September 2005)

In this case, there is an explicit reference to the BBC translation service as having provided the English version of a text which was then used by other journalists in their own reports.

BBC translation service actually refers to the UK's *BBC Monitoring Service*. *BBC Monitoring* is part of the *BBC World Service*, a directorate of the BBC, the British Broadcasting Corporation. It was set up in 1939, the year which saw the beginning of World War Two, and was initially designed to monitor and translate open sources from Germany. Today, *BBC Monitoring* monitors nearly everything which is in the public domain, with a special focus on material appearing in languages other than English. On its website (http://www.monitor.bbc.co.uk/), *BBC Monitoring* describes its work as follows:

> *BBC Monitoring* supplies news, information and comment gathered from the mass media around the world.
> We operate around the clock to monitor more than 3,000 radio, TV, press, internet and news agency sources, translating from up to 100 languages.

Their main stakeholders are the Foreign and Commonwealth Office (FCO) and the Ministry of Defence (MoD), as the two providers of most of the core funding, the Cabinet Office, journalists and academics, but also governments, embassies, multinational companies, charities and media clients around the world. In a promotional leaflet about its work between 2003 and 2006, *BBC Monitoring* comments that since 9/11, the so called war on terror had been at the centre of global coverage. A "campaign against terrorism" coverage was developed, especially monitoring media and other open sources from the Middle East, South Asia, and Africa. Satisfied customers are quoted on the front page of the promotional brochure as follows:

> "BBCM material consistently gave me a better understanding of how the "war on terror" is reported and debated in the Middle East" (FCO).
> "Timely, accurate, excellent" (MoD).

BBC Monitoring describes its task as "rigorously selecting vital information on behalf of our customers" and "translating reports accurately into English and delivering online for immediacy and ease of access" (promotional brochure, also on the website as accessed in November 2005).

Expert selection and accurate translation are thus two of the most significant principles for information processing at *BBC Monitoring*, and the main tasks thus comprise listening, selecting, translating and transmitting information. The translation method is presented on the *BBC Monitoring* website like this:

> They translate reports in a way that preserves the tone of the original, allowing subscribers to draw their own conclusions from what they read. (http://www. monitor.bbc./co.uk - as accessed in November 2005)

In a Debate in April 2005, this view of translation was further specified by Dr Ali Chokri, in charge of the Western Europe and Latin American team at *BBC Monitoring Service*, as "the accurate reproduction of the original in English, capturing the full meaning, style, register and nuances of the original" (see http://www2.warwick.ac.uk/fac/arts/ctccs/research/

tgn/events/gt/prog/ for a report on this Debate). He characterised the *BBC Monitoring Service* as an organisation which gives "the horse's mouth" to its clients, since its objective is to transmit original texts and not to produce an interpretation. Editorial intervention is therefore reduced to the minimum required to make texts more user-friendly (for example, providing a headline and subheadings).

Sample texts that are available on the website illustrate this practice. These samples are arranged according to a common pattern: a main title provided by the *BBC Monitoring Service*, a reference to the original text, the translation of the text, the original source, including an indication of the source language. Three examples will suffice, two from the section on Terrorism samples (accessed in November 2005 and November 2006, resp.), and one from the section on Iraq samples (accessed in November 2007), with the actual texts not reproduced below in the first two cases (as indicated by [...]):

(1) Al-Aqsa Brigades reject disarmament, urge international probe into Arafat death
Text of report by pro-Hamas Palestinian Information Centre website on 17 November
[...]
Source: Palestinian Information Centre website in Arabic 17 Nov 05

(2) Tamil Tigers condemn assassination of Sri Lankan MP Raviraj
Text of unattributed report entitled: "LTTE condemns killing of Tamil National Alliance MP, Raviraj" by Sri Lankan newspaper Virakesari on 11 November
[...]
Source: Virakesari, Colombo, in Tamil 11 Nov 06

(3) Iraqi Turkoman group denies opposition to Turkish offensive against Kurdistan
Text of report headlined: "The Turkoman Notables' Council deny their opposition to Turkish offensive", published by Sbay media website on 3 November
The Turkoman Notables' Council has denied [reports] that it is opposed to a Turkish military offensive against Kurdistan Region. It has also denied its opposition to [the Turkish] decision [given by the Turkish parliament to take military action against the PKK in northern Iraq].
Sbay has obtained a copy of a statement by the Turkoman Notables' Council which rejects a report published by [the Kurdistan Democratic Party's daily newspaper in Arabic language] Al-Ta'akhi on 29 October stating that the council is against the Turkish offensive.
Source: Sbay media website, in Sorani Kurdish 3 Nov 07

The third example above illustrates editorial interventions, which in this particular case may be said to be more than minimal since information is actually added to help the readers understand references to culture-specific items (e.g. Al-Ta'akhi) and to background events (e.g. the specification of the Turkish parliament's decision in the second sentence).

The translation practice of trying to capture "the full meaning, style, register and nuances of the original" can be illustrated with another example: the English translation of a speech by Osama Bin Laden, broadcast in Arabic on the Al-Jazeera TV station. I only give the first sentences below, together with the additional information provided at the very beginning to contextualise the text (the formatting below is the same as in the original texts).

> http://news.bbc.co.uk/2/low/south_asia/1585636.stm (accessed November 2005)
> BBC News Online: World: South Asia
> Sunday, 7 October, 2001, 22:31 GMT 23:31 UK
> Bin Laden's warning: full text
>
> Message first broadcast on Arabic station Al Jazeera
> *Osama Bin Laden has issued a strongly-worded warning to the United States in a recorded statement broadcast on al-Jazeera television. Below is the full text of his statement.*
>
> Praise be to God and we beseech Him for help and forgiveness.
> We seek refuge with the Lord of our bad and evildoing. He whom God guides is rightly guided but he whom God leaves to stray, for him wilt thou find no protector to lead him to the right way.
> I witness that there is no God but God and Mohammed is His slave and Prophet.
> God Almighty hit the United States at its most vulnerable spot. He destroyed its greatest buildings. Praise be to God.
> Here is the United States. It was filled with terror from its north to its south and from its east to its west. Praise be to God. […]

There are several other translations of this speech, including one by the US-American news agency CNN. The beginning of the text on their website (accessed in November 2005) is as follows (the formatting below is the same as in the original texts):

> http://archives.cnn.com/2001/WORLD/asiapcf/central/10/07/ret.binladen.tr anscript/ (accessed in November 2005)
> Bin Laden: America "filled with fear"
>
> *DOHA, Qatar (CNN)* – The Arab television news network al Jazeera broadcast a speech from Osama bin Laden Sunday after the United States

and Britain launched their attack on Afghanistan. It is unclear when the videotaped statement was recorded, but it does refer to the September 11 attacks on the World Trade Center and the Pentagon.

The following is a transcript of the translated statement:

> Thanks to God, he who God guides will never lose. And I believe that there's only one God. And I declare I believe there's no prophet but Mohammed.
> This is America, God has sent one of the attacks by God and has attacked one of its best buildings. And this is America filled with fear from the north to south and east to west, thank God. [...]

In the introductory comments to the CNN text, it is said explicitly that the English version is a "transcript of the translated statement", although there is no indication of the translation agents (and the word "transcript" in all probability hides editorial interventions). The BBC version above just speaks of the "full text of his statement", i.e. translation here is totally invisible (on media representations of texts see also Holland 2006).

There is also an example of editorial intervention in the BBC translation later in the text:

> One million Iraqi children have thus far died in Iraq although they did not do anything wrong.
> Despite this, we heard no denunciation by anyone in the world or a fatwa by the rulers' ulema [body of Muslim scholars].

The CNN text, in contrast, reads as follows:

> And there are civilians, innocent children being killed every day in Iraq without any guilt, and we never hear anybody. We never hear any fatwah from the clergymen of the government.

These two translations create a different impression as a result of different strategies employed. The BBC version sounds more foreign than the CNN one. This foreignisation method is in line with the *BBC Monitoring's* policy of "giving the horse's mouth". The CNN version reflects a translation method of domestication. Bielsa (2007: 151) argues that "news translation is doubly invisible, not just because of the need to adopt a domesticating strategy that values fluency and hides its very intervention, but also because of the fact that translation has been successfully integrated within journalism." As the examples above show, the reality is even more complex. A domestication method may hide the fact that the text is a translation, but the paratext (e.g. introductory comments as above, but also footnotes, a translator's note) may make an explicit reference to translation. It can also be the case, that a method of foreignisation which is meant to let the source text "shine through" and which is thus meant to make translation visible, does not appear to be visible at all to a reader if there is no indication of translation in the paratext. In any case, textual differences can give readers different impressions of politicians and thus lead them in different directions (cf. also Bassnett's comparative analysis of different reports in British newspapers about Saddam Hussein's court trial—Bassnett 2004). That is, texts can take on different functions, quite independently of any original intentions, and even one and the same text allows for a plurality of possible interpretations, since text interpretation is determined by socio-cultural contexts. Research in Critical Discourse Analysis has shown "different implications of different readings for social action" (Fairclough and Wodak 1997: 279) with reference to various examples. In a cross-cultural perspective, different (readings of) translations too may result in different social actions on the part of readers—just think of decisions taken by politicians in response to statements by other politicians (which were often presented in translation).

What all the examples illustrated above have in common, is that they have been produced in line with an explicitly acknowledged translation policy: fluent translations for *Spiegel International*, and accurate translations that capture the full meaning, style and nuances of the original for the *BBC Monitoring Service*. The dominant practices with regard to translations produced by these two media institutions may be characterised as domestication for *Spiegel International*, and foreignisation for the *BBC Monitoring Service*. *Spiegel International* wants to brings *Spiegel's* "unique voice" to English readers, as stated on its website, and the *BBC Monitoring Service* wants to give its readers "the horse's mouth", as explained by Chokri. Both views reflect a priority for the message as expressed by the author in the original text. In view of the translation strategies identified, the question then is: whose voice do the readers actually hear? I will attempt to answer this question in the following section.

Selected and refracted voices

As I have illustrated above, the journalists as translators at *Spiegel International* regularly pay attention to the knowledge of their English-speaking readers and resort to translation strategies of addition, explicitation, generalisation and/or omission. It is therefore not the linguistic make-up of the English translations which lets the readers see the "unique voice", since they will not see any traces of a different "other" in the texts they read. But does my initial argument hold that it is as a result of the very text selection that a different view on an ideologically controversial topic can be got across to English-speaking readers?

In one of the examples above, we saw that the various occurrences of "Pentagonchef" (literally: the chief of the Pentagon) in the German source text had been rendered by "Defense Secretary Donald Rumsfeld" or only by giving the name Rumsfeld in the target text. One consequence of this translation strategy is that the attitude changes. "Pentagonchef" reflects not only a rather informal way of referring to people but also an attitude of less respect and critical distance. In the German texts, the journalists usually opt for more lexical variation, and prefer more informal labels in addition to the official title. However, using the official title in the target text predominantly or exclusively can be interpreted as a sign of respect.

There are a number of associations and groups that see their task in monitoring the media and expose cases of misrepresentation and biased reporting. One of them, *Davids Medienkritik* (http://www.dmko.info/), says in its mission statement:

> This weblog is a watchdog site dedicated to the documentation of anti-Americanism in German media and the negative influence it has on Germans' perception of the United States.
> (http://medienkritik.typepad.com/blog/2006/11 /mission_stateme.html)

Spiegel International is criticised regularly for its supposedly anti-Americanism and its mistranslations. There are regular comments on "significant discrepancies" between the English and the German versions of texts. Here are two extracts critically commenting on a text on the Iraq war. The original German text is entitled "Experten-Ohrfeigen für Bushs Irak-Politik" (literally: Experts' slap in the face for Bush's Iraq policy, http://www.spiegel.de/politik/ausland/0,1518,405135,00.html), and the English version is entitled "When Democracy Looks Like Civil War" (http://www.spiegel.de/international/0,1518,405306,00.html). *Davids Medienritik* comments as follows:

> The final sentence in the second paragraph of the English version is a direct quote from Kenneth Pollack: "A six- to 12-month window of opportunity may be all that remains before the spiral toward possible chaos

and civil war is beyond control." The German translation omits the word "possible."

The first line of the fifth paragraph of the English version states: "According to some experts, in fact, the situation in Iraq has deteriorated so far that a completely new approach to the problem is required." The German states: "Nach Einschätzung einiger Experten ist die Situation im Irak mittlerweile so desaströs, dass sie nach einem ganz neuen Blick auf das Problem verlangt:" Translated that means: "According to some experts' estimation the situation in Iraq is, in the meantime, so disastrous that it requires a completely new approach to (look at) the problem." The word "disastrous" has been left out of the English version.
(http://medienkritik.typepad.com/blog/2006/03/index.html)

The general argument is that the anti-Americanism in the German texts is stronger than in the English ones. As the critical comments above show, the underlying concept of translation is one of literal translation, where each word in the source text is expected to be accounted for in the target text. Although from the point of view of Translation Studies, such comments as e.g. "the word 'disastrous' has been left out" (actually, it had been turned into "has deteriorated so far that"), or "omits the word 'possible'" (the German text had added "im schlimmsten Fall", i.e. in the worst case scenario) can equally be criticised, the overall political argument cannot so easily be rejected. In the case of another text, examples of omissions are identified in an interview which *Der Spiegel* had conducted with Karen Hughes, the US Undersecretary for Public Diplomacy and Public Affairs. Phrases such as "our historic friendship", "this is our fervent hope", "such a close friend" were omitted in the German version, which makes *Davids Medienkritik* come to the following evaluation (bold in the original):

> **And the lesson is this: If you lop off enough sentences and references to friendship, hope and understanding, any interview can fit your distorted worldview.** In this case, a perfectly amicable interview has been twisted into a public relations nightmare by disingenuous journalists with an ideological axe to grind.
> (http://medienkritik.typepad.com/blog/2006/02/spiegels_karen_.html)

For *BBC Monitoring Service*, we have seen that the translators' (i.e. monitors') work includes providing headlines and editorial insertions. If we look again at some of the examples given above, we can say that they are not at all neutral and value-free. For example, the characterisation of the Palestinian Information Centre website as a "pro-Hamas Palestinian Information Centre website" adds a political-ideological affiliation and thus sets the readers up for one particular interpretation of the text. In another example, the choice of "assassination" (Tamil Tigers condemn assassination of Sri Lankan MP Raviraj) in the main headline provided by *BBC Monitoring* enhances the politically motivated nature of the killing compared to the original's title (which had been literally translated as "LTTE condemns killing of Tamil National Alliance MP, Raviraj" in the information bit about the source text). And finally, the choice of the more general word "Iraqi Turkoman group" for "Turkoman Notables' Council" which signifies the official position , somehow degrades the importance and role of this political body. Although the translations produced by *BBC Monitoring* often do reflect foreignisation, due to the intention to give the horse's mouth, such editorial interventions can in fact be described as domestication.

What these practices then show is that for both *Spiegel International* and the *BBC Monitoring Service*, the voices readers actually hear are refracted voices, refracted by translation policies of these two media institutions (on "refraction" see Lefevere 2000). As a result of particular translation strategies, both at the paratextual level (e.g. providing new main titles, adding explanations in brackets) and at the microstructural level of lexical or syntactic choices (e.g. choice of a more general word, opting for a politician's official title), the message in the target text may be "toned down" or "exaggerated". Kang (2007) arrived at similar findings in her study of news translation for a South Korean newspaper. Her study equally showed that translated news discourse contributes to normalising particular ideological understandings of political events or maintaining those already held by the target addressees.

Conclusion: Communication vs conflict

In autumn 2005, *BBC Monitoring* had the following statement on its website:

> As the recent conflict in Iraq illustrates well, the world's mass media not only reflect and report on world events, but influence minds and increasingly shape the agenda of public debate and action.

This applies as well to media texts which are provided in translation. The journalists-qua-translators for *Spiegel International* and for *BBC Monitoring* themselves claim that translated news reports and also speeches by and interviews with politicians are published in order to inform readers accurately and objectively about (opinions about) policies in other countries. For *Spiegel International*, a German voice is to be brought to English-speaking readers, in particular targetting an audience in the USA, i.e. the translators export the texts. In respect of the topic of "the war on terror", texts are selected which the journalists perceive to be of particular interest to the US readers. The intention is to let US readers see that German politicians and large groups of the German people are critical and do not show admiration for the US administration. That is, the ideological position of social groups in Germany is in conflict with the ideological position of the US administration and some social groups of the US public. For *BBC Monitoring*, voices from outside the UK are brought to the UK government and the UK public (although the wider public often has access to the texts only when they are taken up by and published in other media), i.e. the translators import the texts. In respect of the "war on terror", journalists-qua-translators monitor and select texts which are seen as important for the alerting of the UK government. That is, there is usually a conflict between the ideological position of the UK government and the ideological position of governments and/or political groups in the selected countries. In any case, the selection of topics and texts for translation is ideologically determined.

Moreover, both arguments, i.e. bringing the "unique voice" of the source culture news magazine to the target readers, and giving the readers the "horse's mouth", reflect an idealization of representation (Pym 2004: 11). For both media institutions, the source text is seen as dominant and thus to be rendered accurately. For *Spiegel International*, accuracy in content goes hand in hand with fluency and good English style, whereas for *BBC Monitoring*, accuracy is largely equated with literal translation. The underlying assumption is that accuracy in the message ensures objectivity. As the discussion of the sample texts has shown, both of these global strategies in fact amount to ideological appropriation.

As already said above, the journalists' daily work includes translation, but they do not describe their work as translation. The team working for *Spiegel International* stress that they are journalists, and that their text production is governed by the journalistic values of excellent news sense and good writing skills. *BBC Monitoring* recruits monitors, not translators, because "a translator does not have to use so much decision-making in the selection of the story" (Chokri, as quoted on http://www2.warwick.ac.uk/fac/arts/ctccs/research/tgn/events/gt/prog/). What we see here is a discrepancy in what journalists-qua-translators think translation is about and what they themselves actually do, but which they think is something different from translation. Their own discourse reveals a view of translation as a more mechanical linguistic activity, which does not require decision-making beyond linguistic choices. The kinds of editorial intervention, as illustrated above, are perceived to be evidence of a more responsible role of the agent, which is reflected in labels such as editor, monitor, or transeditor (Stetting 1990, also Bielsa 2007). However, from the perspective of modern Translation Studies, all strategies involved in the processes from source text selection to target text delivery are an integral part of translatorial action (Holz-Mänttäri 1984). News translation, in the widest sense of the word, can thus legitimately be called translation.

Translation shapes our knowledge of other cultures, bearing in mind that cultures are not stable and homogeneous entities but rather experienced phenomena. As Koskinen (2004: 147) argues, cultures "are not neutral accounts of a natural state of the world but constructions that carry ideological implications". Translations in the media institutions *Spiegel International* and *BBC Monitoring* contribute to the construction of national and cultural identities, and also to the preservation and maintenance of ideologies. *Spiegel International's* translation strategies of domestication, which, as we have seen, often result in a weakened critical comment, equally contribute more often to maintaining ideological views of large groups of the US readers than to actually challenging them. The journalists as translators are thus by no means neutral cultural mediators who help to bring two cultures together, or who help to bridge gaps between cultures. In other words, they do not operate in an ideologically void "intercultural space" or in a neutral space in-between, they are rather positioned firmly within the social spaces of their respective media institutions (on "intercultural spaces" see also Pym 1998, Tymoczko 2003, and Inghilleri 2005 with reference to interpreters in political asylum adjudication). It has to be acknowledged, however, that decisions taken by journalists (or monitors) in their translation work are determined not only by ideological considerations, but also by other factors such as the individual translator's reflections about style, about target readers' knowledge, and also by wider institutional practices (although they can be described as largely ideological in nature).

As said above, the *BBC Monitoring Service* is part of the *BBC World Service*. The *BBC World Service* itself also operates outside the UK and provides international news, analysis and information in English and 42 other languages (cf. http://www.bbc.co.uk/worldservice/index.shtml). In the autumn of 2005, it was reported that the *BBC World Service* was to stop broadcasting in several Eastern European languages (e.g. Polish, Czech,

Hungarian) and to close a total of ten foreign language radio services. Since the fall of Communism, Eastern European countries have developed democratic societies and their governments do not propagate different ideological views to those in the West anymore—there was therefore no perceived need anymore to broadcast to these countries in their own languages. The money thus saved is meant to help to fund a £20 million-a-year Arabic television service. In an editorial, the British daily newspaper *The Times* commented as follows on these developments:

> Broadcasting is a powerful arm of diplomacy, a fact recognised by the Foreign Office, which funds the BBC World Service. [...] Where will reliable, unbiased news pack the greatest diplomatic punch? Unquestionably, in Iraq and the Arab world. A total of £20 million is not a lot to go head to head with Al-Jazeera (itself about to challenge the BBC in English). (*The Times*, 26 October 2005, p. 19)

This quote conveys an ideological message in two respects. The first one concerns the recognition of the significant role of the media for constructing cultures and influencing ideological positions. Such an awareness of the increasing role of the media can also be seen in a comment by Philip Fiske de Gouveia, from the London-based Foreign Policy Centre, quoted in the *European Voice* in an article that reported about plans within the European Union to launch an Arabic-language television station to promote European ideas in the Middle East and North Africa:

> [...] according to Philip Fiske de Gouveia, from the London-based Foreign Policy Centre, the channel would fit with a growing trend for countries to project their world-view beyond their national borders. "In recent years there has been an increasing realisation in the corridors of power that information and media has to be a strategic priority" he said.
> (*European Voice* 6 October 2005 p.1)

The second point in respect of ideology is the reference to "unbiased news" in the extract from *The Times*. The news to be brought to the Arab world will be in Arabic, i.e. translation will play a significant role. Although translation is not mentioned explicitly in the article from which I quoted above, the argument nevertheless reveals a view of pure and unspoilt message transfer (cf. "the horse's mouth"), and the assumption that "unbiased news" transfer results in the new readers accepting the news presented and the ideological perspective. Such a more traditional view of communication—and by extension of translation—as promoting understanding between different cultures is too limited by far since it ignores the political and ideological determination of any act of communication. As Baker (2005: 4) argues, it is unproductive to "explain away the politics of language and translation by portraying a world in which cultural misunderstanding is unintended, innocent and can be avoided once we are sensitised to cultural differences and have a well-trained group of professionals who can mediate between different cultures in a non-biased and responsible manner."

Ideological aspects of translation have also been highlighted by postmodern and postcolonial translation theories. This is illustrated for example by Tymoczko and Gentzler in the following quote:

> Translation thus is not simply an act of faithful reproduction but, rather, a deliberate and conscious act of selection, assemblage, structuration and fabrication —and even, in some cases of falsification, refusal of information, counterfeiting, and the creation of secret codes. (Tymoczko and Gentzler 2002: xxi)

In the case of *Spiegel International* and *BBC Monitoring*, we have not actually seen extreme examples of falsification or counterfeiting (despite the critical comments of *Davids Medienkritik*), but conscious acts of information selection are mentioned by the journalists-qua-translators themselves when they speak about their work, and examples of assemblage, structuration and fabrication can easily be detected if a comparative analysis of source texts and target texts is undertaken.

Research in Translation Studies has recently shown an increasing interest in studying the actual practices and behaviour of translators in institutional, political and ideological contexts. In this way, the interrelations between social and/or institutional conditions of target text production, the textual profiles, and the effects which translations have on their addressees can be identified. A description and understanding of such causal relationships (see Chesterman 1998) is the precondition for evaluating translation practices in institutions and the effects they have on translations as products. An analysis of the translation practices in news media organisations, together with an analysis of content and textual-linguistic structures of translations as products will therefore raise awareness of the complexities of news translation and also of the underlying, and more or less transparent, power relations in media institutions. Such research then also contributes to Critical Translation

Studies, a label which unifies most recent approaches to translation whose proponents share the belief, as Koskinen (2004: 153) says, "that the task of the researcher is not only to describe and explain but also to attempt to improve the situation or to offer solutions to a perceived problem." In this chapter I have tried to describe and explain the perceived problem that news translation often maintains existing ideologies, independently of whether the overall translation method is one of domestication or of foreignisation. This phenomenon is closely linked to the practices of translation being done by journalists and governed by journalistic values, and a more traditional understanding of translation which is not in line with modern views in the discipline of Translation Studies. To overcome this problem, interdisciplinary research between Translation Studies and Media Studies is required. Raising awareness within both Translation Studies and Media Studies of the practices of news translation, and awareness of the fact that these very practices are determined by wider institutional, ideological, and socio-political conditions, is a first step in this direction, but more research will have to follow before actual changes can be achieved.

References

Baker, Mona. 2005. "Narratives in and of Translation". *SKASE Journal of Translation and Interpretation* 1.1: 4-13.
— 2006. *Translation and Conflict: A Narrative Account.* New York and London: Routledge.
Bassnett, Susan. 2004. "Trusting Reporters: What Exactly Did Saddam Say?" *The Linguist* 43.6: 176-178.
Bielsa, Esperança. 2007. "Translation in global news agencies". *Target* 19.1: 135-155.
Chesterman, Andrew. 1998. "Causes, Translations, Effects". *Target* 10.2: 201-230.
Fairclough, Norman and Ruth Wodak. 1997. "Critical discourse analysis". In *Discourse Studies: A Multidisciplinary Introduction. vol. 2: Discourse as Social Interaction.* Ed. Teun van Dijk. London: Sage. 258-284.
Holland, Robert. 2006. "Language(s) in the global news: Translation, Audience Design and Discourse (Mis)representation". *Target* 18.2: 229-259.
Holz-Mänttäri, Justa. 1984. *Translatorisches Handeln. Theorie und Methode.* Helsinki: Suomalainen Tiedeakatemia.

Inghilleri, Moira. 2005. "Mediating Zones of Uncertainty: Interpreter Agency, the Interpreting Habitus and Political Asylum Adjudication". *The Translator* 11.1: 69-85.
Kang, Ji-Hae. 2007. "Recontextualization of News Discourse: A Case Study of Translation of News Discourse on North Korea". *The Translator* 13.2: 219-242.
Koskinen, Kaisa. 2004. "Shared culture? Reflections on recent trends in Translation Studies". *Target* 16.1: 143-156.
Lefevere, André. 2000. "Mother Courage's cucumbers: Text, System and Refraction in a Theory of Literature". In *The Translation Studies Reader.* Ed. Lawrence Venuti. London and New York: Routledge. 233-249.
Lu, Xing. 1999. "An Ideological/Cultural Analysis of Political Slogans in Communist China". *Discourse & Society* 10.4: 487-508.
Pym, Anthony. 1998. *Method in Translation History*. Manchester: St. Jerome.
— 2004. "Propositions on Cross-Cultural Communication and Translation". *Target* 16.1: 1-28.
Reiss, Katharina. 1989. "Text types, translation types and translation assessment". In *Readings in Translation Theory*. Ed. Andrew Chesterman. Helsinki: Oy Finn Lectura Ab. 105-115.
Schäffner, Christina. 2005. "Bringing a German voice to English-speaking readers: *Spiegel International*". *Language and Intercultural Communication* 5.2: 154-167. (Special issue on Global News Translation, guest editor: Susan Bassnett).
Stetting, Karen. 1990. "Transediting – a new term for coping with the grey area between editing and translating". In *Proceedings from the Fourth Nordic Conference for English Studies*. Eds. Graham Caie *et al.* Copenhagen: University of Copenhagen. 371-382.
Tymoczko, Maria. 2003. "Ideology and the position of the translator: In what sense is a translator 'in-between'?" In *Apropos of Ideology. Translation Studies on Ideology - Ideologies in Translation Studies.* Ed. Maria Calzada-Perez. Manchester: St. Jerome. 181-201.
— and Edwin Gentzler, eds. 2002. *Translation and Power*. Amherst: University of Massachusetts Press.
Van Dijk, Teun. 1998. *Ideology. A Multidisciplinary Approach*. London: Sage.
Venuti, Lawrence. 1995. *The Translator's Invisibility*. London: Routledge.
— (ed.). 1998. *Translation and Minority*. Special issue of *The Translator* 4.2.
Vermeer, Hans J. 1986. "Übersetzen als kultureller Transfer". In *Übersetzungswissenschaft. Eine Neuorientierung*. Ed. Mary Snell-Hornby. Tübingen: Franke. 30-53.

CHAPTER SIX

BUILDING TRACE[1] (TRANSLATIONS CENSORED) THEATRE CORPUS: SOME METHODOLOGICAL QUESTIONS ON TEXT SELECTION

RAQUEL MERINO ÁLVAREZ

1. Translation and censorship in Spain: the history of (theatre) translations 1960-1985

When tackling the study of translations from a historical point of view one of the basic sources for research are usually libraries, bibliographies, archives and databases. In TRACE we have been drawing data from a variety of sources and soon found out that the most complex and richest source of information for most of the 20th century in Spain seemed to be the AGA, *Archivo General de la Administración* (http://www.mcu.es/archivos/MC/AGA/index.html).

The fact that all cultural products (including translations) had been filtered through censorship offices and had consequently left abundant documental traces led us to use the AGA as the main source of data and to use censorship as a privileged standpoint from which to observe and describe the history of translations in Franco's time.

In the AGA archives translations are filed along with native production. They are organized by type (books, theatre, films) and catalogued by year, title or author[2]. AGA files may hold contextual information (reports, notes,

---

1 TRACE projects, BFF2003-07597-C02-01/02 and FFI2008-05479-C02-02 (TRAducciones CEnsuradas INGLÉS/ALEMÁN-ESPAÑOL (TRACE 1939-1985): estudios sobre catálogos y corpus), funded by the Spanish *Ministerio de Educación y Ciencia y Tecnología*. Fondo Europeo de Desarrollo Regional, FEDER. Proyecto TRACE (www.ehu.es/trace): TRAducciones CEnsuradas INGLÉS/ALEMÁN-ESPAÑOL (TRACE 1939-1985): estudios sobre catálogos y corpus. FFI2008-05479-C02-02.
2 Appendix 2.1. shows the information held in AGA (Archivo General de la Administración, Alcalá de Henares, Madrid) index cards, on authors mentioned here. Appendix 2.2 contains information gathered from direct access to AGA complete files (not only index files) as well as from other sources.

minutes of board meetings) and texts (printed books or typed manuscripts). You may find just one version of, for example, a theatre play[3] or different draft versions of the same translation[4] and/or published translated texts[5]. There is also information on theatre groups and the cities they toured with a specific play, from premiere through various performances[6].

The different TRACE catalogues have been compiled using a variety of sources[7], applying two main search procedures: direct use of AGA title or author index files and databases (guided search), and/or extensive sampling on the box files themselves by year or years (random search)[8]. The latter is a slower procedure but renders more accurate results and does not rely on an *a priori* checklist of authors or titles. This is the reason why such procedure was used in the research on theatre translations in the 1960s through to 1985.

The catalogue of theatre translations that underwent censorship in this period (TRACEti 1960-1985) is therefore the result of sampling and

---

3   Labelled "TTce", target text censored. We may find just one translation in a censorship record, but when a play became popular, or when it underwent difficulties when asking for permission, we might find more than one censored translation of a ST ("TTce1", "TTce2"...) by different translators.
4   When we come across various versions of a given translation we label them consecutively: "TTce1.1", "TTce1.2"... They are usually the result of cuts and modifications suggested by censors or of rewriting processes derived from the negotiation that preceded authorization of a theatrical production. They are usually printed manuscripts. Jaime Salom's translation of Crowley's *The boys in the band* is a case in point (see 3 below).
5   We use "TTpub" when the text found is a published play as opposed to other types of printed manuscripts.
6   Theatre files for the period 1938-1985 can be found in AGA archives. The reason why filing went on until 1985 may be that it was precisely that year that the structure of the Ministry of Culture changed almost overnight and former Censorship (later on renamed "Ordenación" and "Calificación") Theatre Sections ceased to exist. In the register book for theatre plays corresponding to 1985 the last entry is June 19th, 1985 (Merino 2000: 123).
7   Elena Bandín in her PhD on Classical English Theatre applies TRACE methodology to research sources. She explains how they have been used to compile TRACEtci, the catalogue of Classical English Theatre performed and published in Spain between 1939 and 1985.
    The following are research sources used in TRACE investigations: AGA General Administration Archives, Index Translationum, El Libro Español, Bibliografía Española, Spanish National Library's database (ARIADNA), Spanish University Libraries network (REBIUN), Spanish Public Libraries Catalogue (REBECA), Spanish ISBN online, Francisco Álvaro's 1958-1985 yearly volumes on theatre performed in Spain, Spanish Theatre Documentation Centre (CDT), and various bibliographies published by theatre scholars (Bandín 2007: 94-102). See also http://trace.unileon.es/.
8   Other theatre TRACE researchers have used both procedures (Pérez 2004) or have started from a checklist of classical authors (Bandín 2007).

contains information about authors or plays that would not have been necessarily deemed representative in histories of theatre in Spain[9] or histories of theatre in the various source cultures. The TRACEti 1960-1985 catalogue also contains information from non-AGA/censorship sources[10].

Since the choice of object of study and corpus does not derive from external criteria (e.g. importance of an author in source culture) but rather it is based on empirical evidence gathered from direct access to sources of information, it is often the case that we end up studying Crowley, Greene or Albee rather than Wilde or Shakespeare. The case study I will be analysing below (*The Boys in the Band*) may serve as an illustration.

The results of the analysis of the TRACEti 1960-1985 catalogue have been presented in previous publications. I have also gone into detail about some representative translated theatre corpus[11] derived from such analysis. So in this paper I would like to address some methodological questions that have arisen when selecting a corpus as an object of study and when drawing textual corpus as objects of study from catalogues.

2.1 Mapping areas of the history of translation in 20th century Spain

In TRACE we have gradually "distributed" among researchers areas of the history of translations in 20th century Spain that were blurred or simply not yet explored. The chart below shows a general break-up of areas of the "map" of TRACE investigations as of 2007.

---

[9] Translated theatre is not usually dealt with in Histories of Theatre in Spain. It is just not mentioned. Even in the most thorough study on censorship of Spanish theatre to date (Muñoz Cáliz, 2005) only a few translations done by the Spanish playwrights under study are mentioned. See also O'Leary (2005).
 In the last decade some publications have tackled the question of translated drama as part of Spanish theatre (London 1997) but they are the exception.
[10] Appendix 2.2 contains information from non-AGA sources merged with information from censorship AGA archives gathered from direct access to box files.
[11] See Merino 2003, http://www.ehu.es/trace/publicaciones/2003bRMA_Catalogo_Corpus_TRACE.pdf and Merino 2005, http://www.ehu.es/trace/publicaciones/2005aRMA_RCEI.pdf.

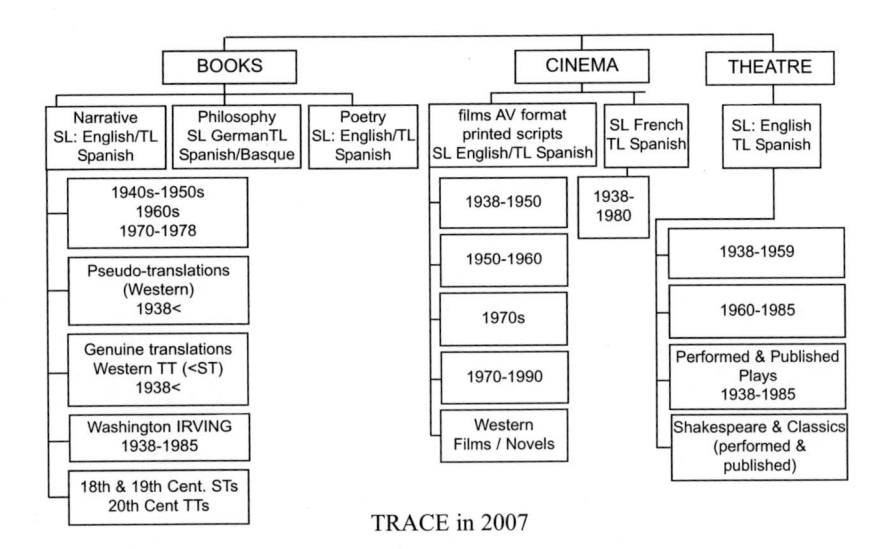

```
                        ┌──────────────────┬──────────────────┐
                     BOOKS                CINEMA            THEATRE
    ┌────────┬───────┴───┬────────┐   ┌──────┴──────┬─────┐      │
  Narrative  Philosophy   Poetry    films AV format   SL French  SL: English
  SL: English/TL SL GermanTL SL: English/TL printed scripts TL Spanish TL Spanish
  Spanish    Spanish/Basque  Spanish   SL English/TL Spanish
```

1940s-1950s 1960s 1970-1978	1938-1950 / 1938-1980
Pseudo-translations (Western) 1938<	1950-1960 / 1938-1959
Genuine translations Western TT (<ST) 1938<	1970s / 1960-1985
Washington IRVING 1938-1985	1970-1990 / Performed & Published Plays 1938-1985
18th & 19th Cent. STs 20th Cent TTs	Western Films / Novels / Shakespeare & Classics (performed & published)

TRACE in 2007

The deeper we went into cataloguing translated culture, the more we could direct researchers on possible areas that might be within their specific expertise. In the last five years at least seven young scholars became members of the group and tackled new genres or periods: translations of narrative (1962-1969 and 1970-1978), English poetry (1939-1978), classical English theatre (1939-1985)[12]. Spanish translations of German philosophy or translations of western novels and films[13] are among the slots added over the past few years.

As I mentioned before sampling proved a fairly productive tool for the first approach to such data as AGA holds. When the results of sampling AGA files were transferred to properly compiled catalogues of narrative (TRACEni), theatre (TRACEti) and cinema (TRACEci)[14], a second generation of studies could be planned and allotted to investigators.

---

12 University of León researchers Rioja (2008) and Gómez Castro (2008) deal with narrative; Lobejón studies poetry and Bandín tackled classical English theatre. http://trace.unileon.es.
13 Uribarri (2008) works on translations of German philosophy and Camus (2008) on Western narrative and films. http://www.ehu.es/trace.
14 The foundations for the catalogue of translations of narrative censored (TRACEni) were laid by Rosa Rabadán (2000) and José Miguel Santamaría (2000). Eterio Pajares is in charge of 20th century translations of 18th century British novelists (Pajares 2008).
  TRACE narrative catalogues were enlarged with Merino's search for translations into Spanish of Washington Irving's *The Alhambra* in AGA book files. The catalogue compiled

Building TRACE (translations censored) Theatre Corpus:... 133

The second wave of TRACE researchers have compiled more thorough catalogues for sub-periods based on the results rendered by the information analyzed in initial TRACE (-ni, -ti, ci) catalogues. Such catalogues are in all cases the source of textual corpus that have ultimately been selected and studied in detail.

2.2 What renders a corpus/set of texts representative?

In dealing with descriptive studies, criteria for selecting well-defined[15] (non-random) corpus are derived from the analysis of TRACE catalogues, such as TRACEti for theatre. Certain authors, directors or translators may prove representative of a period. In the same way each type of theatre (official, mainstream commercial theatres, *teatros de cámara*) can be studied in detail, since they represent different ways of approaching various kinds of audiences, from the bulk of middle-class theatregoers to the avant-garde minorities.

The censors' procedures took for granted that a theatre production could expose audiences to topics that might clash with their morals. Censors were designed to domesticate the plays by means of text selection and adaptation. In this respect homosexuality and infidelity rated higher than politics.

Certain "banned" topics are no doubt a good starting point for selecting a corpus, since plot and sensitive topics are always present in censors' reports as well as in the producers' directors' or translators' attempts to counteract bans and cuts and to get their plays shown to as big an audience as possible.

(TRACEniir) was part of a wider project but helped corroborate that censorship records were the richest and most thorough source of information. http://www.ehu.es/trace/publicaciones/2004RMA_ProgresionMetodolog.pdf .

As for theatre, Pérez L. de Heredia and Merino have compiled representative catalogues of drama translations (TRACEti 1939-1985, http://www.ehu.es/trace/catalogos.html) which were the source for various corpus studies. Gutiérrez Lanza (2005 & 2008) has dealt with cinema, and Marta de Miguel (http://www.ehu.es/trace/MiguelGonzalez.pdf) and Luis Serrano complemented Gutiérrez Lanza's studies. Carmen Camus's PhD on translated western narrative and films will contribute to understanding the leading role the western enjoyed both in popular fiction and commercial cinema in Spain (http://www.ehu.es/trace/tesistrace-ccc.html).
15 Our main methodological framework has always been DTS, "a discipline based on programmed empirical discovery rather than quick opinions" (Preface. *Beyond Descriptive Translation Studies. Investigations in homage to Gideon Toury*. John Benjamins, 2008: ix).
In Toury (2004: 71-79) we find a series of concepts and the global approach to basic DTS research that we have applied to building textual corpus from catalogues. Catalogues add the historical dimension that may lead to well-chosen textual corpus.

Box office success, commercial theatres vs. *teatros de cámara*, the influence of film adaptations of a given play in the final decision of censorship boards are criteria derived from regularities observed in the catalogue that may be used when selecting representative corpus.

The notion of regularity is used when analyzing catalogues and selecting cases to be studied in detail. Those cases tend to be built around complex and complete censorship records, as will be shown below. A censorship record comes into existence when a producer or director applies for permission to perform. A series of interventions by censors, authors or translators leave traces in the form of numerous documents around a given text. Reports, letters, chains of corrected versions of the translated playtext pile up. But whether a play ever gets to the stage or is filed along with other documents does not rule out its being a potential object of study.

A brief example may illustrate this: Peter Shaffer's *The Royal Hunt of the Sun* (record no. 3/69), a play about the Spanish conquest of Peru, was not exactly felt to be pro-regime propaganda. Over eighty documents make up that record: application forms, reports, letters and the printed manuscript of the translation. The Spanish text submitted to censorship has never been published or performed, possibly because of the various bans issued, but also because when it was finally authorized in 1974 the producer did not choose it for the stage. Among the documents found in the record we find evidence of a British film based on this play that was shot in Spain with the necessary prior approval of the cinema board.

Complex records such as 3/69 laden with all kinds of documents await further study including the comparative analysis of both ST-TT and TT-TT pairs. A similar record in terms of richness of the documents found is *Who's Afraid of Virigina Woolf?* (record no. 215/65). In this case the play, after a long process of cuts and threats of total ban, was staged. A huge success was followed by strong reactions from critics and audiences. This case was analyzed as a pre-textual corpus: access to the full text of the translation was not possible (Merino 2003). It was just not available either in AGA or elsewhere[16].

---

16 In pre-textual corpus we usually have access to numerous references to the texts: censors quoting cuts and certain problematic passages, or letters by the director asking for a few more taboo words to be allowed in the final authorized version, even telegrams, hand-written informal notes. All these text fragments are part of the censorship record as such, and they have been used by some researchers (Muñoz Cáliz 2005) as textual evidence in their studies.

Neither Shaffer's nor Albee's play were ruled out as objects of study. The lack of a production or the fact that the Spanish text was not available weighed less than other traits that made those cases representative.

Other case studies can be tackled since the full range of potential documents are available. This was the case with Graham Greene's *The Complaisant Lover* (record no. 299/62 & 238-65). More than one director sought permission to perform this play between 1962 and 1968. There were various versions of the play by different translators or adaptors and after a few attempts the play reached both the stage and the page (an acting edition of the text approved was published in 1969). This case is rich and complex both from a contextual, pre-textual point of view and from a textual stance (various versions by different target authors). The main topic, adultery, once again can be found at the root of its complexity as regards censorship.

One more case that has already been investigated and analyzed in detail is Albee's *The Zoo Story* (record no. 75/63). The history of this play in Spanish theatre can be traced from 1963 to the present. This case was recorded thoroughly and some of the AGA documents that were related to the play were scattered in different files. This is probably due to the fact that the text was sent back and forth on many occasions. The play was banned on account of its topic, homosexuality, after extremely fierce attacks by some censors. Nevertheless, after certain cuts and modifications were made in the text, permission was granted for one-night *teatro de cámara* production. There were many such productions until permission was given for commercial theatres in 1973. And from then on William Layton's translation, the only version of the play into Spanish, has often been staged in different Spanish cities and it has also been published in an acting edition[17].

The case study below, *The Boys in the Band*, has been thoroughly documented and may serve as example of a specific play and author, neither particularly relevant in the history of Spanish theatre (or even of American theatre) but sufficiently illustrative of a certain year (1975) and sub-period (1969-1975) and of the way a taboo topic had gradually entered Spanish theatre via translations.

---

17 The published version (Albee 1991) includes the paragraph that underwent censorship cuts, and the translator, William Layton, also added the fragment modified by a theatre group for their production of the play. The Spanish translation is assumed to have gone through numerous rewriting processes, nevertheless full comparison of all censorship (TTce) and published (TTpub) versions shows that changes were kept to a minimum and that Layton's text remained quite unchanged from 1963 to 1991 (Merino 2003: 658-659).

What most of the corpus derived from the TRACEti catalogue share is the notion of regularity, recurrent traits yield well justified selection criteria that help build well-defined corpus[18].

3. Case Study: Homosexuality enters Spanish stages via TRA_CE[19]

In TRACE theatre catalogues there is abundant contextual censorship (CE) information on plays by foreign authors who were usually granted a more lenient treatment by Spanish censors than native authors or plays. In actual fact anything foreign was justified more easily, this being the favourite counter argument used by censors, producers or translators alike. Of all potentially pernicious topics carefully filtered by censorship boards, the most outstanding was homosexuality. The Spanish production of Mart Crowley's *The Boys in the Band* in 1975 was a landmark; rather than the beginning it marked the coming of age of a topic that had shrewdly bypassed bans and cuts since 1950, when the first permission to stage *A Streetcar Named Desire* was filed in censorship records (record no. 217/50).

Mart Crowley's was not the first nor was it the last play to show homosexuals on Spanish stages, but its premier in 1975 was probably the

---

18   In actual fact it is regularities found in each new analysis of additional pre-textual and textual information that pushes the investigations forward. Enlarging a corpus or selecting new corpus to be studied can only be done using criteria derived from regularities:
— most common censorship resolution or most extreme (prohibition)
— source author/title/country with the greatest presence on Spanish stages
— target author (translator/adaptor) with the largest production or the biggest success in getting his versions through censorship, or any other similar recurrent and or prominent trait
— topic
— period
— complex censorship cases
— complex textual cases
— a combination of any of the above (e.g *The Boys in the Band* case study).
19   Appendix 1 shows a chronological list of the translated plays that dealt with homosexuality, recorded in TRACEti catalogues. All of them were censored and staged. This list is open-ended and might have to be revised as more empirical evidence is found.

In Appendix 2.1 and 2.2 we can find all the plays by the authors mentioned in Appendix 1. It seems obvious that once an author had any problems with censorship authorities, or became notorious for dealing with a taboo topic, the chances that his plays would become more popular increased.

drama production that showed for the first time homosexuality in a more carefree way with the biggest impact on theatregoers and critics alike (Álvaro 1975: 86-90, Crowley 1975: III-XII). Never before had this "banned" topic been treated as openly in Spain.

To be sure, this play was staged in a key year for Spanish history (Franco died 20th November 1975), at a time when official censorship found it quite difficult to withstand increasing pressure from abroad in virtually every walk of life. But still the question may linger as to why and how this play has been chosen as a TRACE case study.

The great impact and success of the Spanish production, sanctioned by the necessary prior authorization by censors, was the result of a long history of foreign plays that helped import a "pernicious" topic. The first cases we have been able to trace back are *A Streetcar Named Desire* (1950) or *Tea and Sympathy* (1955), as is shown in Appendix 1.

In no cases was gaining approval by the authorities an easy matter, neither was it with the first application to perform Crowley's play sought by playwright-translator Jaime Salom back in 1970 (record no. 267/70). Both his first 1970 translation and his second 1972 revision were banned[20] and remain "forgotten pages" only accessible in AGA files.

A second record was filed when Artime and Azpilicueta submitted their translation to censorship offices two years later (record no. 533/74). This time, some cuts and modifications in the Spanish translation suggest that there was some degree of intervention in the text, which saw its debut in October 1975.

Both sets of texts (Salom's manuscripts–TTce1.1 & TTce1.2- and Artime and Azpilicueta's–TTce2- together with the 1975 published translation-TTpub) have been thoroughly compared along with the complete sets of censorship documents available[21]. All other metatextual

---

20 It is worth mentioning that the ban was final after all member of the Theatre Censorship Board voted and a "technical" draw was reached. The votes against of the Director General and Secretary of the Board were decisive.

This, along with the fact that the second Salom manuscript was ready for publication (it was preceded by the "Antecrítica", a standard Escelicer Publisher's Introduction to acting editions, and careful proofreading of the text), indicate that censors in favour of recommending the play for performance were at least as strong in their beliefs as those against. Resistance from within the Theatre Censorship Board is very obvious in this case.

21 For a detailed description of censorship record 267/70 see Merino 2008: 279-285. Censorship record no. 533/74 documents have not been found. The only trace of this record found in AGA is the manuscript identified as record no. 533/74 which has been used in the textual comparison.

information from secondary non-AGA sources (Álvaro 1975, Crowley 1975)[22] has been used to reconstruct this case study.

4 Methodological questions

In this type of descriptive-explanatory textual studies there are some key methodological issues at stake. The first may be how many texts to include in the corpus. If it is feasible, it seems advisable to study as many texts as are available. But then the next obvious question is how much text to select for the descriptive-comparative stage and how to select text fragments (Toury 2004: 85).

Another additional question, when dealing with theatre, is how to compare drama texts at the macro and micro level. In this respect using the *replique*[23] or utterance as the minimal structural unit has been useful. Each TT or ST can be broken up into small units that are then numbered and "maps" of *repliques* may be drawn for each text, but more importantly, for each pair of texts (either TT-TT or ST-TT). In this way pairing text segments becomes much easier, and so does identifying comparable text segments.

When we proceed to number (tag) each minimal drama unit (macro-structural stage), in every text available, we end up with a chart like this:

| Act II, ST (or TTx) | 1 | 2 | 3 | 4 | 5 | 6 | 7 | 8 | 9 | ... |

The descriptive-comparative textual study of *The Boys in the Band/Los chicos de la banda* can be found in Merino (2008: 249-259). All available texts (TTce1.1, TTce1.2, TTce2, TTpub) have been compared, and all potential text relations have been explored (between target texts, TT-TT as well as between source text-target text, ST-TT).

22 The published Spanish version of *The Boys in the Band* reproduced many of the theatre reviews and reactions in the press. Álvaro (1975: 86-90) gives a fairly complete account of the reactions of drama critics.

23 See Merino 2008: 266, note 31. This drama unit, "réplica", was defined in Merino (1994: 41-48) and it was a key methodological aid in analysing hundreds of theatre bi-texts at the macro as well as the micro level (see also http://www.ehu.es/trace/publicaciones/2005 cRMA_Cadernos.pdf).

M. J. Serrano (2003), Pérez L. De Heredia (2004) and Bandín (2007) have used *repliques* for anayilising theatre and Romero (2005) for film subtitles.

Rioja (2008: 181) discusses the *replique* as a potential unit for aligning texts.

For computer corpora of Spanish Golden Age theatre, see: http://www.uqtr.ca/teatro/brocense/bro.html.

This allows us to establish maps of potentially comparable pairs (whole texts, or text fragments). Text fragments are coupled to check where they might coincide and whether there are any additions or deletions at the macro-level (see selection of comparable segments ST 200-207, TTce1.1 175-181, TTce1.2 159-160 in Appendix 3). Maps of comparable units in complete sets of texts may then be drawn in order to identify text fragments that might be submitted to further analysis.

In a prototypical case like *The Boys in the Band* all the texts available have been submitted to descriptive-comparative analysis. The first necessary task had to do with the reconstruction of the process of text generation. Extra textual information helps to identify texts as having been produced at a certain stage. In this way we have plenty of information gathered from the censorship record of the modifications Jaime Salom was asked to make in his text after the first ban had been issued. After comparing ST-TTce1.1, TTce1.1-TTce1.2 (and also ST-TTce1.2), using comparable pairs of text segments (either *repliques* or fragments that could be broken up in *repliques*), we were able to establish the final structural map for ST>TTce1.1>TTce1.2.

ST	1	2	3	4	5	6	7	8	9
TTce1.1	1	2	3	4	5	6	7	8	9

ST	200	201	202	203	204	205	206	207
TTce1.1	175	176	177	178	179		180	181

TTce1.1	1	2	3	4	5	6	7	8	9
TTce1.2	1	2	3	4	5	6	7	8	9

TTce1.1	175	176	177	178	179		180	181
TTce1.2				159	160			

Maps of repliques (ST, TTce1.1, TTce1.2, Act II). Macro level. Selection[24]

Macro-level text fragments comparison may render surprising results. This was the case with Artime and Azpilicueta's translation. The only evidence of this Spanish version that we could find was the published text (Crowley 1975, TTpub), and judging by critics' reviews reproduced in the publication of the Spanish text, it was certain that it had been a great theatrical success (and that it would have been approved by censorship authorities).

---

24 ST-Source text (Crowley 1969), TTce1.1/1.2 Salom's AGA Ms.

140 Raquel Merino Álvarez

Direct AGA search rendered surprising results. For a long time neither AGA index files by author or title, or any other guided search yielded any results. It remained a "lost file" for a long time. At long last we found a trace: a manuscript of the Spanish translation identified as part of record no. 533/74.

| ST | 1 | 2 | 3 | 4 | 5 | 6 | 7 | 8 | 9 | 10 | 11 | 12 |
| TTpub | 1 | 2 | 3 | 4 | 5 | 6 | 7 | | | 8 | 9 | 10 |

| TTpub | 1 | 2 | 3 | 4 | 5 | 6 | 7 | | | 8 | 9 | 10 |
| TTce2 | 1 | 2 | 3 | 4 | 5 | 6 | 7 | | | 8 | 9 | 10 |

| ST | 200 | 201 | 202 | 203 | | | 204 | 205 | 206 | 207 |
| TTpub | 170 | 171 | 172 | 173 | 174 | 175 | 176 | 177 | 178 | |

| TTpub | 170 | 171 | 172 | 173 | 174 | 175 | 176 | 177 | 178 | |
| TTce2 | 153 | | | | | | | 154 | 155≠ | |

Maps of repliques (ST, TTpub, TTce2, Act II). Macro level. Selection[25]

So we had access to two versions identified as being the translation by Artime and Azpilicueta. The obvious sequence of text production would in principle be: ST>TTce2>TTpub[26]. In this case numbering *repliques* and drawing comparative structural maps for every potential text pair helped establishing the only probable sequence of text production: ST>TTpub>TTce2. Textual evidence is overwhelming in refuting the first hypothesis based on external information[27].

---

25 *ST-Source text (Crowley 1969), TTpub (Crowley 1975), TTce2 Artime & Azpilicueta's AGA Ms*
26 We even contemplated the possibility of a different chain of text production: TTce1 >TTpub > TTce2. It is not at all uncommon to find that a play in Spanish does not derive from its assumed source text in English, but rather from an existing translation into Spanish: usually a reading edition of the play published in Argentina, or any other previous translation (manuscript or published text). See Merino 1994 for a tradition of plagiarism in Spanish theatre.
27 The most outstanding evidence can be seen in the number of *repliques* deleted in TTce2, when compared with TTpub. See the TTpub 170-178, TTce2 153-155 selection above. In Appendix 3 the text corresponding to that selection is reproduced.
   The sequence ST>TTpub>TTce2 that we have so far reconstructed may become more complex if there were more than one AGA TTce2 manuscript. TTce2 would be labelled "TTce2.2" in a hypothetical TTce2.1*>TTce2.2 chain. TTce2.1* could very well be the manuscript first presented to censorship, and it could have been used for publication. This might be a plausible explanation since censorship of plays in book form was dealt with by a different independent section, and usually earlier versions of a text were chosen by translators as the final manuscript for publication.

In Merino 2008 (251-253 for Salom's texts, and 254-259 for Artime and Azpilicueta's) we have presented the results of a thorough comparative study of all texts of *The Boys in the Band* and have related them to the censorship records when they were available or to extra-textual information (critics' reviews, audience reaction...).

The overall conclusion is that translations were modified by following some of the censors' direct suggestions (deletion of certain words), not all of them. Censorship cuts were surprisingly low given the language and topics in this play. The translations presented for censorship showed some traces of self-censorship, but there are also shifts from the original that do not seem to be related to censorship of any type but rather to more general phenomena observed in translations from English into Spanish.

With respect to the use of computer programs that may help in the automatic alignment and comparison of theatre texts, we have tried a few and have explored possibilities for aligning drama texts based on the *replique*, but there are still a few problems to be overcome before we can present all the texts that have been digitilized in TRACEti as a proper parallel corpus[28]. When this TRACEti parallel corpus is finally made available its potential will extend beyond the boundaries of censorship proper. In point of fact the texts digitilized, those found in AGA as well as all published material compiled, have been analyzed to find out what got censored (key anchor words and phrases may be used for this purpose), but the potential of TRACE textual corpus is much greater.

All cultural products from the period under study, plays as well as films and books, with very few updates, are still part and parcel of Spanish culture. Many of the translations that were published, performed or shown then are still part of our culture now. This means that texts compiled for the TRACE parallel corpus may be used for future descriptive and contrastive textual studies.

---

[28] My own experience trying *Multiconcord* and *Wordsmith Tools* with *The Zoo Story* and *The Boys* corpus, led me to discuss with Knut Hoffland (AKSIS, Bergen) the possibility of adapting the program used in ACTRES (http://actres.unileon.es/inicio.php?elementoID=12) so that instead of paragraphs we would use *repliques* (TRACE-ACTRES Symposium, May 2007).

In the last TRACE PhD presented in 2008, Rioja applied ACTRES tools (e.g. the Translation Corpus Aligner, TCA) to align a lager corpus of censored translated novels.

In the University of the Basque Country TRACE group Uribarri has successfully used *Wordsmith Tools* to compare multiple translations of a given source text (narrative). In the same line Elizabete Manterola is comparing multiple published translations from Basque novels in her PhD. http://www.ehu.es/ibon_uribarri/aleuska-ikerketa-corpusa.htm.

References

Albee, Edward. 1991. *Historia del zoo*. Transl. William Layton. Madrid: La Avispa.
Álvaro, F. 1959. *El Espectador y la crítica. El teatro en España en 1959*. Valladolid: Author's edition.
— 1975. *El Espectador y la crítica. El teatro en España en 1975*. Valladolid: Author's edition.
Bandín, Elena. 2007. *Traducción, recepción y censura de teatro clásico inglés en la España de Franco. Estudio descriptivo-comparativo del Corpus TRACEtci (1939-1985) / Translation, reception and censorship of classical English theatre in Franco's Spain. A descriptive-comparative analysis of the Corpus TRACEtci (1939-1985)*. León: Universidad de León. PhD dissertation.
Camus, Carmen. 2008. "Pseudonyms, pseudotranslation and self-censorship in the narrative of the West during the Franco dictatorship". In *Translation and Censorship in Different Times and Landscapes*. Eds. Teresa Seruya and Maria Lin Moniz. Newcastle: Cambridge Scholars Publishing. 147-162.
Crowley, M. 1968. *The Boys in the Band*. London/Toronto: Samuel French.
— 1975. *Los chicos de la banda*. Transl. Ignacio Artime and Jaime Azpilicueta. Madrid: MK Ediciones.
Gómez Castro, Cristina. 2008. "The Francoist censorship casts a long shadow: translations from the period of the dictatorship on sale nowadays". In *Translation and Censorship in Different Times and Landscapes*. Eds. Teresa Seruya and Maria Lin Moniz. Newcastle: Cambridge Scholars Publishing. 184-195.
Gutiérrez Lanza, Camino. 2005. "La labor del equipo TRACE: metodología descriptiva de la censura en traducción". In *Trasvases culturales: literatura, cine y traducción, 4*. Eds. R. Merino, J. M. Santamaría, E. Pajares. Bilbao: Universidad del País Vasco. 55-64. http://www.represura.es/represura_4_octubre_2007_articulo2.html
— Camino. 2008. "Traducción inglés-español y censura de textos cinematográficos: definición, construcción y análisis del Corpus 0/Catálogo TRACEci (1951-1981)". In *Traducción y censura en España (1939-1985). Estudios sobre corpus TRACE: cine, narrativa, teatro*. Ed. R. Merino. Bilbao: Universidad del País Vasco/Universidad de León. 197-240. http://www. ehu.es/servicios/ se_az/trace.pdf.
http://www.ehu.es/trace/ [TRACE, UPV/EHU]
http://trace.unileon.es/ [TRACE, ULE]

London, John. 1997. *Reception and Renewal in Modern Spanish Theatre: 1939-1963.* Leeds: W. S. Maney and Son Ltd, Modern Humanities Research Association.
— "Drama in the Spanish Civil War: was There *teatro de urgencia* in the Nationalist Zone?". In *Spanish Film, Theatre and Literature in the Twentieth Century. Essays in Honour of Derek Gagen.* Eds. D. George and J. London. Cardiff: University of Wales Press. 205-236.
Merino, Raquel. 1994. *Traducción, tradición y manipulación. Teatro inglés en España 1950-90.* León: Universidad de León and Universidad del País Vasco.
— 2000. "El teatro inglés traducido desde 1960: censura, ordenación, calificación". In *Traducción y censura inglés-español, 1939-1985. Estudio Preliminar.* Ed. R. Rabadán. León: Universidad de León. 121-151.
— 2001. "Presentación de la base de datos TRACE (Traducciones Censuradas inglés-español)". In *Trasvases Culturales. Literatura, cine y traducción, 3.* Eds. E. Pajares, R. Merino and J. M. Santamaría. Bilbao: Universidad del País Vasco. 287-295.
— 2003. "TRAducciones CEnsuradas inglés-español: del catálogo al corpus TRACE (teatro)". In *Primer congreso internacional de la Asociación Ibérica de Estudios de Traducción e Interpretación, AIETI.* Ed. R. Muñoz. Granada: Universidad de Granada. 641-670. http://www.ehu.es/trace/publicaciones/2003bRMA_Catalogo_Corpus_TRACE.pdf
— 2005 "From catalogue to corpus in DTS. Translations censored under Franco: the TRACE Project". In *Revista Canaria de Estudios Ingleses* 29. Ed. C. Toledano. 129-138.
— 2008. "La homosexualidad censurada: estudio sobre corpus de teatro TRACEti (desde 1960)". In *Traducción y censura en España (1939-1985). Estudios sobre corpus TRACE: cine, narrativa, teatro.* Ed. R. Merino. Bilbao: Universidad del País Vasco / Universidad de León. 243-286. http://www.ehu.es/servicios/se_az/trace.pdf
Muñoz Cáliz, Berta. 2005. *El teatro crítico español durante el franquismo visto por sus censores.* Madrid: Fundación Universitaria Española.
O'Leary, Catherine. 2005. *The theatre of Antonio Buero Vallejo: Ideology, Politics and Censorship.* Woodbridge: Támesis.
Pajares, Eterio. 2008. "Censorship and Self-Censorship in English Narrative Fiction Translated into Spanish during the Eighteenth Century". In *Translation and Censorship in Different Times and Landscapes.* Eds. Teresa Seruya and Maria Lin Moniz. Newcastle: Cambridge Scholars Publishing. 289-297.
Pérez López de Heredia, María. 2004. *Traducciones censuradas de teatro norteamericano en la España de Franco (1939-1963).* Bilbao: Universidad del País Vasco.

Pérez López de Heredia, María. 2005. "Inventario de las traducciones censuradas de teatro norteamericano en la España de Franco (1939-1963)". In *Trasvases culturales: literatura, cine y traducción, 4*. Eds. R. Merino, J. M. Santamaría, E. Pajares. Bilbao: Universidad del País Vasco. 97-112.

Rabadán, Rosa. 2000. "Modelos importados, modelos adaptados: pseudotraducciones de narrativa popular inglés-español (1955-1981)". In *Traducción y censura inglés-español: 1939-1985. Estudio preliminar*. Ed. R. Rabadán. León: Universidad de León. 255-277.

— and Raquel Merino. 2004. "Introducción". In *Los estudios descriptivos de traducción, y más allá. Metodología de la investigación en estudios de traducción. (Descriptive Translation Studies, and beyond)*. Gideon Toury. Madrid: Cátedra.17-33.

Rioja, Marta. 2008. *English-Spanish translation and Censorship of narrative texts in Franco's Spain: TRACEni (1962-1969)*. León: Universidad de León. PhD dissertation.

Romero, Lupe. 2005. "La traducción de dialectos sociales en la subtitulación: Mecanismos de compensación y tendencia a la estandarización". In *Trasvases culturales: literatura, cine y traducción, 4*. Eds. R. Merino, J. M. Santamaría, E. Pajares. Bilbao: Universidad del País Vasco. 243-259.

Santamaría, J. M. 2000. "La traducción de obras narrativas en la España franquista: panorama preliminar". In *Traducción y censura inglés-español, 1939-1985. Estudio Preliminar*. Ed. R. Rabadán. León: Universidad de León. 207-225.

Serrano, Mario-Juan. 2003. "La traducción al español de las referencias culturales en *Who's Afraid of Virginia Woolf?* de Edward Albee". *Translation Journal* 7: 4. http://accurapid.com/journal/26liter1.htm.

Toury, Gideon. 2004. *Los estudios descriptivos de traducción, y más allá. Metodología de la investigación en estudios de traducción*. Translation, introduction and notes: R. Rabadán and R. Merino. Madrid: Cátedra.

Uribarri, Ibon. 2008. "Translations of German philosophy into Spanish and Censorship: a new line of research within the TRACE (TRAnslations CEnsored) project". In *Translation and Censorship in Different Times and Landscapes*. Eds. Teresa Seruya and Maria Lin Moniz. Newcastle: Cambridge Scholars Publishing. 103-118.

APPENDIX 1:
Homosexuality appears on Spanish stages via censored translations

1950-1951	A Streetcar Named Desire / Un tranvía llamado deseo[29] Tennessee Williams	Record no. 217/50. José Méndez Herrera (Banned 1950, Teatro de Cámara y Ensayo / Chamber Theatre 1951)
1956	A Streetcar Named Desire / Un tranvía llamado deseo	Record no. 300/56. Juan Guerrero Zamora. Commercial Theatres. Audiences over 18. (1956 Film adaptation)
1955-1956	Tea & Sympathy / Té y simpatía Robert A. Anderson[30]	Record no. 358/55. M. L. Regás. (Banned). (record no. 118/56) Performance in Teatro de Cámara y Ensayo / Chamber Theatre.
1956	Tea & Sympathy / Té y simpatía	Record no. 338/56. J. I. Luca de Tena. Commercial Theatres. Audiences over 18.
1957	Tea & Sympathy / Té y simpatía	Record no. 61/57. V. de Asís. Commercial Theatres. Audiences over 18.
1958	Tea & Sympathy / Té y simpatía	New production (Pastora Peña Theatre Company) Record no. 338/56 Trad. Luca de Tena Victoriano de Asís 61/57
1958	Cat on a Hot Tin Roof / La gata sobre el tejado de zinc. Tennessee Williams[31]	Record no. 228/58. Antonio de Cabo & Luis Saenz (Banned)
1958	Cat on a Hot Tin Roof / La gata sobre el tejado de zinc[32].	Record no. 7/59
1959	Five Finger Exercise / Ejercicio para cinco dedos Peter Shaffer[33]	Peter Shaffer attends Spanish premiere
1962	Tea & Sympathy / Té y simpatía	Record no. 299/62
1963	The Zoo Story / Historia del Zoo. Edward Albee	Record no. 75/63. Teatro de Cámara y Ensayo / Chamber Theatre
1969	The Zoo Story/ Historia del Zoo	Record no. 118/69
1970	The Boys in the Band / Los chicos de la banda. Mart Crowley	Record no. 267/70. Jaime Salom (Banned 1970 & 1972)
1972	The Zoo Story / Historia del zoo	Record no. 593/72. Terenci Moix (Catalan)
1973	The Zoo Story / Historia del zoo	6 September 1973. First peformance in Commercial Theatres
1975	The Boys in the Band / Los chicos de la banda[34].	Record no. 533/74. I. Artime & J. Azpilicueta. First peformance in Commercial Theatres. Box office success.
1975	The Zoo Story / Historia del Zoo[35]	
1975	Equus Peter Shaffer[36]	Record no. 323/74. First male and female nudes on stage. Commercial theatre.
1979	Cat on a Hot Tin Roof / La gata sobre el tejado de zinc[37].	Record no. 334/79. La gata sobre el tejado de zinc caliente. New version by Ana Diosdado

---

29 Pérez L. De Heredia, 2004: 162-169, 220-222. See also London 1997: 98-103.
30 Pérez L. De Heredia, 2004: 179-184.
31 Pérez L. De Heredia, 2004: 184-192, 358-383. "*Cat* had to be performed under club conditions and was instrumental in breaking ground in the serious theatrical treatment of homosexuals (London 1997: 100-101).
32 Pérez L. De Heredia, 2004: 190-191.
33 Álvaro 1959: 98-101.
34 Álvaro 1975: 86-90.
35 Álvaro 1975. New Productions of *Historia del Zoo* can be found in Spanish theatres almost every year until 2003.
36 Álvaro 1975: 107-111.
37 Authorized for young people over 14. Plays were classified following so-called Censorship procedures under "ordenación" or "calificación" until May 1985 (Merino 2000).

APPENDIX 2.1
Plays by Albee, Anderson, Crowley, Shaffer and Williams in AGA theatre DB (03)046.000

Author	Title	CE Record	Init. Year	Last Year	Trans. Adapt	Ms. on Record	AGA Books
Albee, Edward	La historia del Zoo	0075/63	1963	1973	García Rey, Miguel	Yes	
	La caja de arena	0076/63	1963	1963	Layton, William (trad.)	Yes	
	Zoo o El asesino filántropo	0228/64	1964	1969	Yzaguirre Romero, J. Luis		
	Quién teme a Virginia Woolf	0215/65	1965	1966	Osuna, José	Yes	
	El sueño de América	0050/66	1966	1966		Yes	
	The Sandbox	0061/66	1966	1966	Franfelder, Fran		
	Un delicado equilibrio	0288/67	1967	1967		Yes	
	Un delicado equilibrio	0119/69	1969	1969	Mara, Susana	Yes	
	La historia del Zoo	0118/69	1969	1969	Martínez Trives, Trino	Yes	
	Todo en el jardín o La culpa fue del jardín	0188/70	1970	1972	Hurtado, Ricardo	Yes	
	Quién teme a Virginia Woolf	0368/72	1972	1972	De Ridder, Marcelo	Yes	
	Una historia del zoo o Zoo story	0593/72	1972	1972	Moix, Ramón (sic.)	Yes English	
	Besties de mar	1011/76	1976	1976	Terenci Moix, Ramón (sic.)	Yes	
Anderson, Robert A.	Té y simpatía	0358/55	1955	1956	Regás, María Luz	2 ms 0118/56	
	Té y simpatía	0338/56	1956	1956		Yes	
	Té y simpatía	0061/57	1957	1968	Peña, Pastora	Yes	
	Cómo quieres que te escuche con el grifo abierto	0504/74	1974	1974	Kaufmann, Julio	Yes	
Crowley, Mart	Los chicos de la banda	0267/70	1970	1970	Salom, Jaime	Yes	
	Los chicos de la banda	0533/74	1974	1975	Artime	Yes	MK, 1975
Shaffer, Peter	Ejercicio para cinco dedos	0006/59	1959	1972	Guillot Calatayud, Mariano		
	Ejercicio para cinco dedos	0006/59	1959	1966	López Matheu, Luis	Yes	Escelicer, 1961
	El oido privado y el ojo público	0062/64	1964	1964	Rubio, Miguel	Yes	
	El apagón	0362/67	1967	1968		Yes	
	La caza real del sol	0003/69	1969	1974	Marsillach, Adolfo	Yes	
	The private Ear	0450/70	1970	1970	Clarck, John M.	Yes English	
	The public eye	0451/70	1970	1970	Clarck, John M.	Yes	
	Equus	0323/74	1974	1974		Yes	

Williams, Tennessee	Un tranvía llamado deseo	0217/50	1950	1957	Méndez Herrera, José/ Fresno, Maruchi - Guerrero.	Yes
	El zoo de cristal	0274/50	1950	1978	Vazquez Vigo, Carme/ Gordon, J. / De Quinto, Jose María-	Yes
	Verano y Humo	0342/52	1952	1961	Montes, Conchita	Yes
	El ángel de piedra	0199/55	1955	1955	Cabo, Antonio de (adap.)	Yes
	Figuretes de vidre	0134/56	1956	1966		Yes
	Un tranvía llamado Deseo	0300/56	1956	1956	Guerrero Zamora, Juan	Yes
	La rosa tatuada	0015/57	1957	1958	Cabo, Antonio de (adap.)	Yes
	Una gata sobre un tejado de zinc caliente	0228/58	1958	1958	Frade Almohalia, José	
	Camino real	0003/58	1958	1958	Vila Selma, Enrique	Yes
	Una gata sobre un tejado de zinc caliente	0017/59	1959	1962	Orce, Ramón	Yes
	La caída de Orfeo	0003/60	1960	1968		Yes
	Dulce pájaro de juventud	0152/60	1960	1962	Alonso, Justo	Yes
	Hasta llegar a entenderse	0167/63	1963	1965	Lorente Muñoz, Rafael	
	La noche de la iguana	0007/64	1964	1967		
	El caso de las petunias pisoteadas	0177/68	1968	1968		Yes
	El largo adiós	0356/68	1968	1972		Yes
	El más extraño idilio	0395/68	1968	1969		Yes
	La marquesa de Larkspurtlotion	0176/68	1968	1970	López de Cervera, María Dolores	Yes
	Auto da fe	0369/69	1969	1969	Adan Sánchez, Pedro	Yes
	Háblame de la lluvia y déjame escuchar	0027/69	1969	1972	Espada Díaz, José de	
	Lo que no se dice	0497/70	1970	1970	López Cervera, Dolores	
	Cena desagradable	0651/71	1971	1971		
	Repentinamente el pasado verano	0256/71	1971	1971	Borrel, Carlos	Yes
	Veintisiete vagones de algodón	0339/72	1972	1972		Yes
	La marquesa de Larkspurtlotion	0516/72	1972	1972	San Miguel Sánchez, Francisco	Yes
	Súbitamente el último verano	0554/74	1974	1974		Yes

APPENDIX 2.2
Plays by Albee, Anderson, Crowley, Shaffer and Williams recorded in TRACEti database[38]

Author	Title	CE Record no./Year	CE classification	Theatre	Translator Adaptor	Publishing House	Public. Year
Albee, Edward	CAJA DE ARENA, LA	75/63		Valle Inclán	Layton, William y García Rey, Miguel García Rey, Miguel	La avispa	1991
	HISTORIA DEL ZOO	75/63	Approved	Eslava	Layton, William		
	LO QUE PASÓ EN EL ZOO	75/63	Approved Teatros de cámara (One session)	Eslava	Layton, William		
	HISTORIA DEL ZOO	75/65	Approved Teatros de cámara (One session)		Layton, William García del Rey, Miguel		
	¿QUIÉN TEME A VIRGINIA WOOLF?	215/63	Approved 18+ Cuts	Marquina	Méndez Herrera, José		
	DELICADO EQUILIBRIO, UN	119/69	Approved 18+ Cuts	Barcelona, Barcelona	Gala, Antonio Gala, Antonio		
	LA HISTORIA DEL ZOO	118/69	Approved Teatros de cámara (One session)	Ateneo de Bilbao	Martínez Trives, Trino		
	UNA HISTORIA DEL ZOO (Catalan)	593/72	Approved 18+	Poliorama de Barcelona	Moix Meseguer, Ramón		
	¿QUIÉN LE TEME A VIRGINIA WOOLF?				Ridder, Marcelo de	Nueva Visión	1985
Anderson, Robert A.	TÉ Y SIMPATÍA	358/55	Approved Teatros de cámara (One session)		Regás, Mª Luz		
.	TÉ Y SIMPATÍA	118/56	Approved		Regás, Mª Luz		
.	TÉ Y SIMPATÍA	338/56	Approved 18+ Cuts		Luca de Tena, Juan Ignacio		
.	TÉ Y SIMPATÍA	61/57	Approved 18+ Cuts	Cómico	Asis, Victoriano de		
Crowley, Mart	CHICOS DE LA BANDA, LOS	267/70	Banned 1970, 1972	Beatriz de Madrid	Salom, Jaime Salom, Jaime		
	CHICOS DE LA BANDA, LOS	533/74		Barceló (Madrid)	Ignacio Artime Jaime Azpilicueta	MK Ediciones	1975
	CHICOS DE LA BANDA, LOS				Artime, Ignacio y Azpilicueta, Jaime	MK Ediciones	1975
Shaffer, Peter	EJERCICIO PARA CINCO DEDOS	6/59	Approved 18+ Cuts	Infanta Beatriz	Martínez Adell, Alberto González Vergel, Alberto	Escelicer	1961
	OÍDO PÚBLICO Y EL OJO PRIVADO, EL	62/64	Approved 18+ Cuts	Teatro Club de Madrid	Rubio, Miguel y González Vergel, Alberto		

---

38 http://www.ehu.es/trace/catalogos.html. Eight out of 35 fields that make up the TRACEti (translations censored- theatre English> Spanish) catalogue have been chosen for this Appendix. See Merino 2001 & Pérez L. de Heredia 2005 for more information on the design of TRACEti catalogues and use of databases.

Author	Title	CE Record no./Year	CE classification	Theatre	Translator Adaptor	Publishing House	Public. Year
	APAGÓN, EL	362/67	Approved 18+ Cuts	Eslava	Balart, Vicente		
	CAZA REAL DEL SOL, LA	3/69	Banned	Bellas Artes	Balart, Vicente		
	CAZA REAL DEL SOL, LA	3/69	Approved 18+	Beatriz, Madrid	Balart, Vicente		
	EQUUS	323/74	Approved with Cuts		Balart, Vicente	Aymá	1978
	AMADEUS	85			Pilar Salsó y Paredes Sansón	MK Ediciones	1981
Williams, Tennessee	ZOOLÓGICO DE CRISTAL, EL	/45			Mirlas, León		1953
	VERANO Y HUMO	/48			Mirlás, León y Barberá, Manuel	Losada	1979
	TRANVÍA LLAMA-DO DESEO, UN	217/50	Approved	Reina Victoria	Méndez Herrera, José	Escelicer	1962
	TRANVÍA LLAMA-DO DESEO, UN	217/50	Approved only for Teatros de cámara Oficial de Cámara del Español		Méndez Herrera, José	Alfil	1962
	ZOO DE CRISTAL, EL	274/50	Approved 18+ Cuts		Gordón, José	Escelicer	1960
	TRANVÍA LLAMA-DO DESEO, UN	217/50	Approved Teatros de cámara		Méndez Herrera, José	Alfil	1962
	TRANVÍA LLAMA-DO DESEO, UN	217/50	Banned	en Barcelona	Méndez Herrera, José	Alfil	1962
	VERANO Y HUMO	342/52	Approved 18+, Teatros de cámara (One session)	Cámara y Ensayo del María Guerrero	Cabo, Antonio de Gordon, José		
	ÁNGEL DE PIEDRA, EL	199/55	Banned Commercial Theatre, Approved Teatros de cámara	Windsor (Barcelona)	Cabo, Antonio de y Maseras, Margarita		
	TRANVÍA LLAMA-DO DESEO, UN	300/56	Approved		Guerrero Zamora, Juan	Alfil nº 320 (1962)	
	TRANVÍA LLAMA-DO DESEO, UN	300/56	Approved 18+	Windsor (Barcelona)	Guerrero Zamora, Juan		
	TRANVÍA LLAMA-DO DESEO, UN	300/56	Approved 18+	Windsor (Barcelona)	Guerrero Zamora, Juan	Alfil	1962
	FIGURETES DE VIDRE	134/56	Banned		Vallespinosa, B.		
	ZOO DE CRISTAL, EL	/57		Eslava	Gordón, José		
	TRANVÍA LLAMA-DO DESEO, UN	217/57	Approved	Reina Victoria	Méndez Herrera, José	Alfil nº 320 (1962)	
	ROSA TATUADA, LA	15/57	Approved	Beatriz	Cabo, Antonio de	Primer Acto nº8 (1959)	
	ROSA TATUADA, LA	15/57	Approved	Teatro de Cámara y Ensayo	Cabo, Antonio de	Primer Acto nº8 (1959)	
	GATA SOBRE EL TEJADO (DE CINC) CALIENTE, LA	228/58			Cabo, Antonio de y Saez, Luis	Alfil	1962
	CAMINO REAL	228/58	Approved Chamber Theatre	Cámara y Ensayo del María Guerrero	Hurtado, Diego	Escelicer	1963
	GATA SOBRE EL TEJADO DE ZINC LA	228/58	Banned		Cabo, Antonio de y Luis Saenz	Alfil	1962

Author	Title	CE Record no./Year	CE classification	Theatre	Translator Adaptor	Publishing House	Public. Year
	GATA SOBRE EL TEJADO DE ZINC, LA	7/59	Approved 18+	Eslava	Cabo, Antonio de y Luis Saénz	Escelicer	1962
	DULCE PÁJARO DE JUVENTUD	152/60	Approved	Eslava	Cabo, Antonio de		
	DULCE PÁJARO DE JUVENTUD	152/60	Approved	Eslava	Cabo, Antonio de		
	DULCE PÁJARO DE JUVENTUD	152/60	Banned		Cabo, Antonio de		
	CAÍDA DE ORFEO, LA	3/60	Approved	Alcázar	Cabo, Antonio de	Escelicer	1962
	ZOO DE CRISTAL, EL	/61					
	KRISTALESKO IRU-DITXOAK (Basque)	485/62	Approved (one session)	Principal (San Sebastián)	Beobide, Ignacio		
	HASTA LLEGAR A ENTENDERSE	167/63	Approved	Teatro Club	Paso, Alfonso	Escelicer	1964
	HASTA LLEGAR A ENTENDERSE	167/63	Approved 18+ Cuts	Gira por provincias	Paso, Alfonso Julio Mathias	Escelicer	1964
	HASTA LLEGAR A ENTENDERSE	167/63	Approved 18+ Cuts	Teatro ARA-Málaga	Paso, Alfonso Julio Mathias	Escelicer	1964
	NOCHE DE LA IGUANA, LA	7/64	Approved 18+ Cuts	Cómico	Méndez Herrera, José	Escelicer	1965
	NOCHE DE LA IGUANA, LA				Barberá, Manuel	Losada	1979 1964 1ª ed
	CASO DE LAS PETUNIAS PISOTEADAS, EL	177/68	Approved 14+	Montepío Comercial e Industrial de Madrid		Alianza	
	LARGO ADIÓS, EL	356/68	Approved				
	MARQUESA DE LARKSPURLOTION, LA	176/68	Approved	Montepío Comercial e Indistrial	López Cervera, Mª Dolores	Alianza Editorial	
	MARQUESA DE LARKSPURLOTION, LA	176/68	Approved	Salón Parroquial de los Desamparados	López Cervera, Mª Dolores	Alianza Editorial	
	MARQUESA DE LARKSPURLOTION, LA	176/68	Approved	Círculo de Bellas Artes de Santa Cruz de Tenerife	López Cervera, Mª Dolores	Alianza Editorial	
	MÁS EXTRAÑO IDILIO, EL	395/68	Approved				
	HÁBLAME COMO LA LLUVIA Y DÉJAME ESCUCHAR	27/69	Approved 18+	Montepío	López de Cervero, María Dolores		
	HÁBLAME COMO LA LLUVIA Y DÉJAME ESCUCHAR	27/69	Approved 18+	Casa Municipal de Cultura de Avilés	López de Cervero, María Dolores	Alianza	
	HÁBLAME COMO LA LLUVIA Y DÉJAME ESCUCHAR	27/69	Approved 18+	Teatro del Círculo de Bellas Artes de Santa Cruz de Tenerife	López de Cervero, María Dolores	Alianza	
	AUTO-DA-FE	27/69					

Building TRACE (translations censored) Theatre Corpus:... 151

Author	Title	CE Record no./Year	CE classification	Theatre	Translator Adaptor	Publishing House	Public. Year
	LO QUE NO SE DICE	497/70	Approved		López Cervera, Mª Dolores		
	REPENTINAMENTE, EL VERANO	256/71	Approved		Saénz Montaner, Luis		
	VEINTISIETE VAGONES DE ALGODÓN	339/72	Approved				
	MARQUESA DE LARKSPURLOTION, LA	516/72			Balsino, Mª Luisa		
	SÚBITAMENTE, EL ÚLTIMO VERANO	554/74	Approved				
	GATA SOBRE EL TEJADO DE ZINC CALIENTE, LA	554/79	"Calificación" 14+	Marquina	Diosdado, Ana	MK Ediciones	1984
	ZOO DE CRISTAL, EL	150/81		Marquina	Vázquez Vigo, Carmen		
	ZOO DE CRISTAL, EL	150/81	"Calificación" 14+		Schurjin		
	NO PUEDO IMAGINAR MAÑANA	113/83	"Calificación" 14+		Tabares Soriano, Mercedes		
	ADVERTENCIA PER A EMBARCACION PETITES	59/83	"Calificación" 16+		Melendres, Jaume		
	ZOOLÓGICO DE CRISTAL, EL	403/83	"Calificación" No age restriction		Gordon, José	Escelicer	1964
	VEINTISIETE VAGONES DE ALGODÓN	146/83	"Calificación" 16+		López Cervera, Mª Dolores		
	GATA SOBRE EL TEJADO DE ZINC CALIENTE, LA	37/84	Approved 14+	Reina Victoria de Madrid	Gandolfo, Carlos y Maldonado, Salvador		
	EL ZOOLÓGICO DE CRISTAL	118/84	Approved No age restriction	En Sástago (Zaragoza)	Mirlas, León		
	EN EL BAR DE UN HOTEL DE TOKIO	284/84	Approved 16+	Madrid & Rest of Spain	Producciones Divinas		
	TRANVÍA LLAMADO DESEO, UN	/88			Llovet, Enrique	MK Ediciones	1988

APPENDIX 3
Maps of repliques. Selection.
ST, act II, r. 200-207 (Crowley 1968), TTce1.1 & TTce1.2 (Jaime Salom's translation, AGA)

ST	200	201	202	203	204	205	206	207
TTce1.1	175	176	177	178	179		180	181
TTce1.2				159	160			

ST	TTce1.1	TTce1.2
200 EMORY- He was a steal.	175 EMORY- Barato. Era un saldo.	
201 MICHAEL- He's a ham sandwich-fifty cents any time of the day or night. *(Crosses to bar via below coffee table.)* (DONALD *rises, crosses to Left table with plate.)*	176 MICHAEL- Pues todavía es caro. ¡Qué tipo!	
202 HAROLD- King of the Pig People. *(MICHAEL gives him a look.)*	177 HAROLD- Y tú, ¡qué cerdo! (MICHAEL LE ECHA UNA MIRADA. DONALD LLEVA SU PLATO, YA VACIO, A LA MESA)	
203 EMORY- (To DONALD.) Would you like some more?	178 EMORY- (A DONALD) ¿Quieres un poco más?	159 EMORY- (A DONALD) ¿Quieres un poco más?
204 DONALD- No, thank you, Emory. It was very good.	179 DONALD- No gracias, Emory. Muy bueno.	160 DONALD- No gracias, Emory. Muy bueno.
205 EMORY- Did you like it?		
206 COWBOY- I'm not a steal. I cost twenty dollars. (DONALD *returns to stool.* BERNARD *returns his Plate to* EMORY-)	180 VAQUERO- ¡ No soy un saldo! Me han dado veinte dólares para que viniera.	
207 EMORY- More?	181 EMORY- (ABERNARD) ¿Un poco más?	

Building TRACE (translations censored) Theatre Corpus:... 153

ST, act II, r. 200-207 (Crowley 1968), TTce2 (Artime and Azpilicueta's translation, AGA) & TTpub (Artime and Azpilicueta's translation, Crowley 1975)

ST	200	201	202	203			204	205	206	207
TTpub	170	171	172	173	174	175	176	177	178	
TTce2	153							154	155≠	

ST	TTce1.1	TTce1.2
200 EMORY- He was a steal.	170 EMORY- ¡Uyyyy, un robo!	153 EMORY- ¡Uyyyy, un robo!
201 MICHAEL- He's a ham sandwich-fifty cents any time of the day or night. *(Crosses to bar via below coffee table.)* (DONALD *rises, crosses to Left table with plate.*)	171 MICHAEL- Encima es caro.	
202 HAROLD- King of the Pig People. (MICHAEL *gives him a look.*)	172 HAROLD- Michael, eres el rey de los cochinos. (BERNARD SE LLEVA EL PLATO DE LA MESA).	
203 EMORY- (To DONALD.) Would you like some more?	173 EMORY-¿Más?	
	174 LARRY-¿Por qué no le sirves?	
	175 EMORY-¿Quieres más?	
204 DONALD- No, thank you, Emory. It was very good.	176 DONALD- No gracias, Emory. Estaba muy bueno.	
205 EMORY- Did you like it?	177 COWBOY- No soy un robo. Me compran por sólo veinte dólares.	154 COWBOY- No soy un robo. Me compran por sólo veinte dólares.
206 COWBOY- I'm not a steal, I cost twenty dollars. (DONALD *returns to stool.* BERNARD *returns his Plate to* EMORY-)	178 EMORY- ¿Te ha gustado?	155 EMORY- ¿Más?
207 EMORY- More?		

Chapter Seven

Some Recent (and More Recent) Myths in Translation Studies: An Essay on the Present and Future of the Discipline[*]

Gideon Toury

In the following pages some issues of identity will be tackled, albeit with a certain twist. Thus, while most of what I will have to say will indeed be concerned with cultural identity, it will not be the object-level (i.e. translating, translators and translations) that will be approached, but so-called Translation Studies, the level from which all phenomena regarded as "translational" are observed and in whose terms they are accounted for. Some of the claims I will be making do not enjoy a consensus of opinions. Indeed, at times I may sound provocative, and more and more so as I go along. I will start with a brief presentation of a number of exemplary cases, which will be followed by an *exposé* of the notion of "myth" and its appropriateness for the current discussion. In conclusion, yet another, quite recent, case will be discussed.

An Extended Case in Point: The Myth of the "Text"

Very often, observations that seem rather trivial may nevertheless form convenient points of entry into a field and supply keys to its understanding. Here is one such observation. It is formulated as a *question*. The answer to our question, when we finally reach one, may well sound almost self-evident, making the question itself look rather trivial. But is it really so? Is there nothing deeper to it? Here is the question, then:

> Can we—in our capacity as translation scholars—assume, and hence take as a point of departure for our studies of the practice of translation, that translators read the so-called source texts before they set out to actually translate them?

---

[*] Two versions of this paper were read in the XIII Susanne Hübner Seminar "Translation and Cultural Identity" (Zaragoza 2005) and "Translation, History and Culture: A Colloquium in tribute to Saliha Paker" (Istanbul, 2008).

Note that those addressed are ourselves *in our capacity as translation scholars*, and not anything else we might also be: active translators, consumers of translations, teachers and critics of translation, students being trained to become translators, etc. Each one of those constitutes a "rôle" in the basic sociological sense, and hence it is defined by a set of connected behaviors, rights and obligations as conceptualized by actors in a social setting. Each rôle is established on the basis of different interests, at least in part, and therefore different answers are expected to our rôle-centered question.

What I am interested in here is the answers that might be given by a translation *scholar*. In other words, the question is not about whether anybody *would like* a would-be translator to first read the text s/he will be translating. Even less is it about whether a translator *"should"* allegedly start by devoting an amount of time and mental effort to reading the so-called source text. The question therefore has no immediate normative implications, nor does it stand for mere wishful thinking. What it calls for, rather, is a *factual* reply, i.e. an account of reality, and its primary mainspring is an attempt to satisfy our curiosity—the true basis for research-qua-research—thus enabling us to collect information and accumulate authentic data about what goes on in real-life translation events,[1] which I have recently characterized as "Conducting Research on a 'Wish-to-Understand' Basis" (Toury 2006).

Then again, the way it was formulated, using the definite article (*"the* text"), the question should be seen as far more demanding than the mere assumption that *some* reading is applied to the source text; it clearly refers to a kind of reading applied to the text *as a whole*. After all, theoretically-speaking, no translation would take place that had not been preceded by at least some processing of source material, which presupposes an act of taking-in, and hence reading. The same holds, *mutatis mutandis*, for an oral message that stands to be translated, for which reason the common designation "simultaneous interpreting" constitutes a contradiction in terms: no act of translation, including interpreting, can commence unless a *minimum amount of source language has been produced (by a speaker) and received (by the would-be translator)*. The question of what might constitute a minimum chunk can be answered by means of a speculative

---

1 I am using the term "translation events" to refer to "acts of translation" within their socio-cultural context. The common expression "translation processes" had better be kept for the mental activities as such, that is, what actually goes on in the little "black box" throughout the act.

study of initial possibilities, i.e. in theoretical terms; what this chunk is in individual acts of translation and in types thereof is one of the riddles research into translation is called upon to solve.

By the same token, at the latest a short while before an act of translation comes to its end, which is marked by the full existence of a target text, the language flow which constitutes the input of the act *will have been read in full at least once*. (To avoid tedious digressions, I shun the intriguing question of whether we would be better off regarding an accumulative reading of this kind as an independent activity or just a phase in the act of translation. In this connection, being "better off" is to be understood in terms of *explanatory power.* No intrinsic "truth value" is implied by the phrase.)

Taking these ramifications to bear on the question we have been struggling with, the latter can now be reformulated and given sharper contours, which will be of great help in any attempt to answer it; for instance, in the following way:

> Can an acting translator be assumed [by translation scholars] to have read the source text in its entirety at least once prior to the application of translation strategies proper?

The following two answers are among the first that come to mind:

> 1. Some do, some don't
> 2. They sometimes do and sometimes don't.

Both answers make a lot of intuitive sense and are difficult to dispute. At the same time, however, any reply that is given at this level of generalization adds very little indeed to the bulk of empirical facts we are trying to collect. It therefore contributes next to nothing to our understanding of translators' behavior in its context. The way out of this impasse seems to be to pose *questions of increasing delicacy and specificity;* namely, questions of WHEN, WHAT and HOW. Here are some of the possible questions that may present themselves at this stage:

— When—that is, under what circumstances—would a translator tend to start the act with a full reading of the source text and when (under what circumstances) would s/he opt for not doing so?
— What would one read to start with, beyond the theoretically necessary minimum, if it is not the text in full?

— In the latter case, how would one go about reading the rest of the source text? The answer would probably be "segment by segment as one goes along", but what would constitute a segment, in this connection, and how would it be determined?

And finally, of utmost importance for any attempt to expose the mythical element in much of our thinking about translation:

— To what extent would a source text be read AS A TEXT (or segments thereof AS TEXTUAL SEGMENTS, that is to say, language sequences in the textual relations they enter into and the ensuing [*ad hoc*] functions these sequences acquire in the text they are part of)?

What underlies this last question is that it is possible to apply a reading to a text, even in its entirety, without the reading being necessarily and automatically of a TEXTUAL nature. This assumption rests on the observation (which has taken many shapes and has had many alternative formulations in different communicational approaches to language and text) that *a text is a two-plane structure* whose reading involves two combined, and partly simultaneous movements. One of the readings is *linear*, a unidirectional move forward, along the verbal flow as such, whereas the other one is *non-linear*, an interrupted movement occurring over and above the language continuum and following no fixed direction. These two planes, and the different kinds of reading they generate, have also been called "serial" and "structural", respectively. Some authors (in relation to text processing in translation too, most notably James S Holmes) have likened what presumably goes on in the second movement to the gradual creation in the consumer's mind of a "map" of the text, hence Holmes' suggestion that translation be described as a "two-plane, two-map" operation, as the target text is presumably generated as a mirror image of the way the source text was read (Holmes 1988).)

If this is a true account, then the better the balance between the two movements with respect to the text (the claim goes), the more "textual" the reading will be. Conversely, in cases when the two levels are combined but the ensuing combination is not well balanced, the reading, while still there, becomes less and less "textual". The possibility that, in the process, the verbal flow which constitutes the text will have been covered in its entirety changes very little here. Finally, when the only movement is serial—if such a thing is conceivable at all—there would still be some kind of "reading" going on, which may however be said to border on the pathological. (The opposite situation—drawing a mental "map" of the text with no serial reading whatsoever—is unimaginable. After all, at least *some* "raw material" collected in and through the "linear" reading is required for the "map" to be created.) The bottom line is clear, then: *reading a text "in full"* is not just another name for a *"full reading" of a text.*

It is clear that the reading my question referred to was of the second kind: what is at stake, then, is the extent to which a source text is read AS A TEXT, not just as a concatenation of successive verbal items. The question can thus be reformulated once again:

> Can a translator be assumed to have given the source text at least one full textual reading prior to the application of translation strategies proper?

The shift towards focusing on the *text* as the ultimate unit of translation is not very new, but it is not all that old either. It took place mainly in the 1970s-1980s, when there were a substantial number of scholars who agreed that a *positive* answer should be given to the question we are dealing with. The centralization of the text as a unit gave rise to the notion of "textuality", which was placed at the centre of the discussion and soon gained a train of followers. Some of them even went further. Two quotes follow, which were picked at random from a book by two translation scholars, Albrecht Neubert and Gregory Shreve. The book was published in 1992, when the notion of the "text" reigned supreme in Translation Studies, but most of its claims had already been made earlier:

(1) The text has to be considered the primary object of translation study. (Neubert and Shreve 1992: 10)

(2) In the context of translation studies, the principle of textuality can be used to define the conditions under which an L_1 text and its L_2 counterpart can be said to be textually equivalent. (ibid: 70)

The book's title spells out the authors' intention very clearly, owing to its slogan-like nature. It reads: *Translation as Text.* I will soon have some more to say about the significance of slogans in mythical thinking.

Obviously enough, when one uses formulations of this kind, one is not necessarily making a *declarative* statement. One may just as well be expressing an *opinion*, a personal one, or that of the group one belongs to, or maybe *recommending* a particular kind of behavior. Both are not only legitimate; they are also highly commendable goals. What they do not do is constitute a *theoretical* basis and framework for the study of translation behavior as it is performed "in the real world". Unfortunately, formulations of this kind are often not even presented as *hypotheses* (which invite the application of procedures of verification/refutation/modification), but as *truisms,* a status they cannot possibly have. For any such statement is not just *refutable* (in principle); it is very often de facto *refuted* by instances of actual practice.

Nor does this exhaust the difficulties. Many translation scholars of a "textual" denomination go on to build an elaborate house-of-theory on the shaky sands of the assumption that an act of translation always—by definition, so to speak (see next section)—starts with a fully "textual" reading of the whole source text. Some of them go so far as to claim that this reading can be given a shape and systematized: what they call "text analysis for the specific purpose of translation", which is a transferable skill that can be transmitted in an attempt to make others into translators "in their own likeness, after their image" (Genesis 5:3).

This is precisely where the proverbial cat is finally out of the bag: it is very often a wish to satisfy the needs of the translation *teacher* that is the mainspring of the textually-oriented scholar, who is often the same person wearing two different masks. One of the most elaborate attempts in this direction is of course Christiane Nord's classical book. The cover page reveals it all, especially the subtitle, in both German and English (1988 and 1991, respectively, that is, almost the same publication date as Neubert and Shreve's book): *Theoretische Grundlagen, Methode und didaktische Anwendung einer übersetzungsrelevanten Textanalyse—Theory, Methodology, and Didactic Application of a Model for Translation-Oriented Text Analysis.* Nord's book is to be (and has indeed been) commended for its intricate internal logic, even as it builds on the problematic assumption that texts standing for translation are unconditionally read "as texts" during the process. The book is thus one of a whole array of realizations of what I now wish to call the "myth of the text" in Translation Studies, as is the Neubert-Shreve book.[2]

Second Case: "Translation Should First Be Defined"

Another, much older myth in the field can be summed up in the claim that, should one try hard enough, a *definition* of translation would finally emerge, and that, when this goal has been achieved, many of the difficulties facing translation scholars will have disappeared for good. The most

---

2   Of course, I could also have started at the end (e.g. with the question "Is the result of a translation act necessarily a text?") and gone all the way back.

extreme requirement, in this respect, has been that the definition will have an a-historical and a-social format, that is, be valid for all times, all places, all modes of translation and all possible circumstances. Such an extreme goal-setting for a definition of translation seems rather dated now. True, there is the occasional scholar who still expresses a wish to finally have such a definition, but now, elements of newer myths—including the "myth of the 'text'"—often intervene, which makes it next to impossible to actually come up with a definition, let alone one that would use essentialist terms, i.e. enumerate necessary and sufficient conditions for its application.

Here are one and a half examples of the quest for a definition of translation and the difficulties it may involve:

In the year 1996, the Russian scholar Vilen Komissarov claimed again that devising a definition is a *sine qua non* for the discipline. Proceeding from his own previous work (in Russian) and mixing into it a number of arguments from my (quite different) presentation of the notion of "assumed translation", Komissarov discussed at some length the criteria that the required definition would have to satisfy. However, what he was unable to do, and in fact never tried to do, was to arrive at a concrete formulation which would satisfy those criteria and be in a position to serve as the coveted definition.

Eight years later, Sandra Halverson (2004) managed to show quite convincingly why Komissarov's efforts had failed. She then ventured to offer a reconciliation between Komissarov's approach and mine, which she believed to be a small step forward in the right direction. What was still missing was... the definition itself.

Occasional attempts of this kind notwithstanding, I believe that the wish to start research with a definition of translation has not only assumed mythical dimensions, but the quest for "definition" can be said to have been petered out. Efforts seem to have wandered from the more general issues to lower-level, more specific ones. Or has the hunt for a definition just become dormant? Only the future will tell if and how it will come to life again.

Yet another Case: What about "Translation Universals"?

Nor is the future too far away. In fact, for all practical purposes, it is already here and it has some interesting new things to tell us. Thus, in the last few years, a new myth has been emerging, next to, or instead of some of the older ones. This myth, which has been gaining ground and momentum, winning more and more adherents in various circles, makes use of the notion of "universals". The assumption here is that there are phenomena which can be found only in translations, and which can (some say: should) therefore be regarded as *intrinsic* to the activity and its results; "by definition", so to speak, even though the quest for that definition itself has been dwindling (see above).

This new conviction gave rise to attempts to actually discover (or uncover) such universal features. Recently, there have even been two conferences devoted to the hunt for universals in translation, both in the same year (2001), which resulted in two seminal collections of articles: *Translation Universals: Do They Exist?* (Mauranen and Kujamäki 2004) and a special Section in *Claims, Changes and Challenges in Translation Studies* (Hansen *et al.* 2004).

Quite a number of phenomena, on various levels, have been suggested as candidates for the status of "universals", some on the basis of the findings of earlier descriptive-explanatory studies, others on a speculative basis. These candidates include: explicitation, disambiguation, simplification, conventionalisation, avoidance of repetition, and exaggeration of features of the target language. These hypothetical candidates are all under study now, waiting to be verified, falsified or moderated on the basis of systematic analysis of genuine data using a variety of different research modes.

I have my own position *vis-à-vis* the quest for translation universals, which can be found in the articles I contributed to the two collections I have just mentioned (Toury 2004a and 2004b). However, I think it is about time that we stepped back and asked ourselves a more general question: Why have all these cases been subsumed under the title of "myths"? What was I trying to say about them that is served—or at least *better* served—by recourse to that notion? In brief, how does the introduction of the concept of "myth" into the discussion contribute to the point I am trying to make? A brief survey of the way the concept is used may supply an answer to that question and help clarify my intentions.

What is in a "Myth"?

The way I'm using the notion of "myth" is in tune with what has been going on in the social sciences for many years. There is really nothing new to it, except for its application to Translation Studies and the ways it is tackled there. Thus, in academic parlance and in daily language use alike, the word "myth" is often used to refer to a commonly held but faulty, if not erroneous belief. However, this is only scratching the surface, and the notion goes way deeper and has many important implications.

Basically, what we are dealing with here is a kind of *story* which is *adopted by a group and granted authority over the group and its individual members*. Interestingly, such an authority can be granted to a "story" irrespective of how much "truth" it contains. In fact, more often than not, myths are based on an admixture of fact and fiction. Thus, for those who have adopted one (i.e. decided to join the group in question), the myth is *axiomatically valid*, that is, even when there is little or no evidence to support it; in fact, even if reality (or history) may *disprove* it. A myth simply has functions other than to reflect "reality" or give a "true" report on it. The power of a myth lies in another kind of "truth", then, which is different from the historicity of the (real or possible) story underlying it.

One of the main functions of myths in the socio-cultural domain is indeed the *demarcation of groups* (i.e. distinguishing being "in" vs. from being "out" of it), which goes hand in hand with the establishment of *group identity*. It is thus *constitutive* in nature. At the same time it also serves as a *stabilizing factor* for the group in question. In the long run, this second function makes the adoption of myths highly beneficial for every community wishing to distinguish itself from other groups, especially if those other groups are conceived of as competitors struggling for the same "territory" as is the case in disciplines such as Translation Studies.

To be sure, it is not the myth itself—its contents, that is—which creates the dividing line between those who are "in the group" and those who are outside of it, often in another group, entertaining a different set of myths. Rather, it is first and foremost the fact that a story is SHARED by the members of one group and NOT SHARED by the members of another. (In reality, borderlines are often blurred and there may be some overlap between the myths of adjacent communities such as alternative schools of translation scholars. However, such an overlap can only be partial: there cannot be two *different* communities which entertain the exact *same* mythology.)

One way of conceptualizing the transformation of a mere story, be it factual or fictive, into a true myth, is to view "myths" as lying at the far end of a continuum ranging from a "dispassionate account" to "legendary occurrence" to "mythical status". While the story progresses towards the mythical end of this continuum, what people think, feel and say about it becomes less and less fact-sensitive. Consequently, by the time the mythical end of the spectrum has actually been reached, the story will have taken on a life of its own and the facts of the original state of affairs, if there have been such facts, in the first place, will have become almost irrelevant. "This process often leads to interpretation of myths as 'disguised propaganda' in the service of powerful individuals", and the purpose of myths is seen as to allow the "social order" to establish "its permanence on the illusion of a natural order" (Mâche 1992: 10).

This brings us to another important feature of mythologies; namely, the role of "gods" and "heroes", which was so typical of "classical" myths. Even though I won't devote any time to this issue, *vis-à-vis* any particular myth, I would certainly argue that in Translation Studies too, a lot hangs on the AUTHORITY attributed to those whose names have become associated, sometimes even identified with certain myths; whether they actually introduced, or helped propagate them, or just gave them names or formulated popular catch phrases in connection with them.

* * *

Let us go back to Translation Studies now and devote some attention to the ways the notion of "myth" may help understand what is going on in our discipline.

Myths in/and Translation Studies

Translation scholars have long had a wish to belong; to rise above the position of a mere rabble of individuals with a vaguely common interest and become more of a *community*. This wish is attested, for example, by the formation of a number of scholarly societies, local, regional and international, as well as the creation of publishing venues and various other kinds of networking. It may even be claimed that, to a certain extent, some sense of community has already emerged. To be more precise, I believe what we have in today's Translation Studies is better accounted for as an *aggregate of [sub-]communities* loosely held together, each one seeking (internally) a common denominator and (externally) a demarcation line between it and other sub-communities which pertain to the discipline, in some way or another. As part of the development of group identity, those sub-communities will be found to have adopted one or another myth to enhance their internal coherence and distinguish them from all neighbouring groups. Try to think in "mythical" terms about, for instance, "functionalists" vs. "structuralists", or "linguists" vs. "literary scholars", or "descriptivists" vs. "prescriptivists", and you will have a glimpse of what I have in mind.

This is one important reason why attempts to establish some "common grounds" for all the communities of translation scholars and their constitutive myths tend to fail, as has been shown by a debate which went on in several issues of *Target* a few years ago (2000-2002) about the possibility of finding such grounds. Over ten scholars, among them some of the leading figures of the discipline, took part in this debate, which makes excellent reading material and can serve as a basis for many an eye-opening discussion. At the same time, it cannot be said to have resulted in too much consensus.

An important conclusion of the debate was that not everybody in the field is so much as interested in *searching* for common grounds. What many do instead is hope (or even actually try) to convince others of their own myth, often without telling them it is just a myth, and hence not necessarily true-to-facts. In a sense, what we are witnessing here is a kind of a *missionary* activity, that is, an attempt to beget belief in non-believers, or at least to persuade them to accept the external behavior of the believer. Of course, there is nothing wrong with indulging in missionary work, as long as one is aware that this is what one is doing.

In common language the word "myth" is often used *pejoratively* in reference to common beliefs of a culture, to imply that a constitutive story is both fanciful and fictional, and that it deserves to be exploded. It is well known that a myth is often recognized for what it is only after it has been exploded.

From the way I have been talking about myths in Translation Studies, and especially from my account of the "myth of the text" and the "myth of the definition", it might have been concluded that I had something against particular myths, or perhaps even against having myths in general. This is simply not true. In fact, I am very well aware of my own share in the introduction of myths to our discipline, most notably the one that is usually summed up in the slogan-like sentence "translations are facts of one system only"; a direct quotation from one of my texts which however bears only a vague resemblance of a much more complex argument.

This is indeed typical of the fate of myths: a myth is very often only known to the public—certainly to laymen, but often to experts too—in its nutshell form. As already noted, along the time axis, myths tend to be reduced to *catch-phrases* which, at best, are quoted from an authorized version of the "story" and at worst constitute secondary formulations representing somebody else's summary of the story. Such phrases start as "shorthand" versions of the myth, or cues to it, and anyone exposed to a slogan is expected to evoke the "story" behind it and be able to reconstruct a whole line of argumentation. However, with time, the catch-phrase tends to assume a life of its own and come to totally replace the original story. Little by little, the "story" simply melts away and is replaced by the slogan as an entity in itself.

As it turns out, the wish to explode somebody else's myth, which is so characteristic of the struggle between different groups fighting for the same, or similar territory, is very well served by having the myth trivialized through its reduction to a mere slogan: "the ultimate unit of translation is the text", "a definition of translation is a *sine qua non* for the discipline", "there are universals of translation", and the like. What an elegant way of killing a scholarly initiative!

Third Case: "Translation is a Political Act"

One of the newest, and most popular myths among today's translation scholars involves the relationships between translation and ideology, mainly in its political attire. One extreme catch-phrase designed to evoke this myth is: "Translation is always a political act".

Just as scholars clinging to the myth of the text purport to know—and teach to others—what they regard as the "appropriate" ways of identifying text-types and analyzing texts in the context of translation, so those subscribing to one of the many varieties of the "ideology" (or "politics") myth tend to import from without a notion of "political appropriateness" and bring it to bear on the kind of Translation Studies they wish to promote. Inasmuch as they regard descriptive-explanatory research as relevant, or even legitimate, in the first place, the imported notion exerts a strong effect on it: all too often, research does not proceed from "bare facts", but from facts which have already been filtered through an ideological (or political) sieve, which bears a striking resemblance to the positions they themselves hold with respect to the world, society or culture. The way religion used to act, to be sure.

For instance, a scholar who chooses to identify himself—and especially herself—with the feminist cause and who checks everything in the light of its principles will tend to regard as unsatisfactory those studies—and scholars—who neglect to extol this aspect or tackle it "wrongly" (in terms of the dominant ideology). They would certainly condemn those who have failed to adopt a feminist outlook altogether or those who entertain a different ideology, whether it is merely non-feminist or—God forbid—anti-feminist. Similarly, scholars adopting a "post-colonial" stance towards society, be it defiant or apologetic, will quite naturally tend to focus on phenomena which concur with the position they have adopted and reject other points of view, especially those that can be shown to have "ignored" the post-colonial element.

In my opinion, the worst outcome of this approach is that, in the majority of cases, translations, translators and instances of translational behavior are not really studied, in the way I understand the term. Rather, they are recruited in the service of a particular ideology, to serve as *weapons in a socio-political struggle*. This struggle has the commendable aim of "improving" reality (with an eye to the future), or condemning it (with regard to the past and present). By contrast, studies carried out in the framework of such a struggle thus focus on criticizing reality or attempting to repair it. Consequently, the way the struggled is conducted, it has precious little to do with a systematic attempt to explain reality. Thus, while making us aware of *questions* which may have remained unasked, the new "paradigm" (to use Kuhn's term) added precious little in terms of research *methodology*, or indeed translation *theory*. Its proponents did, however, attain the coveted status of a "community", having myths of its own, including (already) a myriad of slogans.

Final Case: Translation Studies as an Arena for Political Struggles

Politicization seems to be contagious: it lends itself quite easily to transfer from accounts of translation events, translating personae, translational strategies and translated texts to Translation *Studies*. Now it is no longer translation that is targeted, but translation scholars and their behavior as such. In this phase, not only approaches and positions, but the *individuals* who adopt them as well, may find themselves and their work judged and sentenced according to whether or not such approaches and positions are "politically correct".

If this transfer is done consistently, it will not be long before a dividing line appears between what is politically "acceptable" and what is "unacceptable", what is "done" and what is "not to be done" in translation research. Sectarian politics *vis-à-vis* translation very easily become an offshoot of general politics, and dubious decisions start being made which create the impression that a cult has been born.

Today's Translation Studies seem to be well on their way to such a situation. Some would even say that we have reached a point of no return. What comes to mind immediately is something that started as a boycott of Translation Studies performed in a particular country whose *state* politics came under severe attack; that is, it was not even the political positions of the researchers working in that country that brought about the attack, which would have been bad enough. Rather, researchers were boycotted on one and only one ground: their affiliation with an institute of higher learning in that particular place. Consequently, people living and working in that country started to be treated as if they no longer represented themselves, or even any internal faction struggling for domination within Translation Studies (such factions do exist), but rather the state as a political entity, or, even more narrowly, the official politics of its government.

To realize the boycott, a variety of measures were applied, most of them potentially harmful to our discipline and detrimental for its future. Here are some of the measures:

— the publication of studies written by scholars based in the boycotted country was banned as long as the scholars in question had not left the country and taken a job somewhere else (or, at least, agreed to suppress their affiliation or adopt a false one);
— certain books and periodicals stopped being sold to university libraries in that country, thus cutting the free flow of information and opinion, which is vital for any academic community; and
— scholars based in that country were warned—explicitly or implicitly—that if they proposed papers for particular conferences and journals, their proposals would be ignored and rejected, irrespective of their intrinsic merits.

Many members of the (loosely knit) Translation Studies community agreed to abide by this political dictate, the majority simply closed their eyes, turned a deaf ear, and kept their mouth shut, like the three infamous monkeys. Luckily enough, there were also scholars who refused to give in, rejecting any attempt to bring politics to intervene in academic work and international cooperation. Some—not too many—even tried to fight the boycott or the boycotters, most notable EST, the European Society of Translation Studies, and its leading team. With very partial success, one would hasten to add…

Soon enough, lo and behold, a dividing line, almost a wall, was formed, defining two groups of translation scholars, basically in terms of their position with respect to that wall. In a sense, what the boycotting lot has actually been doing is *build up a myth for itself*, so that its wish to have special associations of their own, with different reservoirs of functionaries, along with different journals and book series, will assume mythical proportions and will no longer be tied so closely to the original political motive.

The first boycotting measures—the sacking of two Israeli scholars from the boards of two periodicals—were taken in the summer of 2002. In the midst of a heated debate, which took place mainly on the internet but also in the media (newspapers, radio and television), I was asked to contribute a short piece to the *Times Higher Education Supplement* (7 February 2003). This is what I wrote, among other things:

> The next logical step might be to stop abstracting studies by [citizens of that country] in [periodicals edited by members of the boycotting group], or to start purging articles which have been accepted for publication by [those periodicals] of references to scholars [from that particular country], no matter how important their contribution to the discipline.
>
> Even if such a policy is never announced in any official way, I presume there will be scholars who, struggling to get published (or perish), would take a cue from [...]'s previous deeds and refrain from mentioning the repugnant names, hoping that this will buy them favor in the eyes of the boycott [agents] [...].
>
> Others may decide to send nothing [to the boycotting publications], thus rendering [them] sectarian, which won't be any less damaging for Translation Studies.
>
> Whatever the outcome, the prospects look grim.

I have never purported to be a prophet and I'm not going to start making any prophesies now. At the same time, I do believe I have some understanding of cultural processes; and when I look back from where we are standing now, almost six years later, I have to say—to my regret, to be sure—that I can see my forecast coming true. Thus, in spite of partial overlaps, there are noticeable differences between the audiences attending different conferences, organized by different institutions and individuals, and these differences seem to be growing. Suffice it to compare the lists of active participants in the last Congresses of EST in Lisbon (2004) and Ljubljana (2007) vs. the first two conferences of IATIS (Seoul 2004 and Capetown 2006). The differences are even more striking when it comes to the big "names": the officers of the two associations, the members of the scientific committees of the conferences, the plenary speakers, and the like. In contradistinction to the "simple" participants, there is very little overlap in the realm of leadership.

Luckily enough, in spite of the fact that colleagues were strongly encouraged to take sides in the underlying political dispute and urged to make a (the?) "politically correct" decision, there is still a massive number of scholars who have retained their innocence (and I am using this word in the most positive sense), who take part in conferences on both sides of the dividing line, thus acting as potential *mediators* bridging the ever-growing gap between the two detached groups and their constitutive myths. The point of no return may have not been reached, after all. Still, it seems to be close enough. It is time to revive the old myth of academic freedom and tolerance and leave global politics out of the scientific game. The internal politics of the community of translation scholars itself is more than enough!

References

Halverson, Sandra. 2004. "Assumed Translation: Reconciling Komissarov and Toury and Moving a Step forward". *Target* 16.2: 341-354.
Hansen, Gyde, Kirsten Malmkjær and Daniel Gile. Eds. 2004. *Claims, Changes and Challenges in Translation Studies: Selected contributions from the EST Congress, Copenhagen 2001*. Amsterdam-Philadelphia: John Benjamins.
Holmes, James S. 1988. *Translated!: Papers on Literary Translation and Translation Studies*. Amsterdam: Rodopi.
Komissarov, Vilen. 1996. "Assumed Translation: Continuing the Discussion". *Target* 8.2: 365-274.
Kuhn, Thomas. 1962. *The Structure of Scientific Revolutions*. Chicago: University of Chicago Press.
Mâche, François-Bernard. 1992. *Music, Myth and Nature, or The Dolphins of Arion*, tr. Susan Delaney. Harwood Academic Publishers.
Mauranen, Anna and Pekka Kujamäki. Eds. 2004. *Translation Universals: Do They Exist?*. Amsterdam and Philadelphia: John Benjamins.
Neubert, Albrecht and Gregory M. Shreve. 1992. *Translation as Text*. Kent, Ohio: Kent State University Press.
Nord, Christiane. 1988. *Textanalyse und Übersetzen: Theoretische Grundlagen, Methode und didaktische Anwendung einer übersetzungsrelevanten Textanalyse*. Tübingen: Groos.
— 1991. *Text Analysis in Translation: Theory, Methodology, and*

Didactic Application of a Model for Translation-Oriented Text Analysis. Amsterdam and Atlanta: Rodopi.
Toury, Gideon. 2003. "Mona Baker's double standard". *Times Higher Education Supplement*. 7 February.
— 2004a. "Probabilistic Explanations in Translation Studies: Welcome As They Are, Would They Qualify as Universals?". In *Translation Universals: Do They Exist?*. Eds. Mauranen and Kujamäki. Amsterdam and Philadelphia: John Benjamins. 15-32.
— 2004b. "Probabilistic Explanations in Translation Studies: Universals – or a Challenge to the Very Concept?". In *Claims, Changes and Challenges in Translation Studies: Selected contributions from the EST Congress, Copenhagen 2001*. Eds. Hansen et al. Amsterdam-Philadelphia: John Benjamins.15-25.
— 2006. "Conducting Research on a 'Wish-to-Understand' Basis". In *Translation Studies at the Interface of Disciplines*. Eds. João Ferreira Duarte, Alexandra Assis Rosa and Teresa Seruya. Amsterdam and Philadelphia: John Benjamins. 55-66.

NOTES ON CONTRIBUTORS

José Lambert is a Professor emeritus at the Catholic University of Leuven, a specialist in (Comparative) Literary Studies. As the father of several international initiatives in Translation Studies such as the journal *Target* (John Benjamins, 1989-), he created and edited together with Gideon Toury (Tel-Aviv) and currently with Kirsten Malmkjaer, the research training centre CETRA (1989-), which attracts talents from five continents, and, finally, the PhD curriculum in the same discipline. How he moved from Comparative Literature and Literary Studies, German-French languages relationships etc., into the interdisciplinary study of translation as a component of cultural dynamics on the basis of the historical 1976 Symposium *Literature and Translation. New Perspectives in Literary Studies* (James S Holmes *et al.* Eds. 1978), can be studied in the selection of papers edited in 2006 by three of his disciples, Dirk Delabastita, Lieven D'hulst and Reine Meylaerts (*Functional Approaches to Culture and Translation. Selected Papers by José Lambert.* Amsterdam & Philadelphia: John Benjamins (Benjamins Translation Library 69). See also the interview: *Language International* 7, 5 (1995, 7-9 (Geoffrey Kingscott). Jose.Lambert@arts.kuleuven.be

Raquel Merino Álvarez is a Full Professor of Translation at the Department of English, German and Translation at the University of the Basque Country in Spain. Her research areas are drama and screen translation, translation and censorship and descriptive translation studies. She is the author of *Traducción, tradición y manipulación. Teatro inglés en España 1950-1990* (1994) and editor of *Traducción y censura en España (1939-1985). Estudios sobre corpus TRACE: cine, narrativa, teatro* (2008), as coordinator of TRACE (www.ehu.es/trace). She has co-organized the series of conferences *Trasvases Culturales: literatura, cine y traducción* (1993, 1996, 2000, 2004). Her publications have appeared in journals such as Babel and TTR and collective volumes (*Translation today, trends and perspectives*). She has translated into Spanish, with J.M. Santamaría, Washington Irving's *Tales of the Alhambra* (1996) and, with R. Rabadán, G. Toury's *Descriptive Translation Studies and Beyond* (2004). Dr. Merino is currently supervising research on screen translation in ETB-Basque television.
raquel.merino@ehu.es

Rosa Rabadán is a Full Professor of English at the Department of Modern Languages at the University of León in Spain. Her areas of interest include translation theory, translation, linguistic applications and corpus-based contrastive grammar English-Spanish. She has authored *Equivalencia y traducción* (1991) and co-authored, with P. Fernández-Nistal, *La traducción ingles-español: fundamentos, herramientas, aplicaciones* (2002). Her publications have also appeared in *Languages in Contrast*, *Meta* and *TTR*, among others, and she has contributed to a number of scholarly volumes in her areas of expertise. She has translated into Spanish, with J. L. Chamosa, Walt Whitman's *Leaves of Grass* (1999) and, with R. Merino, Gideon Toury's *Descriptive Translation Studies and Beyond* (2004). As a founding member of TRACE (Translations Censored) http://trace.unileon.es/, she served as the editor of the collective volume *Traducción y censura ingles-español: 1939-1985. Estudio preliminar* (2000). Currently she is the leader of the research team ACTRES (Contrastive Analysis and Translation English-Spanish) http://actres.unileon.es/, which focuses on the design of applications for translation quality assessment (TQA) and professional writing among others. She has been a Visiting Researcher at the universities of Ottawa, Canada, and, Brighton, U.K., and serves as an advisory board member for a series of academic book series and journals including Benjamins Translation Library.
rosa.rabadan@unileon.es

Julio-César Santoyo has been since 1981 a full Professor of English and Translation at the Department of Modern Languages at the University of León in Spain. He has authored, among other books, *Ediciones y traducciones inglesas del 'Lazarillo de Tormes' 1568-1977* (1978), *La cultura traducida* (1983), *El delito de traducir* (1985), *De clásicos y traducciones* (1987), *Teoría y crítica de la traducción: Antología* (1987), *Bibliografía española de la traducción* (1996), *Las páginas olvidadas: Reflexiones sobre canon, literatura y traducción* (1998), *Historia de la traducción: Quince apuntes* (1999), *Historia de la traducción: Viejos y nuevos apuntes* (2008), *La traducción medieval en la Península Ibérica* (2009), etc. He is author of more than 130 articles and chapters of books on the theory and history of translation, bibliography of translation, English literature and history of the printing press, published in journals such as *Meta*, *Babel*, *Atlantis*, *Cuadernos de Teatro Clásico*, *Target*, *Hermêneus*, *Translationskompetenz*, *Trans*, *Ibérica*, etc. He has translated into Spanish works by Tolkien, R. L. Stevenson, Oscar Wilde, E. A. Poe, John Donne,

Christopher Marlowe, Rudyard Kipling, Robin Chapman, Flannery O'Connor, Thomas Watts, Willa Cather, Washington Irving and Jonathan Edwards. He has also lectured on his areas of research and interest in Brussels, Winnipeg, Leipzig, Ottawa, Kalamazoo, Amherst (Mass.), Venice, Verona, Lisbon, Sao Paulo, Trier, Hildesheim, London and Paris (La Sorbonne).
jc.santoyo@unileon.es

Christina Schäffner is Professor of Translation Studies at Aston University, Birmingham, England. She obtained a doctorate in English Philology from Leipzig University, Germany. Before joining Aston University in 1992, she had been the head of a research team at the Saxon Academy of Arts and Sciences at Leipzig, which conducted research in the fields of political vocabulary, text linguistics, and translation studies. At Aston, she has taught undergraduate and postgraduate courses in translation studies, interpreting, text analysis. Her main research interests are political discourse and translation, metaphor research, and translation didactics. She has published widely in these areas. She is the Aston representative on the National Network for Translation, and a member of the EMT expert group set up by the Directorate General for Translation (DGT) of the European Commission whose main task is to make specific proposals with a view to implementing a European Master's in Translation (EMT) throughout the European Union.
c.schaeffner@aston.ac.uk

Gideon Toury is Professor of Poetics, Comparative Literature and Translation Studies at Tel Aviv University, where he holds the M. Bernstein Chair of Translation Theory. He founded *Target: International Journal of Translation Studies* (1989) and served as its first General Editor (until 2008). For years he was also General Editor of the important Benjamins Translation Library (BTL). He has published three authored books: *Translational Norms and Literary Translation into Hebrew, 1930-1945* (in Hebrew; 1977), *In Search of a Theory of Translation* (1980), and *Descriptive Translation Studies and Beyond* (1995), a number of edited volumes and numerous articles, in both English and Hebrew, in the fields of translation theory, linguistics and comparative literature. His articles have also appeared in translation in many other languages, and he is himself an active translator too, especially of English and German literature into Hebrew, with some 30 books and many articles to his credit. He is a member of the editorial or advisory boards of a number of

international journals. In 2000, he was awarded an honorary doctorate by Middlesex University, London. In 2008 he was honoured with a Festschrift (*Beyond Descriptive Translation Studies: Investigations in homage to Gideon Toury*), edited by Anthony Pym, Miriam Shlesinger and Daniel Simeoni.
toury@post.tau.ac.il

Patrick Zabalbeascoa is a tenured lecturer at the Pompeu Fabra University in Barcelona (Spain). He is a specialist in translation theory and audiovisual translation studies. In these areas he has published numerous papers and book chapters, participated in international conferences and research projects. He has contributed to a number of scholarly volumes and journals in his areas of expertise like *Sintagma: Revista de Lingüística, Traducción & comunicación, Miscelanae, etc.*
He has also lectured in Phd and Master's programmes of many other universities in several countries over a period of twenty years.
patrick.zabalbeascoa@upf.edu

NOTES ON EDITORS

MICAELA MUÑOZ-CALVO is a senior lecturer in English Philology at the English and German Department of the University of Zaragoza, Spain. She teaches Scientific English at the Faculty of Sciences and gives doctoral courses on Translation. Her fields of interest are Literary Translation, Translation of Humour, Translation and Culture and Scientific English. She co-edited *New Trends in Translation and Cultural Identity*, published in 2008 by Cambridge Scholars Publishing. Email: micaela@unizar.es

CARMEN BUESA-GÓMEZ is a senior lecturer in English at the Department of English and German Studies of the University of Zaragoza, Spain. She teaches English for Specific Studies to students of Library Studies at the Faculty of Arts. Her fields of interest are English for Specific Purposes, Translation Studies, literary translation and corpus and contrastive studies applied to academic and other registers. She co-edited *New Trends in Translation and Cultural Identity*, published in 2008 by Cambridge Scholars Publishing. Email: cbuesa@unizar.es

INDEX

A
ABC newspaper, 24
Abril, Pedro Simón, 22
academic
  community, 54, 168
  dialogues, 48
  disciplines, 13, 34
  discourse, 50
  freedom, 170
  institutions, 97
  parlance, 162
  publications, 54
  research, 34, 42
  text genres, 44
  translations, 54
  work, 168
  world(s), 54, 55
acceptability, 98, 99
ACTRES tools, 141
adaptation, 16, 22, 23, 42, 67, 133-134, 145
adequacy, 67, 95
  cultural, 67
  literary, 67
advertising, 55, 96
aesthetic elements, 102
AGA, 153
Agyeya, 29
Aitmatov, Chingiz, 18
Al-Jazeera, 116, 124
Albee, Edward, 131, 135, 142, 145-146, 148
alliteration, 86
ambition, 94, 96, 102-103
appropriation, 122
Arias Montano, Benito, 19
Arrabal, Fernand, 25
Artime and Azpilicueta, 137-141, 145-146, 148, 153
assessment of identity reinforcement, 76

"assumed translation", 161
Atxaga, Bernardo, 19
audiences, 5, 49-50, 133-134, 169
audiovisual media, 56
  products, 67
  translation, 64, 176
author-translator, 13, 20
authorial intentionality, 17
authority, 163-164
autotranslation, 30
avoidance of repetition, 162

B
Baker, Mona, 7, 107, 125, 171
Ballester, Xaverio, 1
Balliu, Chistian, 19
Bassnett, Susan, 110, 118
Bassnett, Susan and Harish Triverdi, 61
Basque authors, 19
BBC Monitoring Service, 8, 108, 113-123
BBC News, 116
Beckett, Samuel, 18, 20, 27
Berman, Antoine, 19
Bernstein, M. , 70, 175
Bielsa, Esperança, 110, 117, 123
Bigirimana, Jean-Baptiste, 53
bilingualism, 30
binary-tree
  analysis, 8, 84, 104,
  diagrams, 88
  mapping, 8, 84, 87
  structure, 91
Blixen, Karen, 18
BoE (Bank of English), 73
"border spaces", 65
Bourdieu, Pierre, 35
Boyden, Michael *et al.*, 52, 57
Boys in the Band, The, 130-145

Bravo, Jose M., 66, 68
Brisset, Annie, 62-63, 67
Brodsky, Joseph, 18
Brossard, Nicole, 29
Bruni, Leonardo, 20
Burundi intellectuals, 53

C
C-ACTRES, 73
can (modal verb), 73-75
cannibalism, 61
canon(s), 48, 51, 52
canonical texts, 49, 53
canonized national language, 53
canonized texts, 45
Carbonell, Eudald and Robert Sala, 1, 2
Cardinal Bembo, 20
Carrier, Roch, 63
Casares, Carlos, 19
Catalan authors, 19
categorization
    type-within-type, 87-88
Catford, J.C., 15, 33, 46
censorship, 8-9, 23, 67, 95, 107, 129-141
    archives, 9
    authorities, 136, 139
    boards, 134, 136-137
    offices, 129, 137
    records, 130, 133-137, 139, 141
    Theatre Censorship Board, 137
Chesterman, Andrew, 74, 94-95, 125
Chicano writers, 63
cloned narrative, 67
Coates, J., 74
code
    "restricted", 70
    communication, 1-9, 17, 33-40, 46, 48, 51-56, 62, 107, 121, 124, 158
    act of communication, 125
    (bilateral) mobility of communication, 36, 51, 53-54
    cross-cultural, 1-2, 5-7, 9, 107
    electronic, 39
    human, 1
    intercultural, 6, 54
    international communication policy, 54
    interstellar, 5
    managers, 37
    multilateral, 37
    multilingual, 6, 37, 53
    political, 108
    translated, 36
    verbal, 7, 33-34
Communication Studies, 6, 46
communities, 36-37, 51-54, 66, 163-165
"community interpreting", 35
competence, v, 2, 6, 13, 37
Complaisant Lover, The, 135
computer linguistics, 41-42
Conde, Alfredo, 19, 26
Conner, Steven, 19
contextual censorship (CE), 136
corpus-based
    contrastive (work), 73-74
    empirical studies, 8, 62
    evidence, 76
corpus linguistics, 41, 46-47
Corpus Translation Aligner, 69
Corpus Work Bench browser (CWB), 69
Cotoner, Luisa, 23
CREA (Corpus de Referencia del Español Actual), 73-74
Critical Discourse Análisis, 118
Cronin, Michael, 6, 36, 61
Crowley, Mart, 130-131, 136-140
cultural
    dynamics, 35, 173
    identity, vii, 3-4, 6-7, 9, 13-15, 25-26, 29-30, 38, 155
    milieu, 22
    shifts, 35
    turn, 39, 41, 46
"culture bound" examples, 15
Cunqueiro, Alvaro, 19, 26

D
D'Annunzio, Gabriele, 19
Da Costa, Luis Angélico, 28
Danan, Martine, 55
Davids Medienkritik, 119-120, 125
decoding, 99, 101

De Swaan, Abram, 51
De Toro Santos, Suso, 19, 26
Delabastita, Dirk, vii, 44, 84
Deleuze, Gilles and Felix Guattari, 62-63
demarcation of groups, 163
Descriptive Translation Studies, 19, 34, 41-42, 107, 133, 173-176
devices, 42, 47, 65
  cohesive devices, 86
  rhetorical devices, 88, 93
dialects, 2, 25, 51, 66, 81
diatopic variations, 25
diglossia
  professional, 64
discourse, 7, 33, 36-50, 52-53, 55-57, 61, 95, 100, 102, 123
  academic, 50
  analysis, 6
  legal, 53
  media, 43-44, 121
  on translation, 49, 52, 56
  political, 175
  translated news discourse, 121
  TV discourse, 43
domestication, 56, 61, 110, 113, 117-118, 121, 123, 126
Donne, John, 19-20, 174
DTS (Descriptive Translation Studies), 107, 133, 173
Du Bellay, Joaquim, 20
dubbing, 36, 55-56, 68, 98
dynamics of translation, 7, 40, 55

E
Eckert, Penelope, 65
editorial intervention, 115-117, 121, 123
Elvira Rodriguez, Adoración, 24
equivalence, 2, 14, 29, 85, 89, 94, 100-102
  intentional equivalence, 101-102
  intended equivalence, 101
  interlinguistic lexical, 85
equivalent, 14-15, 17, 23, 30, 159
  formal equivalent(s), 73
  lexical equivalent, 72-73
EST (European Society of Translation Studies), 168

European Union, the, 35, 40, 45, 56, 124, 175
European Voice, 108-109, 112-113, 124
evaluative criteria, 94, 97, 102-103
Even-Zohar, Itamar, 44
explanatory power, 157

F
Fairclough, Norman and Ruth Wodak, 118
fake translation, 66
falsification, 125
Feijoo y Montenegro, Benito Jerónimo, 19
Ferré, Rosario, 14, 26-27
Félix Fernández, Leandro, 15
Fernández de Castro, Félix, 74
fictitious translations, 66
Fitch, Brian T., 17, 30
Flemish translators, 50-52
foreignization, 56, 61
force (parameter of), 98-100, 103
"foreignness", 65, 70, 76
"foreignnizing", 76
formal aspects, 102
formulation(s), 158, 159, 165
  conceptual, 42
  "restricted code", 70
Franco's regime, 9, 63, 67, 129, 137
Frawley, William, 63, 68

G
GAID, 3
GALA (Globalization and Localization Association), 7
Galician authors, 19
Gambier, Yves, 55
García Ripoll, Martí, 64
genre, 9, 43, 46, 66, 102, 110-111, 132
  text genres, 43-44, 49
Gentzler, Edwin, 6, 61-62, 65, 125
geographical-cultural maps, 52
geographical dialects, 25, 66
Gimeno Menéndez and Gimeno Menéndez, 64
Gimferrer, Pere, 19
Glenn, Kathleen M., 20
"global village", 4, 16
globalization, 2-5, 35-36, 52, 55-56

Goatly, Andrew, 85
Gobard's taxonomy, 62, 68
Goldini, Carlo, 19
Gómez Arcos, Agustín, 24
Gómez Castro, Cristina, 67, 132
Gómez Miedes, Bernardino, 21
Gómez Torrego, Leonardo, 73-74
grammatical
    anchor, 72-74
    misuse, 70-71
    traits, 76
Green, Julien, 18
Greene, Graham, 131, 135
group identity, 163-164
Gruen, Erich S., 13
Grutman, Rainier, 30
Gubern, Román and Domènec Font, 67
Gutierrez-Lanza, Camino, 67-68
Gutt, Ernst-August, 94

H
Halverson, Sandra, 161
Hammond, Paul and Patrick Hughes, 89
Hansen *et al.*, 162
Harry Potter, 70
Hatim, Basil and Ian Mason, 6, 102
hierarchical model, 94
Hinojosa, Rolando, 63
Hjorth, Daniel *et al.*, 39
Hobsbawm, Eric, 39, 51
Holland, Robert, 107
Holmes, James S., 34, 158, 173
Hoye, 73
Huston, Nancy, 21, 27

I
IATIS, 6-7, 169
identidad cultural, 13
identity, i, v, vii, 3, 20, 25, 61-68, 155
    cultural identity, 3-7, 9, 13-15, 25-26, 29-30, 38, 155
    group, 62, 163-164
    in translation, 68
    inscription, 69-70, 72
    issues, 8, 65-68
    language, 62
    linguistic, 65
    marking, 7, 61-65, 69-70
    marking tools, 74, 76
    missing hypothesis, 61, 73, 77
    national, 63
    reinforcement, 76
    symbol, 76
    through translation, 66
indirect translation, 43, 50
information load, 101
Inghilleri, Moira, 123
interdisciplinarity, 6-7, 33-34
interlinguistic lexical equivalence, 85
intermediary language(s), 50
internationalization, 35-36, 55, 64
Internet, 2, 4, 13, 36, 40, 50, 52, 54-56, 114, 169
intersemiotic transfer, 67
intertextuality, 62, 90, 97

J
Jakobson, Roman, 67
jargon
    lexical, 43, 67
    translator' jargon, 48
Jiménez Julià, Tomás, 73
Joyce, James, 18-19
Juaristi, Felipe, 19
justification procedures, 94

K
Kálmán, Gyorgy, 19
Kang, Ji-Hae, 121
key anchor word, 141
Kirundi language, 53
Kittel, Harald *et al.*, 39, 44
Komissarov, Vilen, 161
Koskinen, Kaisa, 123, 126
Krzeszowski, Tomasz P., 73
Kumakhova, Zarema, 29

L
Labov, William, 65
Lambert, José, vii, 7, 33-60, 173

language
    global, 63-64
    identity, 65
    manipulation, 68
    multilingual, 65, 76-77
    mythic, 62-63
    referential, 62-63, 68
    vehicular, 62-63
    vernacular, 62-64
law of growing standardization, 72
Lefevere, André, 95,121
legal texts, 49-50
León, Luis de, 19-20
level (parameter of), 98-101
Levý, Jirí 40, 44, 46, 94, 99
lexical jargon, 43, 67
lingua franca, 4, 37, 43-44, 49, 51, 54, 63-64
linguistic
    identity, 65
        markers, 69-70, 72
    "sanitation", 67-68
    variation approach, 65
linguistics, 6, 34, 37-38, 40, 46, 51, 175
    computer linguistics, 41-42
    corpus linguistics, 41, 46-47
    psycho-linguistics, 5
    sociolinguistics, 6, 42, 51
    text linguistics, 175
literal translation, 85, 89, 92-93, 120, 122
loan words, 42, 45, 50
"localization", 35-36, 50, 56
Lu, Xing, 107

M
Madariaga, Salvador de, 19
Mâche, François-Bernard, 164
Maeztu, Ramiro de, 19
Management Theory, 37
mapping, 8, 83, 86-87, 90, 131
    binary-tree mapping model, 8, 84, 87
    metaphor translation, 84
Marí, Antoni, 19
Marquis of Villena, 19
Martínez de la Rosa, Francisco, 19
Marvell, Andrew, 20

Mauranen, Anna and Pekka Kujamäki, 162
may (modal verb), 73-75
McLuhan, Marshall, 4
Media Studies, 126
Media translation, 52
Mendoza-Denton, Norma, 65
Merino Álvarez, Raquel, 129-153
message transfer, 124
Mestre, José María, 22
metaphor, 49, 83-86, 104
    as-unit-approach, 85
    "bare" metaphor, 86
    compound metaphor, 86, 89
    "coupled" metaphor, 86
    non-verbal metaphor, 89
    translation, 84, 87
metaphorical idioms, 86
Merino, Raquel, viii, 9, 66, 129-153
Merino, Raquel and Rosa Rabadán, 66
Meyerhoff, Miriam, 65
Meylaerts, Reine, 52, 54, 173
Milián Massana, Antoni, 64
Miller, Grady, 19
Milosz, Czeslaw, 18
Mistral, Frédéric, 17
misunderstanding
    cultural, 125
mobility of languages, 38-39, 53
model of analysis, 103
    type-within-type binary-branch, 103-104
monitors, 113, 120, 122-123
Monzó, Quim, 19
Mooney, Sinéad, 13
More, Thomas, 20
multiperspectivism, 7, 33
Muñoz Cáliz, Berta, 131, 134
Muñoz-Calvo, M., 1-12
"myth of the text", 160, 165-166
myth(s) in Translation Studies, 9, 155-171
mythic language, 62-63

N
"nativeness", 76
Nabokov, Vladimir, 18

Nebrija, Antonio de, 19
Neubert, Albrecht, 33
Neubert, Albrecht and Gregory Shreve, 159-160
Newmark, Peter, 35, 84, 89
news, 8, 48, 52, 56, 109, 114, 116, 122-124
   agencies, 109, 116
   journalism, 8
   magazine (s), 108-109, 122
   media organisations, 125
   production, 8
   translation, 8, 116-117, 121, 123, 125-126, 128
   "unbiased news", 124
newspaper, 48, 56, 69, 73, 86, 92, 108, 115-116, 118, 124
   language, 64
   reports, 52, 56, 121
Nida, Eugene, 33, 83, 94
Nikolau, Paschalis and Mª Venetia Kyritsi, 61
non-translation, 42, 55
Nord, Christiane, 160
norms, 2-3, 8, 40, 42, 44, 46, 94-95, 98-99, 103, 110
   journalistic, 110
   translation, 40
   translational norms, 8, 103, 175
notion of reinforcement of identity, 76-77

O
Ong, Walter, 37
Organization Theory, 37
Øverås, Linn, 63
overtranslation, 74

P
P-ACTRES (Parallel English-Spanish Contrastive Analysis and Translation corpus), 68-70, 73-75
Palau i Fabre, Josep, 21
parameters of priorities, 100-101
parameters of restrictions, 98-99
Pasolini, Pier Paolo, 19
Pérez-Reverte, Arturo, 63, 65, 76
performance(s), v, 13, 94, 130, 137

Pirandello, Luigi, 18
plane of references, 86-87
   metaphorical plane, 87, 90
Potter, Jonathan, 65
Priorities and Restrictions (model of), 83, 94, 97, 100, 103
priorities of a translation, 99
   ST priorities, 97
   TT priorities, 97, 100
priority sets, 97
procedures, 53, 130, 160
   censors', 133
   censorship, 145
   discovery, 94
   justification, 94
   search, 130
process of semiosis, 65
pseudotranslation, 66, 68
Puig, Valentí, 19
pun(s), 29
   translation, 84
punning, 89
Pym, Anthony, 36, 39, 122-123, 176

Q
Québec, 63
Quebecization, 67
québécois, 63

R
Rabadán, Rosa, v, vii, 8, 61-81, 132, 173-174
Rabadán, Rosa and Noelia Ramón, 73
range, 34, 52, 83, 89, 98-101
rank, 65, 92-94, 97-103
reading
   "linear", 158
   "full", 159
   "serial", 158
   "structural", 158
referential language, 62-63, 68
"refraction", 121
register, 43, 45, 102, 114, 116, 130, 177
   language register, 22
   oral register, 25
Reiss, Katharina, 107

Rener, Frederic, 43
replique(s), 138-152
Resch, Doerte *et al.*, 39
research on translation, 9, 34, 38-39
retranslation, 66-68
rhetoric, 43, 49
rhetorical devices, 88-89, 92-93
    options, 43
    questions, 89
Riera, Carme, 19-20, 23
Rioja, Marta, 132, 138, 141
Rivas, Manuel, 19, 24-25
Royal Hunt of the Sun, The, 134

S
Sáenz, Miguel, 19, 29
Salom, Jaime, 130, 137, 139
Sánchez de las Brozas, 19
Santamaría, José Miguel, vii, 132, 173
Santoyo, Julio-César, v, vii, 7, 13-32, 66, 174
Schäffner, Christina, v, vii, 8, 107-127, 175
scope, 94, 97, 102-103
self-translation(s), 7, 13, 19-20, 22, 28-30
self-translator(s), 7, 19-25, 29-30
semantic translations, 72
Sengupta, Mahasweta, 22
SETI Projects, 5
Shaffer, Peter, 134-135, 145-148
Shread, Carolyn, 21, 27
Shuttleworth, Mark and Moira Cowie, 30
Sidiropoulou, Maria, 61
simile, 86, 93
Simon, Sherry, 61
Singer, Isaac Bashevis, 18
Skopos theory, 34
Snell-Hornby, Mary, 4, 6, 35-36, 41
sociodemographic categorization, 65
sociolects, 89
sociolinguistics, 6, 42, 51
source (parameter of), 98-99
Spiegel International, 8, 108-113, 118-126
Spinoza, Baruch, 19
Stetting, Karen, 123
Steyaert, Chris *et al.*, 39

Streetcar Named Desire, A, 136-137, 145
Stylistique compareé, 42
subgenres, 66
subset(s), 87-91
subtitling, 45, 55-56
subjectivity, 87, 94, 97, 102-103
superset: 87
Suso de Toro, Xesús, 19

T
Tagore, Rabindranath, 17-18, 20, 22
Tanqueiro, Helena, 19
TCA (Translation Corpus Aligner), 141
Tea and Sympathy, 137
telecommunication, 2
terminology, 46-47, 49-50, 56, 83
    electronic, 44
    gastronomic, 50
    legal, 44
tertium comparationis, 73-74
text genres, 43-44, 49
text processing, 101, 158
textual segments, 158
textuality, 159
The Times, 124
The Times Higher Education Supplement, 169
Theatre Censorship Board, 137
"third code", 63, 68
    jargons, 67
    situations, 76
Tirkkonen-Condit, Sonya, 68
Toury, Gideon, vi-vii, 9, 34, 42, 44, 66, 84, 86, 94-95, 97, 99, 133, 138, 155-171, 173-176
Toury's law of growing standardization, 72
TRACE (Translations Censored), vi, 9, 84, 119, 129-153
transeditor, 123
transference, 14, 24, 29-30
    cross-language, 17
    lexical, 64
translation as text, 159
    events, 156, 167
    in freedom (method), 22

process(es), 44, 66, 156
  strategies, 8, 62, 83, 89, 110-111, 113, 118-119, 121, 123, 157, 159
  theories, 34, 40, 42, 46, 125
  training, 34, 42, 45, 49
translational concepts, 61
  criteria, 8, 83
  solutions, 8, 83
  strategies, 167
Translation Studies, vi, 5, 7, 9, 19, 30, 34-35, 37, 41-42, 54, 107, 120, 123, 125-126, 159-171, 173-177
"Translation Universals", 161-162
translationese, 45, 48, 56, 68, 73, 77
translator's paradox(es), the, 47
translator's jargon, 48
TreeTagger, 69
Trudgill, Peter, 65
TT priorities, 97, 100
Tymoczko, Maria, 123
Tymoczko, Maria and Edwin Gentzler, 125
type-within-type categorization, 87, 103-104

U
Ubaldo Ribeiro, Joâo, 27
UNESCO, 19, 35
Ungaretti, Giuseppe, 18

United Nations, 35, 51
University of the People, 3
usage, 46, 48, 75
  grammatical, 74
  language, 70

V
Van Dijk, Teun, 107
Van Gorp, Hendrik, 43
variationist research, 65
Venuti, Lawrence, 56, 61, 107, 110
Vermeer, Hans J., 25, 107
Vinay J. P. and J. Darbelnet, 15, 33, 84
Vintró, Jordi, 23
visibility, 61, 68
Von Flotow, Luise, 61

W
White, Christopher, 17, 20
White, Roger, 85
Who's Afraid of Virginia Woolf, 134
Wolfe, Tom, 91
word games, 25

Z
Zabalbeascoa, Patrick, 83-105
Zoo Story, The, 135, 141, 145